BreakingFREE
From the Chains of Silence

LORRAINE NILON

Illustrations by Katherine Close

First published 2017 by Insight & Awareness Pty Ltd
Copyright ©2011 Lorraine Nilon
No part of this publication may be reproduced, stored in retrieval systems or transmitted in any form by any means without prior written permission of the copyright owner.

Insight & Awareness Pty Ltd
www.insightandawareness.com.au

The information contained in this book is in no way intended to offer medical or psychological advice or treatment. The author is neither a psychologist nor a licensed counsellor. All information is designed as suggestions for soul truth exploration. Individuals using this information, do so on their own volition. The author neither warrants nor guarantees the level of success to be achieved by the application of the information in this book. The author specifically disclaims any liability arising from how others choose to apply the information in this book. The ultimate efficacy is affected by the reader's willingness to be truthfully honest.

National Library of Australia Cataloguing-in-Publication entry:
Author: Nilon, Lorraine Dawn, author.
Title: Breaking Free From the Chains of Silence
Lorraine Dawn Nilon
Illustrator Katherine Close

ISBN: 978-0-9922817-4-8 (paperback) | 978-0-9922817-2-4 (eBook) | 978-0-9922817-5-5 (casebound)
Subjects: Self.
Contributors: Close, Katherine, illustrator.
Dewey Number: 126

This book is also available in paperback and hard cover.

Illustrations by Katherine Close
Cover illustration by Katherine Close
Conceptual design for illustrations by Lorraine Nilon
Conceptual design for illustrations and Assistant to clarity - Leanne McIntyre-Burnes
Editor and Assistant to clarity - Bronwen Prazak
Proofreading and Assistant to clarity - Rachel Dearnley
Internal design and typesetting by Green Hill Publishing
Author photographed by Paul Mathews

www.insightandawareness.com.au

Life is like a river and you may find yourself stuck in a whirlpool and surrounded by murky water. At first, truth may trickle past you, but as you align to truth you find yourself in an expanding stream that refreshes your soul.

This book is dedicated to the souls who have been wounded by the indifference of another.

The chains of silence cannot be broken until they are recognised.

If the content in this book raises any issues, for help please contact:

24-hour helpline (Australia)

- Lifeline - 131 114

- 1800 RESPECT - 1800 732 732

Office hours

Survivors & Mates Support Network (SAMSN) - 1800 472 676
Working with male survivors & their supporters

Victorian-based: Centres Against Sexual Assault - 1800 806 292

Blue Knot - 1300 657 380 or email helpline@blueknot.org.au
9am-5pm Monday to Sunday AEST/ADST

Broken Rites Australia is an excellent reference centre and source of advice:
"Since 1993, these volunteer advocates of abuse victims have been researching the cover-up of sexual abuse in the Catholic Church. Their articles are written in a professional, non-sensational manner. They expose the perpetrator (and the cover-up) but they protect the privacy of victims."
www.brokenrites.org.au

I would like to acknowledge the volunteers and staff, who dedicate themselves to these organisations and assist in breaking the silence.

Contents

Preface 4
Tips for reading *Breaking Free From the Chains of Silence* 6
Abuse 11
Introduction to your energetic system 16
A declaration to be of truth 21

Section One   29

Chapter 1:   To the soul who has been wounded by indifference 30
Chapter 2:   Abuse of a soul 34

Section Two   39

Chapter 3:   Indifference energy in the form of paedophilia 40

               The paedophile's attitude 45
               Struggling human 46
               How paedophiles operate 47
               Abuse is a multifaceted experience 50
               Orchestrating denial 55
               Charades 57
               The victim's torment 59
               Non-believers 61
               The survivor's self-rejection 63

The paedophile's mindset	66
The paedophile's behaviours	68
The victim's confusion and fear	71
The paedophile's manipulative games	74
Cycle of abuse	76
The survivor's pain, and their buffers to reality	78
Emotional overload	81
The victim's misconceptions	85
The paedophile's abuse of innocence	87
Paedophilic networks	89
Silencing the victim	92
Incestuous abuse	96
The survivor's mind chatter	100
The paedophile's depravities	103
The code of silence	105
A paedophile's cult leadership and domination	110
Betrayal of trust	116
False entitlement	119
Reactions to abuse	121
Expectations of recovery	125
The generational impact of abuse	128
The survivor's fear	132
The survivor's fear of intimacy	135
Hangover of degradation	136
Soul carnage	137
Society's struggle	139
Perpetuation	141

Trapped in victim mentality 142

Societal fears 147

Falsely Accused 150

Family shock 154

The ramifications for the victim 155

Looking for justice 160

Child exploitation material 166

Freedom 168

Section Three   171

Chapter 4:	Forgotten Soul	172
Chapter 5:	Curiosity	176
Chapter 6:	Anchoring to the truth of who you are	179
Chapter 7:	Core essence of your soul	189

Glossary 216

Acknowledgements 220

About the Author 222

Preface

Breaking Free From the Chains of Silence is an exploration into indifference. Indifference is a multifaceted energy that has varying degrees of destruction. Paedophilic abuse is an experience of many degrees and facets of indifference, and is an attack on the soul of the abused. Those who embody indifference do not just lack concern and compassion, they disconnect from integrity and are insensitive to the point of being cruel. Those who abuse others with their indifference, narcissistically beguile those who are unsuspecting of their deviancy.

The intent of this book is to broaden the awareness of indifference, explain the layers of trauma resulting from abuse and expose the arrogance of paedophiles who choose an innocent child to be their victim, while relying on the trauma to keep them silent. We as society should be willing to hear the truth of the abused and nurture the integrity of their soul. We should be part of a choir of support and to do that we have to understand the reality of abuse. We can only become informed through the victims' bravery to break free from the chains of silence and share the truth of their experience, and we need to be present in the uncomfortableness of their truth. Understanding empowers us all. Hopefully, as we educate each other on the travesty of indifference and abuse, we can better comfort the innocent and bring the guilty out of the shadows they hide in by reducing the number of places they can hide.

This information is multilayered and you do not need to have experienced paedophilic or sexual abuse, to relate to the various forms of indifference exposed. All traumatic experiences leave a residue of indifference. Indifference is within all types of abuse, such as domestic violence, discrimination, harassment, vilification and sexual assault. Verbal, mental, emotional and physical abuse leaves a residue of indifference. This book was written for survivors of paedophilia, but those who have experienced any type of abuse will gain insight into the reality of indifference.

When the effects of indifference are not acknowledged and addressed, they manifest into a multitude of fears, embedded beliefs and unresolved emotions, becoming emotional prisons that are reinforced by silence. This book sheds light on the reality of that which is left in the wake of indifference and abuse. Paedophilic abuse is insidious and permeates the survivor's self-perception, which has a cumulative effect on their life and others.

Abuse affects not only the abused but also their loved ones. It is difficult to know how to respond to the unfathomable, and yet it is essential to be compassionately present when listening to the recount of what has occurred. Those who become a witness to a survivor's recount of abuse can use the information to understand the rawness of emotions and the fallout that ensues. Providing a survivor with a safe place to be heard and understood is one of the greatest gifts we can give to those who have been left emotionally reeling from the trauma they have endured. Abuse is never deserved, it is an exploitation of innocence and physical disadvantage, which is perceived as an opportunity by the abuser.

Section two addresses being stuck in your own emotional prison from a soul perspective. This section is not just for victims of abuse, but for anyone who has felt lost in their own emotions. Section two is written with the intention of understanding and exploring being confined by confusion and restricted by your own indifference towards the truth of who you naturally are. It is a reminder that you are much more than just what you have experienced and the emotions you feel engulfed by.

When you feel trapped by your own indifference against yourself, regardless of the events that lead to you feeling imprisoned, it is difficult to confront your own reality and yet completely necessary to resolve how you oppress your sense of self. Indifference and despair are like quick sand; you can recognise them and struggle only to find yourself succumbing to the hopelessness that indifference and despair invokes. Being indifferent crushes your curiosity, which can cause you to forget the exquisiteness of your own soul and leave you ensnared by your own unresolved emotions.

Some readers may prefer to read section three first, others may use it from time to time while reading section one. Reading *Breaking Free From the Chains of Silence* is a personal process, be kind to yourself as you explore what is written.

Tips for reading *Breaking Free From the Chains of Silence*

This book raises difficult issues and you will feel uncomfortable. Feeling uncomfortable about abuse is a good thing; when we become comfortable about the indifference motivating those willing to abuse, we become complacent and numb to reality. This allows indifference to flourish. Reading this book will be a personal experience unique to you. You will filter the information through your own life experiences and this can trigger different emotional, energetic or physical reactions within you. Allow yourself the grace to explore how you react and respond to the information. You are embarking on an exploration of the effects of indifference and the trauma of abuse.

This book has been written from an awareness of energy and recognition of how we all respond energetically. Coming to terms with the energy you feel can be quite daunting as paedophilia is a difficult subject matter. Energetically you will feel the reality of your own emotional reactions to being exposed to what is written. You may experience energy that at first confuses you, until you become honest about your awareness of feeling energy. Allow yourself the time and space to contemplate and observe your emotional reactions to the truth of your feelings about what you are exploring within *Breaking Free From the Chains of Silence*.

There are many layers to your emotions and, as you explore the truth of your unresolved emotions, the depths of them may surprise you. You may believe you have accomplished the resolution of an emotion, only to discover another layer of the emotion. This is all part of the process and as your awareness increases so does your ability to truthfully explore the reality that is being exposed to you. Take your time and give yourself the grace to observe the reality of how impacting abuse is to the soul. Allow yourself the grace to feel the truth of your opportunity to resolve. Your negative self-judgement is a hindrance to the opportunity of discovering the truth of yourself.

You may automatically react to the information from your unresolved emotions, try not to tell yourself what you should be feeling or create excuses, and instead take notice of what you are feeling. You reveal information to yourself through your feelings, listen and learn from your own awareness. Indifference invokes an agitation, despair or can make you feel shrouded in oppressive energy. The energy produced by indifference can cause your eyes to feel gritty, you can feel extremely cold and feel 'sick to your stomach'. This book is not graphic about the abuse itself, but the energy can become intense. Saying the '*Self* expose self' declaration, explained on page 21 helps you to clear the energy you are reacting to, and feel. It also helps to anchor you back to yourself and your present moment.

Using this declaration periodically, while reading the book and each time after you stop reading, may be beneficial for managing any invoked emotions, distressing thoughts or unpleasant feelings. The declaration will also help when you experience energetic reactions. Energetic reactions are involuntary movements of your own energy, produced by your emotions or recognition of energy. You may at first be unable to identify the emotion, triggering the energetic reaction, but as you acknowledge the truth of your own reaction, you become more open to explore your emotions. Suppressed emotions and fear create energetic reactions and some people are sensitive to the energy they feel or generate. These examples may help you recognise an energetic reaction.

Fazing out: If you are emotionally reacting to what you are reading, you may faze out, unable to comprehend what you have just read. You can become stuck repeating a line, feeling confused and vacant. You may reread something without at first recognising you have just read it. You may also experience feeling shocked and zone out, causing you to disassociate from being present. These are all energetic reactions and are a signal to take notice of what you are reacting to. You may need to take a break, acknowledge what you are experiencing and allow your own energy to settle.

Overwhelmed: If you are extremely reactive to what you are reading, you may lose all concept of time. You may experience feeling groggy and realise that you have lost consciousness for a while and find yourself waking up, feeling disorientated and confused. This can be a signal that you are emotionally overwhelmed and can indicate that you are discovering something that may have a major effect on how you perceive yourself and your life experiences. This reaction exposes the significance of exploring what you feel uncomfortable about. You may need to acknowledge the truth of your reaction to settle your energy, so you can consciously acknowledge what you have unconsciously orchestrated to resist, deny and avoid.

Agitated: If you are emotionally reactive to what you are reading, you may feel agitated. Your agitation may be a direct result of being made aware of the reality of the indifference energy you are reading about or from a recognition of past indifference. This can trigger an involuntary agitation within you. You may be agitated because your illusion of control is being interfered with, but it is your illusion of control that gets in your way of feeling at peace. Your agitation could stem from your fear of being exposed to that which you want to suppress. You may fear the discovery of truth will cause you to lose how you define yourself. You can use your emotions to fool yourself about the reality of who you naturally are and default to agitation as a protective mechanism to sustain your denial. You may need to take a short break and occupy yourself with something else for a while to settle your energy. At times, you may find it helpful to just read small amounts and give yourself time to digest what you have read and energetically reacted to.

Denial: If you are emotionally reacting to what you are reading, you may attempt to suppress your awareness of your emotional, energetic and physical reactions to the information. You may feel yourself make excuses for your reactions, permitting yourself to retreat from what is being exposed to you. Your own opposition to feeling the truth of your reactions may cause you to become arrogant about your own ignorance. This may make you indifferent to the significance of your honesty about your own reaction to what you are reading. Your emotional, energetic and physical reactions reveal a lot to you. You may need to objectively observe the truth of your reactions to comprehend the reality of your own suppressed emotions.

Tips for reading Breaking Free From the Chains of Silence

Avoiding: If you are emotionally reactive, you may ignore what you are feeling and become oppositional to the process of discovery, acknowledgement and resolution. Trust that you have encountered this book for a reason. Be honest about your emotions as they reveal information to you and create an opportunity to explore and resolve any negativity you feel about yourself.

There will be times you want to explore more deeply and times you may seek a rest from your own exploration. Take notice of your emotional and energetic reactions and be honest about the urge to ignore your own insight.

Try not to engage with the information within *Breaking Free From the Chains of Silence* from fear or denial, be open to discover and explore. Your awareness of yourself will expand as you explore the truth of your own feelings and unresolved emotions.

Acknowledge the questions you contemplate within yourself, and accept the significance of your own soul. You matter to this world and to the origin of your soul. Seek support when needed, find avenues that assist, support and nurture you. There is no shame in needing or wanting help, comfort and support, and all souls deserve to be nurtured.

There are many organisations, support groups and helplines that give practical and emotional assistance. They can help you deal with any triggered memories and emotions. Being emotionally overwhelmed is not a sign of weakness, it is a sign of your humanity and the enormity of what you are dealing with. Humanity describes souls within a physical body, experiencing life, and the experience of abuse can make you feel lost, alone or trapped. Liberating yourself from the shackles of oppression that abuse creates is difficult and the aim of this book is to be an assistant to clarity for you.

Abuse

buse is indifference towards another's natural value, worth and significance. It is the intent to:

- Cause harm
- Control
- Manipulate
- Be cruel
- Be violent
- Oppress
- Humiliate
- Misuse
- Deceive
- Exploit
- Intimidate
- Dominate
- Punish
- Undermine
- Betray trust

Abuse changes how the abused perceive themselves; it changes their experience of life and can be very difficult to resolve. Abuse is never contained to a present moment, it lingers across a person's lifetime and has pervasive long-term ramifications. Abuse creates traumatic memories and emotional scars that the victim has to contend with.

Cyber abuse encompasses a wide variety of abuse. The abuser uses the internet and devices such as a phone or computer to exploit or cause harm to another.

- **Internet stalking** is obsessively targeting a child or adult with unwanted attention via the use of the internet and electronic devices. The stalker has a compulsive drive to monitor those they prey upon, and this is a severe invasion of privacy. This can also include stealing photographs from social media.
- **Online bullying** is using any form of electronic messaging system to send insulting or threatening messages. It is repetitive harassment that can come in many forms of disrespect for the victim's emotional wellbeing and reputation. This can include distributing naked or sexual images of the victim. It is also making false accusations with the intent to humiliate and defame the victim.
- **Online predators** use the internet to locate and lure their victims to become engaged in the illusion of a relationship or friendship, as they seek to procure, groom and engage a child in sexual activities. Predators seek to mislead and coerce their victims to comply with their demands. Some send indecent communication and photos of their own genitals, and others seek to coerce children to post explicit photos of themselves.

- **Online sexual abuse material** is the use of visional material that shows or entices an offence against a child or non-consenting adult. It is an offence to access, possess and distribute child exploitation material. It is also an offence to advertise, solicit or supply a child for pornographic purposes.

Emotional abuse is designed to undermine another's sense of self. It is deliberate humiliation, with the intent to seize control of how others feel about themselves. An emotional abuser coerces the victim to align to the lies they use to create disparaging definitions for them to adopt. An emotional abuser, desires to corrupt the victim's relationship with their own soul, with the intent to have them believe they are worthless.

Emotional abuse affects the victim's sense of identity and confidence, and is used to ensure they remain trapped in low self-esteem and patterns of behaviour that oppress their awareness of their own soul. It also leaves a victim believing they are unlovable and 'not good enough'. Emotional abuse is derived from the intent to silence the victim and to browbeat them into submission. Emotional abuse can leave a victim feeling like a shell of a person, separated from the true essence of who they naturally are. It also leads to a victim feeling tormented and tortured by their own emotions.

Energetic abuse is also known as a psychic attack. It is the intent to cause harm by projecting thoughts, judgement and energy. Those who want to create psychic trauma seek to leave a lasting impression and a residue of their insidious energy. Psychic trauma stems from being aware of, or experiencing, the insidiousness of the abuser. Psychic trauma is the reverberation of the shock at the level of indifference the abuser has for the abused. The purpose of energetic abuse is to create pain for another to carry and to ensure the shock of the abuse has a long-lasting impact. Energetic abuse is derived from the abuser's desire to intimidate and dominate those they want to manipulate, control or have ownership over.

Energetic abuse is an intrusion into another's energy system or a forceful projection of energy at them, with the intent to deprive another of feeling their value, worth and significance. This can be done consciously or unconsciously. The more conscious the abuser is of their own energy, the more intense and repugnant their energy feels. Energetic abuse leaves the victim feeling a foreboding energy that invokes a primal fear, which can develop into psychic trauma.

Extreme indifference produces an energy that feels like there is an energetic shroud; a film, that descends over the victim, which creates an internal sensation of emotional suffocation, or a trapped sensation entwined with the belief that they are damned if they do and damned if they don't. This creates a sense of powerlessness and hopelessness. These sensations can be carried as a memory of what was felt, or can be felt repetitively as the victim ruminates over their history or becomes aware of thoughts produced by suppressed fear. The carried sensations, thoughts and beliefs can invoke a shame shudder coursing through the body, or an inescapable shadow that lurks in the hidden crevasses of the victim's awareness.

Physical abuse is an intentional act to create physical pain, injury or long-lasting bodily harm. It is also the desire to use violence to gain control over whoever the abuser has chosen to victimise. Physical abuse is using brute force to render another incapable of defending themselves. It is also the neglect, enslavement or mistreatment of another in such a way that results in poor health or injury.

Mental abuse also known as bullying or psychological abuse, violence or warfare is a verbal or non-verbal interaction that leaves the victim believing they are worthless. It is the desire to invoke or create insecurities within another to ensure they feel insignificant and distressed about their safety. This creates anxiety that sustains fear. It is also the desire to sustain a power imbalance and to leave the victim questioning their sanity and self-worth.

Mental abuse is using mind games intentionally. It is a series of planned manipulative strategies that steer the victim to be disadvantaged or to be more pliable to the abuser's demands. Mind games cause the victim to be confused and to doubt their own perception or recollection of reality. It is the desire to infiltrate another's thought processes with confusing and degrading beliefs designed to fester within the victim. Mental abuse impacts how the victim thinks about themselves and diminishes their sense of competency. It is used to ensure they perpetuate their own patterns of self-loathing, self-hatred and soul oppression.

Sexual abuse is the crime of executing any sexual acts with a child or with a nonconsenting adult. It is exploitation, motivated by sexual interest. Sexual abusers are lewd and lascivious towards their victims. Sexual abuse is being forced or tricked into sexual activities. It is a violation of another's soul and their freedom.

Soul abuse is any type of abuse that has permeated through every aspect of a person's soul, causing them to lose awareness of the foundation of who they are. It is any abuse that destroys the victims' awareness of the strength of their own soul. It is any abuse that incites the victim to be indifferent to their own truth, and to flood their thoughts, feelings and sense of identity with disparaging self-beliefs. It also diffuses their ability to feel the truth of who they naturally are and leaves them depriving themselves of their own core essences.

Soul abuse is any abuse that becomes a filter that ensures a person remains separated from their awareness of their own soul and truth. It also any abuse that disassociates the victim from feeling unconditionally loved by themselves, others and their origins.

Soul abuse results from the use of indifference to intentionally corrupt another's understanding of their own natural significance. It is the abuse that leaves the victim feeling fractured and fragmented, and deprives them of feeling unity within their soul and at peace with their own life.

Soul carnage is the pain and damage that is carried from one lifetime to another, until it is resolved. Soul carnage is felt within the depths of the soul, due to the severity of the indifference experienced. It results from callous indifference and a complete disregard for the mayhem the victim has to endure.

Verbal abuse is the use of words, mutterings, intonations, snorts or sniggers of condemnation. It is using words, lies and sounds as a weapon to undermine another's self-confidence. This can be loud rants designed to intimidate, or quiet but consistent criticisms. Verbal abuse is communicating in a demeaning way, calculated to make another feel inferior, 'not good enough' and to believe that there is something very wrong with who they are. Verbal abuse incites flawed beliefs and invokes shame, and is always a coercive tactic to ensure greater control over the abused. It is an expression of contempt and is used to ensure the victim is more vulnerable to future attacks, manipulation and exploitation. It is designed to persuade and encourage the belief that the victim is useless and unworthy of rescue or respect.

Verbal abuse is deliberately seeking to create or toy with the victims' insecurities, and can be systematically used to brainwash the victim. Brainwashing is methodical manipulation that alters the victim's attitude to form beliefs that can become so ingrained that the victim believes they are true. Brainwashing can leave the victim devoid of independent thought so that they reject any other opinions or evidence of truth that is contradictory to that which has been infused into their psyche. These beliefs undermine the victim's self-worth and reduce their ability to mentally defend themselves. They often unconsciously align without challenge, to that which they have been indoctrinated to believe. This can also cause victims to blame themselves, not realising that they have been manipulated into believing that the abuse is their fault.

The words **emotional, energetic and physical** have been used throughout this book to delineate the different and intertwining aspects and ramifications of abuse.

Abuse | 15

Introduction to your energetic system

True Source Divine Origin Consciousness is a label for the collective purity of truth and is the collective energy of the origin of your soul and the truth of all souls. This is where you come from and where you will return to after your death. This label is used because you do not have a history with it; it is a way of counteracting what you believe you know and enables you the freedom to explore what you discover about your own origin of truth. *True Source Divine Origin Consciousness* is the source of your soul's consciousness.

Your soul's consciousness is the part of your soul system, which has never abandoned the unconditional love of *True Source Divine Origin Consciousness* (your origin), or the awareness of truth. Your soul's consciousness is the truth of who you are unencumbered by any unconscious energy and is naturally the core of your being.

Your soul's unconsciousness is the part of your soul system, which is unconscious to the unconditional love of *True Source Divine Origin Consciousness*, and is the part of you lost within your willingness to oppress your awareness of truth. Your soul's unconsciousness is the energetic storehouse of your unconscious energy, such as your unresolved emotions, control structures, barriers to truth, framework of soul oppression, fears and beliefs which you use to deny the truth of who you are.

You are the interface between your soul's consciousness and unconsciousness.

Your unresolved emotions are what you use to energetically sustain the vortex of your soul's unconsciousness. These are the emotions you refuse to resolve, or you have become so unconscious to the reality of them, that you deny their existence. All unresolved emotions are unconscious energy. The trauma of abuse creates a myriad of unresolved emotions, and these are sustained by your fear and your inability, or unwillingness to face the truth.

True Source Divine Origin Consciousness
CORE ESSENCES
Grace
Peace
Loyalty
Truthfulness
Appreciation
Acceptance
Clarity
Integrity
Freedom
Patience
Kindness
Harmony
Joy
Independance
Honesty
Uniqueness
Compassion
Serenity
Care
Dynamic
Purity
Individuality
Hope
Trust
Soul's Consciousness
ARROGANCE HATE VICTIM
JEALOUSY BLAME
FEAR HUMILIATION
GUILT
CONTROL INFERIORITY
DISASSOCIATION
INSECURITY RAGE
VICTIM JEALOUSY
AVOIDANCE FEAR
SHAME
OPPOSITIONAL ANGER
FRUSTRATION ENVY
INFERIORITY
REGRET
INDIFFERENCE
DENIAL
RAGE INSECURITY
INDIFFERENCE
DENIAL REGRET
IGNORANCE MANIPULATION
ENVY
ANGER
OPPOSITIONAL
HUMILIATION CONTROL
FRUSTRATION GUILT
HATE ARROGANCE
SHAME
JUDGEMENT
DISASSOCIATION
IGNORANCE
AVOIDANCE
BLAME
SOUL DENIAL
Soul's Unconsciousness

Your soul denial is the foundation and original energy of your soul's unconsciousness and the source of all unconscious energy; all unconscious energy is a mutation of soul denial. Your soul denial energy is your war with the truth of who you are, which enslaves you to exist within the unconsciousness of your soul. Your soul denial consists of your embedded beliefs and fears, which inhibit you from accepting the truth of your natural significance, uniqueness, independence and individuality.

Your soul oppression is the active force of your soul's unconsciousness, you use to emotionally, energetically and physically oppress your awareness of your soul truth. Your soul truth is the reality of both your conscious and unconscious energy.

Barriers to truth maintain your separation from your awareness of your soul. Barriers are part of the energetic structural web of the vortex of your soul's unconsciousness, and are sustained using major collectives of energy that result from opposing truth. The major collectives are:

- Resistance, denial, avoidance and codependency
- Judgement, manipulation, confusion and control
- Images, illusions and controlled identities
- Controlled evolution
- Heresy

Barriers are deceptive control structures formed from your layers of triggered emotional reactions, which you use to prevent your awareness of the flow of truth within you, and to inhibit your ability to recognise and learn from the truth of your reality.

Framework of soul oppression is comprised of your various avenues of indifference, which are sequenced reactions and responses that you use to be and remain indifferent to truth. These avenues of indifference originate from the fears and embedded beliefs within your soul denial. Each avenue of indifference is a cyclic pattern of your soul oppression that ascends from your soul denial to your heresy barrier and descends back to your soul denial. The indifference energy is fueled by your soul control, which is your desire for control and your illusion of having control. The avenues of indifference are:

- Soul abuse
- Soul betrayal
- Soul deception
- Soul defiance
- Soul demise
- Soul illusion
- Soul sabotage
- Soul traitor

You use these to construct a framework of how you oppress the truth of yourself.

Core essences are unique strands of conscious energy that contribute to the purity of who you are. They are the unique strands of conscious energy within unconditional love. Core essences are natural energy that emanate from your soul's consciousness. The core essences explored in Insight and Awareness are:

- *Acceptance*
- *Appreciation*
- *Care*
- *Clarity*
- *Compassion*
- *Dynamism*
- *Freedom*
- *Grace*
- *Harmony*
- *Honesty*
- *Hope*
- *Independence*
- *Individuality*
- *Integrity*
- *Joy*
- *Kindness*
- *Loyalty*
- *Patience*
- *Peace*
- *Purity*
- *Serenity*
- *Trust*
- *Truthfulness*
- *Uniqueness*

The energetic mass energy of mankind is the energetic structure of our collective unconsciousness, which is the unconsciousness of *True Source Divine Origin Consciousness*. It is the energetic storehouse for mankind's varieties and types of soul denial energy, which form energetic collectives out of the reverberation of unresolved emotions and form energetic barriers to truth out of control structures and belief systems. The energetic mass energy of mankind is the collective energy of each individual souls' unresolved emotions combining to create barriers that oppress the awareness of soul truth.

These are explored in more depth in book 1.

Your Insight & Awareness Book
Your life is an expedition to discover the truth of yourself

Introduction to your energetic system

True Source Divine Origin Consciousness

Your Soul's Consciousness

Heresy - Desire to control, indifference to truth, resentment of reality, oppositional energy, programming, conditioning and indoctrinations, guilt, shame, humiliation, denial of reality, disassociation from feeling.

Controlled evolution - desire to control your soul denial with beliefs.

Images, illusions and controlled identities.

Judgement, manipulation, confusion and control.

Resistance, denial, avoidance and co-dependency.

Framework of Soul Oppression

Barriers to Truth

Illusion of control

Desire to control

Soul Denial
Embedded Beliefs and Fears

A declaration to be of truth

***"Self* expose self, RDAC, S and D, DVP, rebalance to origin truth."**

This declaration is a bridge to your awareness of your soul's consciousness, which may make the process of aligning to your truth easier. The declaration assists in clearing the emotional and energetic debris of your unconsciousness. It does not resolve the energy; you only achieve resolution when you are truthful. However, it does assist your ability to be honest. When you choose to say the declaration, you are highlighting to yourself your intention to acknowledge truth and the presence of your soul's consciousness.

When you choose to say the declaration to yourself, you are exposing your willingness to be of truth and your intention to explore the truth of your own emotional, energetic and physical reality. Your willingness to be honest with yourself enables you to align to truth. You may have conditioned yourself with your aversion to truth, to be in opposition to the presence of your soul's consciousness. The declaration is a way of reminding yourself that you are a soul with the intention to resolve and evolve. Resolving and evolving is a choice; this declaration is an expression of your choice.

When the declaration is used as a control structure to avoid responsibility for your unresolved emotions, you tarnish your own intention to be honest and the effectiveness of the declaration will be undermined. However, your soul's consciousness provides grace for your naivety in relation to your control structures. Your soul's consciousness will endeavour to expose you to the truth of your control structures, because they are part of your soul's unconsciousness. The declaration assists you to be honest about your own deception. Your honesty alters your alliance with the energy you have been generating from your unresolved emotions and shifts your allegiance back to your origin truth. You are bridging your awareness to your ability to trust truth and to be honest with yourself. If you are aware of your intent when using the declaration, you will align to your soul's consciousness, enabling yourself to reveal the truth that you need to acknowledge and resolve, to be able to evolve.

Your soul's consciousness supplies the energy of truth; your choice to be honest sustains the space for you to explore truth. Your soul's consciousness cannot be fooled; if your intention is to control energy with this declaration, you will be attempting to alter reality for the purpose of emotionally feeling in control, while you ignore the truth of yourself reacting to reality. This declaration is not meant to alter reality, but to expose you to the truth of reality, enabling you to objectively observe yourself within the truth of your reality. You have the freedom to deceptively believe your own lies; however, your lies cannot corrupt your soul's consciousness. Your soul's consciousness responds to the truth of all energy.

By saying the declaration to yourself, you are acknowledging the intent of your soul's consciousness, which is to be honest with yourself. You are asking yourself to be present in your reality and own the truth of what you are experiencing within yourself. When your desire to control is overriding your willingness to be honest, you inhibit the effectiveness of the declaration.

You do not have to say the declaration aloud; you can internally say the declaration to allow yourself to anchor to your awareness of your present moment. You can use the declaration to calm your emotions and anchor to your awareness, creating the space to observe the truth of your emotional, energetic and physical reaction to your present moment. You can use the declaration when you feel insecure, anxious, scared, overwhelmed or unsure. You can use the declaration when you are seeking the truth of your own feelings and emotions. You can use the declaration when you seek clarity to quieten your mind chatter.

You are not being asked to believe in the declaration; it is there for you to explore and experiment with. While you explore and experiment with the declaration, be mindful of your honesty, your intent, your expectations and your desire to control reality. The effectiveness of the declaration is determined by your willingness to explore the truth of both your consciousness and unconsciousness.

Your soul's consciousness is naturally exposing truth to you and the declaration is a temporary tool to assist you to become honest about the exploration of your ability to trust your awareness of what is being exposed. The declaration is temporary because your honesty will help you to evolve beyond the need to use the declaration. The declaration exposes you to the deception you use to overshadow your own natural awareness of truth.

"*Self* expose self, RDAC, S and D, DVP, rebalance to origin truth."

Self You are acknowledging you are a soul and asking your soul's consciousness to push conscious energy into any barriers or aversions to truth that you have.

Expose You are asking your soul's consciousness to expose truth to you. You are asking for assistance to expose the truth of your unresolved emotions and how they are affecting you. You are asking for assistance to expose how you are controlling yourself to fight your awareness of truth and reality. You are asking for assistance to expose the truth of your soul's consciousness and unconsciousness, and the truth of your feelings and unresolved emotions.

self This is a way to describe the unconsciousness of your soul, which is the combination of your unresolved emotions, barriers to truth, your framework of soul oppression, your desire to control and your soul denial. Your soul's consciousness seeks to expose the deception of your opposition to your soul truth, so you can resolve your own stagnation and feel the truth of yourself as a soul.

RDAC You are asking your soul's consciousness to expose your **R**esistance, **D**enial, **A**voidance and **C**odependency energies, which are barriers to truth. By honestly observing, acknowledging and accepting your **RDAC** energies, you create the space to acknowledge truth, develop your awareness of your soul, resolve unresolved emotions and evolve to unify with truth.

S and D You are asking your soul's consciousness to bridge your **S**eparation from your awareness of your soul, which you have created with your unresolved emotions, and to expose your **D**isassociation from feeling truth.

D **D**isconnect, **D**isengage and **D**isentangle your soul's consciousness from being bombarded by your own unresolved emotional energy, any external source or any mankind energy, that is affecting your awareness of the presence of your soul's consciousness.

V **V**ice **V**ersa is attempting to deal with yours and others' projection of unconscious energy. Your soul's consciousness acknowledges each soul's individuality; you honour their space by not projecting your energy into their energetic system. This part of the declaration is the acknowledgement that you have a choice and can withdraw your unconscious projection of energy from another's system, and that you have the ability to reject another's unconscious projections into your system. You also seek to be able to hold the uniqueness of your space, without the interference of others' emotional projections.

V within the declaration is often overridden by your desire for control, so be aware of what you are emotionally feeling. Are the emotions yours or are they being projected at you? If the emotions are from another, how are they affecting you? What are they triggering within you and why are you hanging on to them? These are the questions that will expose how you deny your individuality, by using another's emotional energy to oppress your awareness of your soul truth. Be mindful of how you use others' projections of unconscious energy to feed your own willingness and ability to oppress yourself. Be mindful of projecting unconscious energy into another's energy system and the intention behind your energetic intrusion. If you are willing to be dishonest with unconscious energy you will override the effectiveness of the declaration.

P If you trusted your soul's consciousness and accepted your truth and reality, what would your **P**otential, **P**ossibilities and **P**robabilities be? How would you utilise your freedom of choice? **P** within the declaration is a representation of the significance of your freedom of choice. It is a choice to seek your true potential. Truth exposes your true potential as a soul. The declaration is the choice to acknowledge you want to become aware of what you are unconscious of. You have the freedom to explore the possibilities within your alignment with truth or to continue your enactment of your unresolved emotions. Your alignment to truth or the enactment of your unresolved emotions is always your choice. You have the freedom to determine the path of your soul journey. You have the freedom to align to the potential, possibilities and probabilities of your soul truth.

By saying the declaration, you are choosing to align to truth and acknowledge the significance of being a soul seeking truth. You are choosing to align to your origin truth and shifting your loyalty back to the truth of your soul and *True Source Divine Origin Consciousness*.

The declaration is a tool to assist you until you can sustain your own awareness of truth. It is a bridge, which supports you until you can support yourself with your own honesty, grace and unconditional love.

There is often an energetic undercurrent to our interactions with each other when we are willing to judge each other and our unique experiences. What we say may be different to what we energetically project. Due to the energetic entanglement, both the receiver and projector of unconscious energy can emotionally, energetically and physically feel drained because of their loss of energetic independence.

I'm going on holidays next week, I'm so excited.
Oh, that's lovely.
I never get anything!
I want what you have!
That's not fair!
How did you do better than me?

Why do I suddenly feel so drained and agitated?
I feel so drained and agitated

When you forget, you have the declaration as a tool to assist you, you are experiencing your disassociation from truth and how easily you can become unconscious of your ability to be honest with yourself about your emotional, energetic and physical reality. You often forget about the declaration:

- When you are swamped by your own unresolved emotions and separated from your awareness of truth.
- When you believe you are in control of life, yourself, others and reality.
- When you believe you do not need to be honest about your emotional, energetic and physical reality.

This is how unconscious energy works and your soul oppressive patterns are cyclic, so you will bring yourself back to the point of wanting the assistance of the declaration.

Your emotional, energetic and physical experiences expose you to the truth of your own soul's consciousness and unconsciousness. The resolution and evolution of your soul is a process you will experience throughout the course of your life. The declaration is not a tool you can use to control yourself to be just conscious energy; it is a tool to expose you to your awareness of the truth of both conscious and unconscious energy within your soul.

Let yourself acknowledge the truth and what you are emotionally, energetically and physically reacting to when reading and exploring *Breaking Free From the Chains of Silence*. Give yourself permission to accept you are exposing yourself to the truth of your soul's unconsciousness and allow yourself to feel the truth of your soul's consciousness. The declaration is there to assist you as you expose yourself to the encyclopaedia of who you are. The declaration supports you while you are unconscious of your own truth. However, as you discover, observe, accept and understand aspects of your conscious and unconscious energy, the declaration returns responsibility for your awareness to you.

For example, think of yourself as a set of encyclopaedias. As you understand the first volume, you become responsible for what is within the first volume and the declaration supports what you are unaware of from volume two onwards. As you understand the second volume, you become responsible for what is within the first two volumes and the declaration supports what you are unaware of, from volume three onwards.

At times, you may feel completely overwhelmed by your own unresolved emotions and may require yourself to anchor to the truth of what the intention of the '*Self* expose self' declaration is. Allow yourself to become aware of what you are saying and why you are saying the '*Self* expose self' declaration. Acknowledge that you are seeking your soul consciousness' energy to expose the truth of your soul's unconsciousness and that you do not want to resist, deny or avoid the truth of yourself. Acknowledge your own codependency on the familiarity of your unresolved emotions and the ease with which you dismiss the importance of your own honesty with yourself. Acknowledge your separation from your awareness of your soul and your disassociation from feeling truth, and explore the reality of your own feelings. Acknowledge the energy affecting your awareness of truth and accept there is more to you than what you have already surmised and believed. You may assist yourself to do this by reading the details of the '*Self* expose self' declaration.

Being responsible is to choose to honestly observe the truth of your own emotional, energetic and physical reactions to yourself, life, others, relationships and your awareness of truth. Being responsible is to choose to use your freedom of choice to participate in your own resolution and evolution.

Section One

CHAPTER ONE

To the soul who has been wounded by indifference

Breaking Free From the Chains of Silence was written with the survivor of sexual abuse in mind. This book is intended to be a respectful exploration into the effects of paedophilic abuse and to explain why the indifference energy produced by those willing to abuse, is so destructive. I want to be very clear with you, I am not a psychologist, and this book has been written from my insight and awareness of energy. I intend to explain indifference and how it affects the soul. I have become a custodian of many wounded souls' accounts of their history and experiences of sexual abuse. As I met many souls living with this history, I was shocked at how prevalent abuse is within our society. Regardless of how many horrific accounts of sexual abuse I hear, I am always shocked. How could one soul do this to another soul, especially a child, when there is not a soul on this planet that deserves to be treated with such indifference? How could anyone ignore the insidious indifference required to hurt another soul in such a manner?

As I listened to many recounts of child abuse and the ongoing effects into adulthood, I energetically tracked the energy and became acutely aware of how the carried victim energy was affecting each abused soul. I realised the victim mentality was built on misconceptions and attempts to conceal fear. One of the consistent misconceptions I heard is the belief that it was the victim's unworthiness that caused the paedophile to choose to abuse them. This is not true; if you have been abused it is not because of a lack of worthiness. It was because a paedophile saw or created an opportunity to control and abuse you.

You cannot change the truth of your history or the ramifications you have experienced because of your history. However you can change how you feel about yourself, especially if how you feel about yourself is built on misconceptions and attempts to conceal your fear. You can rediscover and feel the true value, worth and significance of who you are. This book has been written to illuminate all that I have become privy to, because of the souls who were willing to be honest about their struggle, with the hope of resolving the wounds that paedophilia leaves behind. Paedophilia is an extreme form of indifference towards another soul and the complexities of abuse are difficult to understand and recover from. This book is a way of bringing to the surface that which is hidden in order to help those who want to break free from the chains of silence.

Breaking Free From the Chains of Silence was written to explain how the experience of abuse has such a hold on you and why it is not easy to shake off your past. When you have been wounded by a paedophile's indifference you feel as though you are carrying a stain on your soul. If you are a survivor, you can often feel pressured by yourself, your family and society to ignore your own history of abuse and let the past be the past. You may believe you have to be stoically brave, silently fighting your own internal upheavals, without inconveniencing others with the emotional dilemmas resulting from your sexual abuse. The past is not the past if you carry the pain and feel like there is a stain on your soul. Being aware of the pain carried can cause you to blame yourself for not being able to come to terms with the true extent of the abuse and to immerse yourself in the fear that there is something wrong with you. There is nothing wrong with you; you are in a difficult place, but you always have the potential to recover. However, recovery does require truthful honesty and your willingness to engage in caring for your soul.

The journey of recovery from your history of paedophilic abuse is complicated because it is an experience that is felt within the core of your being, and is often compounded by a myriad of other experiences of indifference. You carry your pain as fear within yourself, so you become fearful of not being in control, and fearful of being in control. You become fearful of being vulnerable, exposed, talked about, shamed and of never being free from your internal torment. The fear entraps you in the carried victim energy and becomes an emotional prison. The way to resolve fear is to become informed and to bring what is hidden in the shadows out into full awareness.

We, as society, do not know how to respond to the reality of sexual abuse and often attempt to avoid the insidiousness of abuse and abusers. This can cause us to struggle to comprehend what the survivor of abuse tries to explain, which is often muffled by their fear and shame. We can overlook the ongoing suffering the survivor endures because it is so unfathomable. The survivor can be painted as damaged beyond our comprehension, which causes us to try to avoid the true impact abuse has on the individual, their family, their community and the fabric of society. Our avoidance of truth is derived from a fear of not knowing how to deal with the emotional, energetic and physical reality of sexual abuse. This fear becomes judgement, which can cause the innocent victim to attempt to hide from their own reality and become a runner who struggles to escape from the truth of their own unresolved emotions.

The stigma of sexual abuse can silence the victim, which is why society needs to be more informed and exposed to the reality of the long-lasting effects of abuse. Sexual abuse can cause the victim to experience anxiety, depression, oversensitivity, obsessions, unreasonable fears and uncontrollable compulsions. These are all symptoms of the fear engulfing the victim and from believing they are unable to escape what they want to run from, which is the emotional upheaval they feel within. This book was written to assist you to choose to stop running and instead walk towards what is within you that needs resolving. It was written with the intention of putting the jigsaw together, in the hope that you will no longer need to carry fear or be indifferent to the truth of your own natural significance, uniqueness, independence and individuality. The intention of this book is for you to use it as an assistant to clarity, and to use your clarity to release yourself from your own indifference to truth and the misconception that you need to remain permanently wounded and broken.

The information is intended to explain why the experience of abuse emotionally feels like it shattered your soul. I say "feels like" because the experience of abuse may have shattered your awareness of your soul, but your soul's consciousness remains unbroken, hidden beneath your self-judgement, hurt, shame and humiliation. It can be a long journey back to rediscover the natural essence of your soul, but it can also be exciting to awaken to the truth and strength of your soul. You will experience a myriad of emotions and feelings that can potentially expose truth to you. Please do not run, trust yourself to explore what is written and be kind to yourself.

You can become so locked into your survival mode that you condition yourself to avoid feeling the joy within your soul or your own natural compassion for yourself and others. As you discover pieces of your unique jigsaw, acknowledge the relief of finding what was previously hidden from you.

The information is confronting. There is no point in soft selling or hiding from the reality of the truth of paedophilia and the effects of carried victim energy. The information is intended to clarify the confusion, explain why the process of recovery is complicated and give hope to those who fear they will never feel safe or feel peaceful within themselves.

Chapter Two
Abuse of a soul

This information refers to all sexual abusers as paedophiles, even though there are subgroups within this collective. (The labels for age preferences are explained in the glossary.) Paedophilia is sexual interest and sexual activity that victimises a child. A paedophile is someone who is sexually interested in and willing to engage in sexual abuse of juveniles, especially children who lack the maturity or ability to protect themselves. Regardless of whether this is rape or molestation of a child, or the viewing of child exploitative material, those who operate with paedophilic energy are all using or supporting the extremes of indifference and control against their victim.

I have never felt an energy as insidious and as separated from truth as paedophilic energy, no matter the age preference of the abuser. It is the epitome of indifference, and created by the choice to operate from the manipulative slyness of their indifference to another soul. A paedophile is narcissistically engulfed by their own indifference. Paedophiles desire ultimate control over others; they desire the power surge they experience by having ultimate control of an innocent child, and feed their own ego by deriving a thrill out of manipulatively deceiving all those around the child. Paedophilia is the desire to disable an innocent child from feeling their own value, worth and significance as a soul of truth. Paedophilia is a person's choice to disregard everything except their own desire to create a surge of power using the energy of indifference. The sexual energy a paedophile craves is the sensation created by feeding their ego and feeling the surge of power they derive from the slyness of being able to sustain control over others and a situation. They inflict their debased desires on an innocent victim and revel in their ability to hide the truth of what they are doing from others.

People who entertain and immerse themselves in paedophilic energy, revel in their denial of the emotional, energetic and physical reality paedophilia creates. They fuel their indifference with denial of reality and are willing to abuse the innocence, beauty and significance of their victims. Paedophiles choose to override their awareness of their own souls' consciousness for an illusion of control, at the expense of another soul. A person with paedophilic tendencies becomes engulfed in their own cesspit of indifference to truth, which is a direct result of being unable to process the reality of their own life experiences or to acknowledge and accept the significance, uniqueness, independence and individuality of all souls. Paedophilia is the emotional, energetic, physical, mental and sexual abuse of another soul.

My understanding of paedophilia has come from feeling the truth of paedophilic energy when victims of paedophilia were willing to share the truth of their experiences with me. Through their truthfulness they exposed the results of paedophilia, the reality of indifference energy and the aftermath resulting from being a victim of abuse. A paedophile knowingly attacks the soul of another. The paedophile directly attacks the core of their victim's being, their soul's consciousness, with the intent of oppressing the victim's ability to feel their own natural significance, uniqueness, independence and individuality. Paedophiles opportunistically prey on the most vulnerable by abusing the soul of a child, expecting the child's initial response to be suppression and to deny how they feel. This traps fear within the child which is their constant background noise that they believe is inescapable. How do you come to terms with the shock, insidiousness and abhorrence of soul abuse when you haven't even had the chance or the time to develop your understanding of the foundation of who you are? The child is being robbed of their awareness of their natural core essences such as joy, hope, trust, grace and unconditional love.

The experience of paedophilia is unique to each child (soul). I have endeavoured to expose a broad spectrum of experiences, encompassing all aspects of the effects paedophilia has on victims, families, society and paedophiles. The paedophile seeks to incite fear reactions within their victim. Paedophilia is the epitome of indifference and exposes what some people are capable of when they become the embodiment of their own indifference. This information is intended to expose you to the truth of indifference. When truth is valued and not shunned, the paedophile loses their greatest protection; secrecy, silence, fear and shame are the paedophiles most important shields, because they allow the paedophile to remain manipulative. Secrecy, silence, fear and shame secure an arena for the paedophile to slyly operate from indifference. When the insidiousness of paedophilia is brought out into the open and truth is valued, it creates the opportunity to protect and nurture the innocent. The victim's greatest protection is to be visible, heard, cared for and nurtured, because indifference flourishes when people are complacent and apathetic about the value of truth.

It is highly likely you will have a reaction to this information, which may cause you to emotionally feel overwhelmed, energetically impacted and physically uncomfortable. When you feel the energetics of paedophilia you may become irritated and agitated, because we all instinctively fear indifference energy. Regardless of whether you are a victim of paedophilia, we have all experienced indifference energy. There are many different types of indifference, which people use to be manipulative and sly as they seek to gain ultimate control of another. Paedophilia is the end of the line for the embodiment of indifference, as it is an attack on the innocence of a child who is vulnerable and defenceless.

When reading this information allow yourself the grace to be honest about what your reactions are exposing to you; your reactions to indifference can expose your fear of indifference, your history of indifference and how you have utilised indifference. Paedophilia is indifference in the extreme, but as you read this information it will also highlight the different components of indifference we all use. It is your recognition and then acknowledgement of the different components of indifference that you use that allows you to embark on the complex process of resolving your own forms of indifference and the effect indifference has had on you. When you value the truth of your feelings, you allow yourself to explore the truth of indifference. When you accept the truth of your own indifference, you confront your fear of being indifferent to your soul. When you acknowledge the significance of your soul, you participate in the resolution of your automatic reactions to your own and others' indifference to truth. Your truthfulness about your awareness of indifference, bridges you back to honouring your natural significance, unconditional love and compassion for self.

There are many ramifications to being abused, one of which is your loss of awareness of your natural significance. However, it is a loss of awareness, not a loss of significance. Resolution of your carried victim energy, restores your awareness of your natural significance and unshackles you from the belief of 'not being good enough' to be significant. Denied fear morphs into indifference energy such as; resentment, guilt, shame or humiliation, which you can use to sustain your self-loathing, self-hatred and self-judgement. Self-loathing, self-hatred and self-judgement are the toxic residues of not being able to freely resonate with the truth of your soul and are sustained by your inability to comprehend the cause and effect of what you carry due to the abuse. Your carried victim energy causes you to remain stuck in the unfathomable void created by the abuse of your soul. Paedophilia is a sexual act that is not just an abuse of the body, it is also an abuse of the victim's soul.

The use of the word sexual in front of the word abuse has been purposely omitted from the majority of the writing, because it restricts the understanding of the magnitude and the extent of the effects caused by the abuse. Paedophilia is sexual, emotional, energetic, physical and mental abuse that attacks the essence of truth within a soul. Paedophilia is soul abuse. Paedophiles willingly abuse all aspects of an innocent soul for the purpose of self-gratification. Regardless of any attempt to deny it, the residue of paedophilic energy continues to impact until it is resolved, because it is a form of indifference to truth. The information is written with the intention to expose the long lasting effect abuse has on the victim, and to dissipate the fear generated by abuse that actually shields and inadvertently protects the paedophile.

Victims become survivors of abuse, and throughout this information the terms victim and survivors of abuse are used interchangeably. The term victim is used under the information about paedophiles and in current abuse situations, because paedophiles deliberately choose to victimise someone who is defenceless. However, there is a blurred line between victim and survivor as you cannot be one without the other. Each of these terms can be acknowledged together as they define how you experience abuse, first as a helpless child and then as a soul who has lived through the abuse. You did not choose to experience being either a victim or a survivor, however they are now both part of your reality and continue to impact how you live your life. Sexual abuse changes your experience of life, and the ramifications of your experience cannot be switched off by choosing which term you use to describe yourself. You are a victim because someone chose to deliberately hurt you and to commit a crime against you; you had no choice, you were unable to protect yourself, it was not your fault, you were victimised. You are a victim as the result of another's choice to use their insidious indifference against you. You are a survivor because despite your abuse ordeal, you continue to live, breathe and maintain your presence within your existence. Acknowledging yourself as a survivor does not dismiss the reality of being a victim, and acknowledging yourself as a victim does not diminish being a survivor. You, as the person who has been abused, get to decide when you no longer feel victimised by the long-lasting impact of the abuse history and when you want to see yourself as a survivor. The impact of sexual abuse is not an experience that you can wake up one day and be suddenly free from. The impact of the abuse will always be an intrinsic part of your experience of life and this is why the term 'victim' is used. However, 'victim' does not have to remain your only self-definition and this is why 'survivor of abuse' is also used. You are not limited by these terms or any other definition of yourself, you are a significant, unique, independent, individual soul, and discovering what that means to you is part of your natural recovery process.

Survivors of abuse are victims who have endured and survived the ordeal of abuse, and are coping or learning to cope with life, themselves and their history. Being a survivor is a process, because a soul can never be defined by one label or type of experience. Despite the trauma they have experienced, a survivor has managed to live through the ordeal of being a victim of another's indifference towards the natural value, worth and significance of who they are, and they have found the courage to survive. Although they may not realise the strength of their soul and struggle to come to terms with the reality of being a victim of abuse, they deserve admiration and respect for enduring that which many of us find unfathomable.

Due to the energetic impact of paedophilic energy, you may find you need to take breaks from reading the information to allow your emotional reactions to settle. If you feel distressed or overwhelmed, reach out to those who can hear, support and nurture you. There are many organisations, support groups and helplines that give practical and emotional assistance.

Section Two

Chapter Three
Indifference energy in the form of paedophilia

Paedophiles seek to destroy the truth within the innocence of a child; they do this to chase the sensation of ultimate control. Abuse comes in many forms, some paedophiles are manipulative and seductive, some are sadistic and revel in being brutal. Whatever abuse the victim endures, their experience of a paedophile always leaves an open wound of pain. The paedophile wants the sensation of gratifying their sexual desires by having ultimate control of another. Children are physically unable to protect themselves and are by nature trusting of adults; the paedophile plays on this and purposely chooses a child because they are the easiest to control and dominate with their perversions. Paedophiles use children's naivety to manipulate them into denying the truth they feel, which causes the child to override their natural instinct to seek help. This can cause the child to align to the belief of being worthless, and their own shock at what they are experiencing and their helplessness leaves them thinking there is no escape, which further disables their ability to determine who to turn to for help.

Some paedophiles use manipulation to dominate their victim and systematically oppress the child's ability to acknowledge the truth that they do not deserve to be treated in such a way. The paedophile creates distortions about the victim's value, worth and significance, which the victim becomes indoctrinated into believing. This creates doubt within the victims about their perception of reality. This doubt haunts the victims' understanding of themselves and their understanding of what they are experiencing or what they have experienced. The victim can become confused about what reality is, and fear not being able to quell their own doubt, fear and anxiety, which is exacerbated by their inability to accept their natural value, worth and significance. The victim's doubt about their own value, worth and significance is carried into all other experiences and infiltrates their ability to trust themselves as a soul. Their inability to trust themselves causes them to disconnect from the truth they feel. This can cause some victims to become codependent on the paedophiles' manipulation of reality, and they can succumb to wanting to believe that what is occurring is not abuse, to create an escape from the internal torture of their own self-judgement and their fear of their reality.

Some paedophiles manipulate those around the child to believe they are honourable, and may at first manipulate the victim to get them alone. However, once they initiate their attack, they do not seek compliance but derive a thrill out of brutally raping the child every opportunity they get. These paedophiles are experts in cornering the child and delight in their own brutality. The paedophile controls their environment, which means the victim is left fearing the savagery of their attacker, as well as believing that there is little chance to seek help.

Paedophiles leave an emotional, energetic and physical stain on their victim's soul. Some paedophiles want to leave a residue of their indifference and malice for the victim to contend with as a way of oppressing and burying the victim's awareness of the truth of themselves. Paedophiles inflict their indifference and seek to be an authority over their victims' perception of themselves. They are determined to distort the victim's sense of their reality. These paedophiles seek to control their victims' perception of what is occurring as well as altering how the victim will perceive their abuse later. The paedophile wants their victim to carry a piece of their indifference as a constant reminder that they had control over them.

If the paedophile is someone the child depends on for survival and who the child wants to be loved by, such as a parent, grandparent, sibling, relative or guardian, the child may feel the need to distort their own perception of reality, to maintain their ability to believe the paedophile is someone who loves and cares for them. In an attempt to sustain their illusion of the paedophile as someone who loves them, some children blame themselves for the abuse and sacrifice their own innocence, taking on and carrying the indifference they feel from the paedophile as an assessment of their own value, worth and significance. For example, the child may want to retain an illusion about their parent, which leaves them distorting their own understanding of the reality of their parent in an attempt to survive, and suppress the indifference felt from the one who they most expected to be loved by. The child attempts to focus on the belief of what a parent should be, because they want to override their awareness of what their parent actually is when no one is watching.

Some paedophiles want to dictate what the victim should have as memories and create illusions to conceal the truth of their actions, often bombarding their victim with tales of good times, while omitting the reality of their abuse. Some paedophiles attempt to control via confusion, distorting facts and often debating what the victim remembers. The victim also becomes confused by the myriad of images they watch the paedophile portray, and realises the image the paedophile performs is determined by who the paedophile wants to impress. As the victim experiences all of the paedophile's images, they at times doubt their own experience of being sexually abused, as they too want to believe in the wholesome image often portrayed. Some victims desperately want to believe there is good in what attacks them, which means they try to convince themselves their abuse is not real, or that it is justified. This means some victims begin to believe it is easier to succumb to a lie than acknowledge the truth, which causes them to become extremely judgemental of themselves. Many victims attempt to use their negative self-judgement as a mechanism to understand what is occurring, blaming themselves and believing they are worthless because the reality of the abuse is incomprehensible.

Some victims create an illusion to conceal the truth of their abuse from themselves. This contributes to the victim's disassociation from reality, even at the time of being abused. The victim can disassociate from feeling reality into an illusory world within their mind to hide from feeling the full force of the experience of the abuse and abuser. Some victims feel themselves disassociating from the experience of abuse and some can consciously observe the abuse from afar, creating a surreal sensation in an attempt to protect themselves. Others can disassociate to the point of complete withdrawal and disconnection from what is occurring. However, the energetic residue of the paedophile's indifference to the abuse they have perpetrated, infiltrates victims' understanding of themselves. They can manifest a veil of denial to avoid feeling infiltrated, which can inadvertently oppress their awareness of being a significant soul. The victim then becomes lost in the emotional labyrinths they create to avoid the truth of their own feelings and awareness of their abuse.

Disassociation from reality creates a fog that becomes a memory haze during and after the abuse. Disassociation from feeling creates a disbelief of the reality being experienced. However, the inability to completely deny what is occurring during the abuse creates emotional and energetic shock, which is carried until resolved. Some victims can feel the paedophile's indifference for their soul. This emotionally and energetically shocks victims, which manifests as carried confusion and disdain for themselves. The experience of abuse deceptively becomes an anchor point for all existing unresolved emotions as well as the unresolved emotions created by the abuse. Some victims attempt to deny reality, which creates emotional labyrinths they use to counteract feeling the truth of their own unresolved emotions. This causes them to spiral further into the energy of their soul's unconsciousness, losing their will to be aware of their soul's consciousness.

The victim's emotional labyrinths are attempted avoidance pathways they use to suppress the truth of their emotions, which actually sustains their denial and confusion. The victim's denial and confusion sustains the unresolved emotions they refuse to acknowledge or do not know how to resolve. The victim has triggers, which create a sequence of emotional reactions and responses that reinforce the carried emotional and energetic shock. The victim fears (often unconsciously) feeling their own emotional and energetic shock. This causes the victim to want to sustain any emotional and energetic barrier to the truth of their own experience. They believe they are protecting themselves from feeling the indifference energy they fear, except they become indifferent to the truth of themselves and become immersed in the protection of their denial. This enables their internal fear and embedded negative beliefs about their own value, worth and significance to fester.

Some victims try to suppress feeling the indifference of the abuser during the abuse, as well as trying to suppress the shock of their reality. When victims disassociate from reality they create veils of denial, in an attempt to protect themselves from feeling the paedophile's evil indifference and sadistic oppression. Some paedophiles' obsession for control is generated from their compulsion to act out the toxic residue carried from their own experience of being a victim of paedophilia. These paedophiles have become what they once despised.

Some survivors of abuse desperately want to protect themselves from feeling the reality of indifference energy and create automatic emotional reactions and responses to feeling indifference energy. This can trigger them to become anxious or paralysed with fear whenever they feel indifference energy. Some survivors attempt to become indifferent and numb to their reaction to indifference, believing their own indifference will shield them from having to experience others' indifference. This can often leave them attempting to avoid their own awareness of their present moment, their reality, their past, their feelings and their fears, believing they can shield themselves from their memories of their experience or experiences of abuse. Some survivors of abuse programme themselves to emotionally shut down and oppose feeling the truth of any experience, fearing they will be unable to control their emotional backlog if they allow themselves to be present within their life experiences. They programme themselves to create charades to hide from feeling the truth of their past and present life experiences, and become their own oppressor, even though they believe they are protecting themselves.

Some survivors attempt to suppress the emotional trauma within themselves with addictions. Their addictions become a way of believing they can control the emotional, energetic and physical barriers they use to avoid acknowledging the truth of their feelings, reality, history, images of themselves and illusions of reality. These survivors of abuse use their images, illusions and addictions to counteract being present in their reality. The survivor can become obsessed with attempting to anticipate what will affect, expose or create more emotional pain. The use of emotional, energetic and physical barriers to truth allows the survivor of abuse to attempt to sustain their own disassociation from feeling their reality and from feeling their awareness of their own history. They numb themselves to reality, anchoring to images of themselves and illusions of reality in an attempt to be devoid of feeling. However, they internally fear losing their ability to sustain their own disassociation from feeling, and this creates a constant struggle from within to suppress their own feelings and awareness of truth. The survivor's addictions are the result of the constant struggle within. These addictions become emotional, energetic and physical traps, which sustain their emotional pain.

Some survivors of abuse fear the loss of their denial, because they have the misconception that their denial keeps them safe from their own unresolved emotions. The survivor's incessant mind chatter manifests from the attempted suppression of their unresolved emotions and desire to repress their own negative beliefs about themselves. The survivor seeks to control the impact their mind chatter has on their ability to deny how their abuse is affecting their experience of life. Some survivors of abuse endeavour to control their mind chatter and become obsessed with their own thoughts. Some survivors' mind chatter is an awareness of their unresolved emotions within their soul's unconsciousness. They become consumed with their obsession to defiantly oppose accepting the truth of their own emotional, energetic and physical reality. Some survivors try to use their mind chatter to repress their awareness of their soul consciousness' ability to guide them to the opportunity for resolution of their unresolved emotions. Our soul's consciousness can guide us to opportunities to be truthful and it is our truthfulness that resolves carried victim energy. The survivor's mind chatter becomes a way of anchoring to the isolation created by their separation from their awareness of their soul and disassociation from feeling truth.

Some survivors of abuse who attempt to hide from their internal reality, suppress their awareness of truth and ruminate about different scenarios of abuse in their mind. They are attempting to alter their perception of reality or to perfect their ability to conceal how they feel about their own past. Survivors of abuse who hide from their reality attempt to deal with their emotional pain with more deceptive emotions, often fighting the reality of their own existence. Some survivors who hide from their reality can attempt to relieve themselves from the frustration of being trapped in their own emotional world by being abusive towards themselves, their siblings, parents, others and pets. Some survivors are swamped with their own emotional torment and the belief that they can hide from their unresolved emotions and memories. This actually immerses them in the fear of confronting the horror of the abuse, which leaves them stagnating in their fear, opposing their own significance.

The paedophile's attitude

Some paedophiles obsess about suppressing their own mind chatter, because their mind chatter exposes the truth of their indifference to children and the ramifications of being an abuser. They justify their own arrogance to themselves with lies and deception. Paedophiles use lies and deception as part of their own seduction of themselves, which can only be sustained by remaining indifferent to acknowledging the equality of all souls and that every soul is significant. Paedophiles use their indifference as a barrier to truth that maintains an emotional, energetic and physical place where they can override their awareness of their soul niggling their conscience about their own indifference, sexual depravity and desire for control.

Due to the indifference and sexual depravity of the paedophile, there is a general perception that a paedophile is easily identified and often thought to be a gruff, creepy, dirty, old man. This is a fallacy; paedophiles cannot be stereotyped, as they are within all personality types, cultures, professions, socio-economic levels, genders and ages. However, they all belong to the same energetic collective of indifference. Our general misconception can aid the deceptive sham the paedophile hides behind. Some paedophiles revel in being seen as model citizens, at the same time as being actively anti-establishment and disregarding society's moral codes for how to engage with children. They arrogantly believe they are entitled to be an authority over whatever and whomever they desire to control. Paedophiles delight in their ability to slyly remain undetected. Paedophiles believe they have the right to determine how a particular child should be treated and view children as commodities that they can use as their merchandise, with a complete disregard for the child's soul. Paedophiles revel in their indifference, believing they are beyond having to take responsibility and accountability for their own actions. Part of a paedophile's thrill is to knowingly abuse the freewill of their victim and deny the ramifications resulting from their decision to abuse an innocent child. Paedophiles deprive and rob innocent children of their freewill and seek to impact their victim's experience of life. The ramifications of paedophilia have long-lasting effects on the victim and insidiously reverberate throughout society.

Some paedophiles delight in exposing their victim to the insidious nature of indifference, knowing it will be an intricate part of how the victim oppresses themselves. The paedophile indoctrinates their victims to be anti-themselves, which leaves them fighting truth and opposing their own natural significance. The paedophile surmises that once the victim is immersed in struggling human energy and the belief that they are 'not good enough', they can be assured the victim will be silenced. The paedophile takes pride in being able to select a victim they can easily silence and derives a thrill out of believing that they are secure within the victim's silence and have got away with the abuse.

Struggling human

The victim's experience of abuse turns into their own immersion in struggling human energy, facilitated by their own heresy against themselves. This causes the victim to be:

- Anti-the existence of their own soul
- Anti-the truth of their soul journey
- Anti-their opportunity for resolution
- Anti-their own intention for evolution
- Anti-being present and honest with their reality
- Anti-this lifetime

All of this causes the victim to become a struggling human and to carry this as their identity.

Examples of victims immersed in struggling human energy:

- Victims can be anti-their own existence and resent being born. This entraps them in an emotional cycle that deprives them of feeling the significance of who they naturally are, constantly aligning themselves to self-destructive behaviours.
- Victims can be anti-their opportunity for resolution and remain stuck in repetitively assigning self-blame and operating from shame. This entraps them in an emotional cycle that deprives them of peace and obliterates any feeling of joy as they constantly fixate on the negativities of life.
- Victims can be anti-being present in their reality, becoming oppositional to everything they encounter. This entraps them in an emotional cycle that deprives them of clarity and of feeling free, which means they constantly override their ability and willingness to accept reality.

Victims' indifference to their truth concretises their unwillingness to express the truth of themselves and deprives them of feeling the core essences of their soul. Victims can fear judgement, which creates barriers to truth that sustain their struggles with life, themselves, the abuse, relationships and reality. The victim emotionally feels isolated and desolated in their own despair, trapped in confusion and their own harsh self-judgement.

How paedophiles operate

Paedophiles operate in different forms. Although their motives are the same, they all seek to emotionally feel ultimate control of another soul. Paedophiles protect images of themselves and seek to conceal their slyness with lies. They become master manipulators because they derive great pride out of their conniving ability to manipulate so deceptively. Some paedophiles are proud of their own arrogance and celebrate validating their illusion that they cannot be interfered with by truth or any type of mankind authority. These paedophiles pride themselves on being able to covertly control and deflect anyone who believes they can stop or hinder the paedophile's perceived right to do as they please, with whoever they please. The paedophile may completely disregard anyone who becomes suspicious and questions their behaviour, and will seek to control the situation back to their status quo, arrogantly believing that they can dictate how everyone should respond to their control.

Paedophiles are hunters. Part of the thrill of the hunt is to look for and choose their victim. They choose their victim by using a selection criteria that assesses their intended prey's vulnerability to being controlled. Paedophiles determine the risk of being exposed and examine the surroundings and the awareness of those connected to the child they prey upon. Paedophiles test the waters and energetically determine which style of approach to use. Part of a paedophile's insolent behaviour is to use their ability to assess the unresolved emotions of their victim, determining how to manipulate their victim's internal alert system to danger, in order to secure opportunities for the gratification of the paedophile's desires. The paedophile grooms the victim to doubt and override their own internal alert system. The paedophile tries to alleviate the victim's fears and to counteract their ability to be suspicious of the paedophile. Not all paedophiles groom their victims, some prefer to sadistically attack, while they groom the adults connected to the victim. They want the adults to believe they are morally sound and someone they can trust.

The conniving manipulation used to groom those they prey upon becomes an exciting mind game for the paedophile. They slyly delight in exploring how good they are at manipulating and creating an environment conducive for their sexual gratification. Paedophiles challenge and test themselves on what they can get away with and justify their manipulation to themselves with lies. Once the paedophile has assessed who their victim is, they believe they have ownership over the reality of the child and become fixated on their devious intention to groom the child out of any of their self-protection mechanisms. The paedophile attempts to groom the child to be responsive to their manipulation. They become hunters who reject moral boundaries and ethics because these would limit or expose the insidious truth of their actions. Paedophiles are opportunists, and manipulation is the tool they use to justify their indifference to the truth of their actions, beliefs and thoughts. Paedophiles are narcissistically consumed with their sly delight in believing they can get away with abuse, while overriding the abhorrent nature of the abuse they are willing to carry out on an innocent child.

Paedophiles disregard the effect they have on their victims and the hideous ramifications the abuse has on the remainder of a victim's life. Paedophiles disregard the effect they have on a victim's family, future partners, friends, children and the cost to society. They are totally indifferent to being the cause of mental illness, depression, self-harm, drug and alcohol abuse, crime and suicide. A paedophile's indifference, mixed with their selfishness, is a lethal combination that creates a narcissistic person, completely driven by their desire to have ultimate control to gratify their own depraved desires.

Paedophiles are complex with varying degrees of intelligence, denial and indifference. Some act out their compulsions and implode with guilt, shame and humiliation, which leaves them feeling out of control. The sense of control they get from abusing a child creates a temporary relief from the guilt, shame and humiliation they feel. This becomes an addictive cycle where they offend again to pacify and gratify their compulsions, regardless of the carnage created. Some paedophiles can emotionally feel like a victim to their own compulsions and justify their actions by believing they are powerless against their desire for sexual gratification at the expense of an innocent child.

Some paedophiles are creepers, sneaking into a sleeping child's bedroom. When the child awakes to the abuse, the shock is so inconceivable they disassociate, and their memories of abuse can be dream-like. Some victims associate their abuse with memories of seeing dark shadows, feeling a presence above them, feeling pressure upon them, smelling odours or feeling physical sensations while being too frightened to look. The victim compartmentalises the abuse experience and only retain vivid memories of different sensations, denying the entirety of their experience. Victims may use denial to protect themselves during their abuse, because they want to disassociate from the reality of their experience preferring to believe it is a recurring nightmare. The child has an inability to cope with or comprehend the experience of abuse; what is occurring is unfathomable to them and disassociation from reality becomes an automatic survival mechanism.

Some paedophiles reject intimacy with an adult, frightened of being judged as inadequate and emotionally feel safer with a child they believe they can control to succumb to the illusion the paedophile wants to construct. The paedophile can go to extreme effort to construct environments conducive to their need for control and conducive to supplying easy accessibility to a child. They often want the child to join their illusory version of love and are anxious about the child discovering the truth of their manipulation and insecurities. These paedophiles deny and avoid the carnage they cause and relentlessly cling to their own distorted belief of loving the child. These paedophiles are dangerous because they believe in their own innocence, and become obsessive about the child and possessive of their relationship with the child. Some paedophiles create illusions within their mind to conceal the truth of their actions, existing in a state of denial, denying and disregarding the pain they cause and the insidiousness of their actions.

Some paedophiles distort their perception of reality and do not associate themselves with the truth that they are a paedophile, falsely believing they are not hurting anyone. In their distorted manipulation of truth, they believe that they have found a deeper love that many cannot handle and that is why society frowns upon their lifestyle. Paedophiles use their distorted beliefs to justify their sense of entitlement that they can coerce an innocent child to endure their sexual and abusive cravings. Some paedophiles use their distorted beliefs to deny the reality of their cravings and compartmentalise their abusive behaviour as separate from who they are, as they attempt to exist straddling their construction of two worlds. Paedophiles ignore the soul carnage created by their selfishness and indifference, and attempt to distance themselves from the true ramifications of their hidden abusive behaviour. However, everyone around the paedophile, regardless of which constructed world they are connected to, becomes covertly and often unknowingly ensnared in the hideousness of the paedophile's deceptive manipulation.

Some paedophiles create an illusory reality in their mind, believing they love the child so much that they cannot help themselves and that the child needs, wants and thrives in the secret world the paedophile creates. If the child's body has a sexual response, the paedophile uses this as evidence that the child is willing and contributing to the experience, regardless of any evidence to the contrary. The paedophile uses their false assessment of the victim to sustain their indifference to the truth that they are victimising an innocent child.

Abuse is a multifaceted experience

If the child's body has a sexual response, the victim becomes very confused by their body's response. This adds to their fear of disclosing the abuse to others, and becomes part of the internal shame they carry. This internalised shame the victim carries causes them to debate that they are actually innocent, and they filter their own awareness of their experience of being sexually abused through the distortion of believing they are guilty of causing the abuse. The carried shame alters how victims perceive themselves and tarnishes their own perception of their innocence and significance. Unfortunately, it may take years, if ever, for victims to realise they should not carry shame as a definition of themselves, they were not the instigator they were the innocent victim. The shame they carry is entwined with their inability to readily assign all responsibility to the paedophile for the abuse they endured. This is because the abuse experience has distorted their perception, and often left them believing they are worthless. Some victims may underestimate the huge ramifications resulting from falsely believing they were in some way responsible for their abuse. This belief distorts victims' perception of the abuse, their perception of the paedophile's accountability and their perception of themselves.

As victims becomes older they distort their perception of what they could have done to help themselves at the time of their abuse, often believing they should have fought back, while omitting the truth of their age, size and situation. This can become mental torture that survivors of abuse use to plague themselves, which has them denying the innocence of being a child. This can reinforce beliefs of 'not being good enough' because they could not protect themselves, which inhibits the survivor from accepting that at that young age there was nothing they could have done to prevent the abuse.

If the child is young enough to be pre-verbal they have no words to describe what they are experiencing and emotionally feeling, and apart from the abuser, the people around the child have no way of comprehending why the child is emotionally reactive.

For example, if the child is being abused in their cot, the cot will trigger an emotional fear reaction from the child. The paedophile knows that others will not automatically be suspicious of sexual abuse and will seek to explain the child's reaction using normal child development such as teething. Nightmare images are the only way the child can process what they are feeling and their memories may be explained as nightmares when they are older. However, something will not feel right to them and they are left with a constant unexplained undercurrent of uneasiness and confusion.

This constant unexplained undercurrent of uneasiness and confusion can be experienced by victims who have been abused when they were too young to comprehend what was happening, those who have been drugged for the purpose of abuse and those children who have been awoken to the abuse from a deep sleep.

The truth is, victims internally carry the energy of abuse whether they were fully conscious at the time of the abuse or not. Victims who are drugged by the paedophile, carry the residue of abuse with intense confusion. Sexual abuse leaves a residual energy and victims can often misinterpret the residual energy as a definition of themselves. The residual energy creates an internal insecurity, which the victim mistakes as part of who they are. Victims can focus on their fear of their insecurity, and attempt to control themselves to avoid the confusion of not understanding what they feel. The confusion of not understanding how and why they feel the way they do, creates an internal battle with their emotional ravine of suppressed unresolved emotions. Victims can struggle to identify their emotions and this causes them to look for escape routes such as drugs, alcohol or sexual promiscuity. Victims can misinterpret what they are feeling because of their inability to label and assess their suppressed unresolved emotions and the origins of these emotions. They judge their suppressed unresolved emotions as proof of their internal failing and judge themselves as inadequate to cope with their own emotional state. This causes victims to bombard themselves with judgement and control structures in an attempt to control and suppress the unidentified, unresolved emotional energy they feel.

When victims bombard themselves with judgement, they create an emotional labyrinth of self-loathing. The victim uses their judgement to create a non-winnable cycle of oppressing the truth of who they are with self-sabotaging patterns, which sustain their own indifference to their natural value, worth and significance. Victims can create a relentless competition against the truth of themselves to suppress their awareness of reality. Victims can compete with reality to test their ability to appease their own desire for control; they want to either dissipate the intensity of their own self-loathing and hatred or justify their judgement of themselves. Victims use the emotional energy created within this cycle to keep devaluing the truth of themselves and the reality of their abuse. Victims can turn on themselves with self-blame, guilt, shame and humiliation, debilitating their ability to have an honest assessment of themselves, others, reality and the abuse. This fuels the intensity of the victim's own self-loathing and hatred, which the victim uses to justify their self-sabotage and struggling human energy.

They become willing to be:

- Anti-their own soul
- Anti-their own soul truth
- Anti-existing in this lifetime
- Anti-their own opportunity for resolution
- Anti-their own potential for evolution
- Anti-being present in their own reality

Some victims sustain their self-hatred by retaining the indifference they felt during the abuse; this is the stain the survivors of abuse feel within themselves. Victims can create an emotional chasm of indifference against the truth of their own soul. They feel they are carrying a stain on their soul, because they mistakenly took the indifference they felt during their abuse as an assessment of their worth. This is a distortion created from the victims' confusion and shock at the indifference one soul can have for another.

The intensity of what the victims feel causes them to implode in their own inability to control the indifference they have felt and perpetuated within themselves. They emotionally shut down and separate from their awareness of their soul, willing to disassociate from feeling truth, to hide in the abyss of their insecurities. This causes some victims to anchor to their ability to disassociate from feeling their reality and immerse themselves in the energy of indifference. Their disassociation from feeling reality causes them to become detached, aloof and rageful. Their disassociation from feeling the truth of their own feelings causes them to be scared of life, unconditional love, truth and their emotional reality. They become stuck in an emotional and energetic idle; emotionally frozen in their own indifference against the truth of their natural value, worth and significance. They use their awareness of the presence of indifference to be indifferent to their own truth. The victim has created emotional cycles that originated from their abuse experience and awareness of their abuser's indifference to them. These cycles continue because the victims cannot comprehend their own indifference to themselves.

Some victims are confused by their reactions and responses to abuse, not realising what is being triggered within themselves, because they have become so disassociated from their own emotional reality. The victim emotionally feels their disassociation as a trance-like, surreal sensation and adopts this as an escape mechanism. The victim uses their ability to disassociate from feeling truth to counteract being overwhelmed by their own confusion; it is a way of numbing their senses to the trauma of their internal emotional torment. The victim is unaware that by anchoring to a constant state of disassociation they are creating their own emotional torment and all aspects of life can then become overwhelming.

Some victims use their thought process to analyse their judgement of reality and are constantly assessing and reassessing their comprehension of reality. This is part of the cycle they attempt to use to protect themselves from experiencing the sensation of losing control, which is what they experienced during their abuse. However, the continuity of their own judgement and their reluctance to trust themselves to feel, causes them to be insecure about their own perception. This insecurity leaves victims immersed in their emotional torment, and their solution to this never-ending cycle of self-abuse is to bury themselves in their own denial of reality. This means some victims remain indifferent to the truth of themselves, and cling to their own illusion of control regardless of the inefficiency of their control. Some victims become indifferent to the reality they create for themselves and remain trapped in their own never-ending cycle of self-abuse. What they try to control ends up controlling them.

The survivor of abuse may succeed in suppressing their conscious memory with their denial, but this denial is unsustainable and the effect of the abuse will manifest, often obscurely, in different aspects of the survivor's life. Different memories may later be triggered by experiencing similar physical, mental, sexual, emotional or energetic sensations as those trapped in the survivor's suppressed memories of abuse. The survivor often automatically suppresses what they feel and denies their triggered reaction to these sensations. They then exert all their effort into denying their own awareness, and this disassociates them from their emotional reality. They want to believe there is a way of securing control over their denial and the suppression of their unresolved emotions. The survivor unconsciously elects to exist, struggling against their own automatic reactions, responses and indifference, at the same time as disregarding the impact their denial and suppression is having on the way they live their life. The survivor attempts to sustain their denial by disassociating from what they feel, which leaves them feeling confused, often numb and consistently aware of their own background fear.

Some survivors react with panic, fear and anxiety when they cannot control the sensations they feel, that remind them of their abuse. They may not be clear about what, in their present moment situation, has triggered the sensations they are unable to control, or why they are so reactive to the sensations they feel. This leaves them engulfed in confusion and fear. Confusion becomes their norm and they end up systematically abusing themselves with their own unresolved emotions, because they believe they should be in complete control of their emotions and fears. Some survivors can carry the belief that if they could have controlled their fear at the time of the abuse, they either would not have been abused or could have done something about it. This becomes a way of crucifying themselves and believing that it was their fault that they were abused. This is a complete falsity and is why the ramifications of paedophilia are so catastrophic to the victim who becomes a survivor of abuse. One such catastrophic ramification is when innocent souls turn on themselves, believing they have no other option.

Guilt, shame and humiliation become constant emotional foes that the survivor battles with as they blame themselves for not being able to have a sense of peace. Emotional triggers cause survivors of abuse to engulf themselves in confusion about their own understanding of themselves, and they lose their awareness of being a significant, unique, independent, individual soul of *True Source Divine Origin Consciousness*. This is catastrophic because it means they identify themselves as someone who is not worthy of discovering, exploring or expressing the truth of who they are. Some survivors identify themselves as unworthy, because they have experienced the indifference of the paedophile's willingness to abuse them and emotionally feel scarred by experiencing the insidiousness of the paedophile's desire to have ultimate control over them. This means they have conditioned themselves to give their abuser the power to determine their worth and become trapped in the vicious cycle of believing the abuse is what defines them. This is a fallacy; none of us are defined just by our experiences.

The survivor of abuse remains shocked at the indifference they have felt during the abuse experience, and this causes them to disassociate from the reality of being a significant soul. The disassociation is felt as a surreal sensation and disorientates the survivor's sense of reality, which impairs their ability to acknowledge truth. During the abuse experience, the paedophile uses the victim's shock to manipulate their perception of reality. This leaves the victim believing they are completely entrapped by the paedophile's control. The paedophile seeks to confuse the victim about the reality of the abuse and the paedophile's capacity to control the victim's life. Some paedophiles will seek to convince the victim that the victim is to blame, which causes the victim to become entrapped in the cycle of believing they are guilty for everything they experience. This cycle of guilt is then automatically used by the survivor to deflect the truth of reality and to avoid confronting the truth of their own unresolved emotions.

The victim's ability to trust their own perception of reality is corrupted by the paedophile deceptively anchoring their manipulation to the confusion the victim is already feeling. This is a control structure used by the paedophile that activates an emotional see-saw within the victim about what reality is, which causes the victim to doubt their own perception of reality and stay immersed in a constant state of shock. The victim is indoctrinated to emotionally believe they are powerless within the presence of the paedophile and the energy of paedophilia. The paedophile's desire to control shrouds the victim in indifference energy, which becomes the energy the victim fears most.

Orchestrating denial

Some paedophiles seek to undermine the integrity of the victim by manipulating them with confusion. Any questions asked by the victim are met with a barrage of confusing and often contradictory answers. This is part of the paedophile's control structure of immersing the victim in various types of denial, lies and illusions. Some paedophiles orchestrate denial for the victim to adopt, which manifests as emotional torment within the victim's mind chatter as they ruminate on what has been said to them, trying to figure out what was true, what was deceptive and what was the paedophile's intention. The victim's mind chatter becomes overwhelming, because they are constantly fighting against what they want to believe, their ability to acknowledge the truth of what they are feeling and their own awareness of truth. The internal battle can intensify for the victim when they attempt to assess and justify the reality of their own confusion. The desire to protect their orchestrated denial creates more confusion within the victim, and this leaves them more susceptible to the paedophile's manipulation. Orchestrated denial creates voids within the victim's memories, which become emotional barriers to accepting the truth of the abuse they have experienced.

Orchestrated denial is the willingness to confabulate a story you tell yourself, that may have elements of truth, but has omitted what you believe is confronting or an interference to controlling your own denial of reality. Denial of reality is a type of indifference to truth that ensures you sustain separation from your awareness of your soul and truth. It also secures your disassociation from feeling the truth of yourself within reality. Denial of reality eventually leads you to being anti-yourself, at the same time as being resentful of your own self-deception.

Orchestrated denial inhibits the victims from feeling their own individuality. Victims engulf themselves in the indifference energy they feel, identifying themselves as someone who either deserves abuse or who will never escape the trauma of abuse. The victim incorporates the paedophiles' indifference as part of their identity, losing awareness of the purity of who they are. When a victim feels indifference energy and seeks to control what they feel with denial, they often revert to harsh self-judgement. Their own harsh self-judgement annihilates any sense of self-worth as they deny their own natural significance, uniqueness, independence and individuality.

Some paedophiles go to great lengths to create internal confusion within the victim, and part of the thrill of the paedophile's devious manipulation is to undermine the victim's perception of their own mental state. The paedophile will do and say whatever they deem necessary to achieve control over the victim's perception. The victim also has to contend with the paedophile's energetic intimidation, which the victim interprets as meaning they have no choice but to remain silent during and after the abuse. The victim has an automatic fear reaction to the energetic intimidation, and even at a very young age understands and fears that there will be consequences if the abuse does not remain a secret. This leaves them believing their only recourse is to exist in their own emotionally tortured secret world.

Some paedophiles arrogantly believe they can remain undetected and free to do as they please, and actually indoctrinate the victim into believing this is a true assessment of reality. The victim is so tormented and overwhelmed by the arrogance of the paedophile that they believe they are powerless to expose the truth. The paedophile manipulates the victim to succumb to the belief that no one would believe or help them if they were to expose the truth. This demoralises the victim's sense of self-worth and cages them in the fear that they are perceived as unworthy by everyone.

Some paedophiles arrogantly go to great lengths and patiently set up a perceived safe emotional arena, in which they can groom the victim to trust them, while hiding their malicious intent. The paedophile orchestrates pulling the victim from the safe arena into progressively more malicious arenas. The paedophile sets up the arenas to instigate a charade for the victim to enact, and the victim is unaware that it is the charade that hides the truth of the paedophile's intentions. In the early arenas where the victim is trusting the paedophile and has yet to be abused, the paedophile orchestrates for the child to crave their attention. When the paedophile believes the victim has completely succumbed to what they are orchestrating, the paedophile makes their next move and pulls the victim into a more dangerous arena. The paedophile is constantly striving to get to the end game which is sexual abuse. Their ability to deceptively run these initial manipulative charades and secure the stepping stone of each arena they orchestrate, is part of the paedophile's thrill of the chase. By the time the victim realises that they are in danger, it is often too late.

Charades

Some experiences of paedophilia instigates a craving within the victim to control their abuser's indifference by using sexual energy. In an attempt to suppress their own humiliation, some victims may feel compelled by the craving to align to charades that are used to hide the truth of what is occurring. This becomes very confusing for the victim because they can be manipulated into emotionally existing in a love-hate relationship with the sexual abuse and the abuser. Some victims feel an excitement in the sexual energy or even from their own nervous tension, and then implode within the reality of indifference and manipulation. These victims use their own momentary excitement as a weapon against themselves and may not acknowledge that they have been sexualised when they were too young to comprehend the reality of being sexualised. Being sexualised means that you are aware of the control that can be exerted over another by using sexual energy. Sexual energy can become a means of controlling another's indifference. However, the victim is also aware of their own implosion of guilt, shame and humiliation when they try to control their own or another's indifference by using their sexual energy.

Some victims fear the truth of their reality and find it easier to align to the charade the paedophile orchestrates to conceal the reality of the abuse. When victims continue to align to the charade, they believe they are keeping themselves safe from the insidious indifference they feel. The charade becomes what they believe is protecting them and they suppress the fear and hurt they feel with their belief that they have no alternative but to protect the charade. This type of abuse creates long term mental torture as the victim becomes the protector of the paedophile, believing they need to protect the charade to conceal their own hurt. The victim fears the loss of the charade and will often refuse to accept that they have been abused. The victim is conditioned to help the paedophile protect and uphold the paedophile's image of being beyond reproach. Children have an innate tendency to feel everything is their fault. An example of this is when parents separate, often the child assumes it is their fault. Only as children mature and develop their independence do they realise they are not to blame. The paedophile's manipulation and abuse interferes with the child's developmental maturity and independence, which leaves them with a very distorted view of themselves.

Some victims align to the paedophile's orchestrated charades, succumbing to the illusions that conceal the reality of the paedophile and the truth of the abuse. Some victims fear the exposure of reality as much as the paedophile, because they want to conceal the humiliation they feel, which was created from and is the residue they carry from the experience of being abused. Some victims remain silent about their abuse because they fear compounding the indifference they have experienced, with the indifference of others' judgement. These victims live in an anxious state of trying to hide from having their reality exposed, fearing their own inability to control or cope with the unjustified stigma associated with being abused. The victim is in a constant state of trying to judge, analyse and assess what they can and cannot control. The victim's disassociation from reality has them obsessing about their ability to be right in their judgement, which creates emotional patterns of torment with their judgment, analysis and assessment of themselves, life, their emotions and the abuse. The victims' judgement of themselves becomes a domineering mind chatter that overshadows their ability to be present within their present moment. The victims' incessant mind chatter can leave them believing they are crazy and insignificant to the world.

Some paedophiles enforce the victim's compliance to their orchestrated charades with various threats of harm to the victim's loved ones, or threats to the victim's life, or by creating an illusion of how the victim will be judged if they disclose the abuse. Some paedophiles have their victim so confused that the threat to not love them is enough to coerce them into complying with the paedophile's control over them. These victims have been conditioned to align to the manipulative illusion the paedophile projects to conceal the reality of the paedophile's vulnerability. These threats and manipulation have the victim taking on the responsibility of concealing the reality of abuse, and this is also part of the abuse. This sense of responsibility compacts the victim's denial of being a victim and disorientates them into believing they are responsible for the abuse. This is the cunning way the paedophile manipulates the victim into believing they are to blame, as well as extracting any ability the victim has to be compassionate for themselves.

Using gifts can be part of the devious manipulation of the paedophile; they often use gifts in an attempt to alter their victims' understanding of themselves and the reality of the abuse. The paedophile uses gifts to confuse the victim and others about the true nature of the relationship between the paedophile and their victim. Some paedophiles use gifts and outings as a way of compounding the victim's confusion about the reality of what they are experiencing, often causing the victim to feel sickened at having to receive rewards from the paedophile. The paedophile can use these gifts to ensure there is a constant reminder of the emotional control the paedophile has over the victim, even when the paedophile is not present. Unfortunately, for these victims the confusion builds up and causes great anxiety. The anxiety is caused by their inability to control what they internally feel when they see the gifts or photos of outings or any other reminder of the abuse or the abuser. Photos can be used by the paedophile as evidence of what they are capable of getting away with and how ignorant others are of the abuse. Unfortunately, the victim feels trapped by the presence of these reminders and can use them to reinforce their own guilt, shame, self-blame and humiliation.

The victim's torment

Some victims never succumb to the paedophile's manipulation and see the insidiousness of the paedophile's indifference from the moment the paedophile attempts to control them and initiate sexual interaction. This can cause the victim to internally battle the anxiety of the inevitable, which is being abused whenever the paedophile gets the opportunity. This may cause the victim to try to limit the opportunity the paedophile has alone with them, and a cat and mouse game begins. This cat and mouse game is part of the thrill for some paedophiles. These paedophiles get a thrill out of creating opportunities that the victim has no ability to counteract. The victim feels haunted by their own inability to control their safety and live on high alert, in a constant state of anxiety and intense tension, and may never experience feeling safe and relaxed in their own reality.

Some survivors of abuse torment themselves with guilt, shame and humiliation for being unable to control their situation to avoid being abused; and later they torture themselves for being unable to create a sense of peace or to control how their history has affected them. The guilt, shame and humiliation causes the survivor to detach and disassociate from understanding they were manipulated before, during and after the abuse, which leaves them judging the abuse as their own fault. These victims who have survived abuse use their own guilt, shame and humiliation as a weapon against themselves.

Some survivors of abuse attempt to suppress their confusion, which has them codependent on their own illusion of control. They believe if they can suppress their confusing emotions they are in control of themselves, creating the illusion that they are unaffected. The survivor starts striving to create the illusion they are unassailable, which can manifest into indifference towards themselves. They seek to control the suppression of every emotion and attempt to repress every thought that interferes with their illusion of being able to control themselves to an image of normality. In an attempt to conceal their hidden secret, the survivor seeks to counter-act their own perception of how they will be judged and becomes obsessed with their fear of judgement. Some survivors want to be indifferent to the emotional, energetic and physical reality that their secret is creating. These survivors either perceive themselves as just insignificant victims or they attempt to deny that what they experienced was abuse. They constantly retreat and remove themselves from their reality, often becoming robotic in their approach to life and relationships. The survivor does not want to feel the ebb and flow of their own emotional energy or the truth of their feelings as they live life, they want to be numb to reality. The survivor seeks to be neutral but is internally experiencing an emotional tidal wave of unresolved emotions, and is relying on their denial or performance of their images to suppress and repress their internal nightmare.

Some survivors of abuse anchor to their indifference towards themselves in an attempt to quell their awareness of the unresolved emotions that they cannot control with denial or deception. This is why many survivors approach life destructively, destroying their ability to naturally feel significant, because they are too frightened to feel. Some survivors create control structures that they apply to life as a way of creating an emulated version of functionality. They adopt charades to hide within, in an attempt to conceal their own internal reality. They seek to control the validation of their charades while undermining any validation they receive, which leaves them immersed in the despair of not feeling the truth of themselves, and disillusioned by their own internal reality.

Some survivors' indifference towards the truth of what they are doing to themselves leaves them vulnerable to more sexual abuse or other types of abuse. These survivors have conditioned themselves to ignore reality and to anchor to their own illusion of reality. They crave proof that they are loveable but seek indifference, because indifference is familiar and they have learnt to tolerate their own reactions to indifference. The survivors use the familiarity of their own tolerance of indifference as a sense of security and can develop a fear of love because they fear letting themselves feel. Survivors can fear their perception of love could be tainted with indifference and they fear that if they open themselves to love and are mislead, they will never recover. Some survivors fear being open to love because they fear what is trapped within them will be exposed, which leaves them retreating to their own internal shame. The survivor struggles with feeling the reality of what they are experiencing and uses indifference as a barrier to accepting the truth of who they are and the truth of their reality. Survivors can be insecure and constantly plagued by their own self-judgement and their awareness of their inability to trust themselves to feel love.

Some survivors become conditioned and compelled by their own desire to sabotage all opportunities to feel their natural significance. They may have an extreme desire to control the reality of their emotions and life, which can feel like their ability to be functional is being encroached by madness. They are aware of their own disassociation. Some survivors are so sensitive to what they feel, and they desire to deny so much, that they become trapped in an internal battle against their own awareness. This causes them to feel overwhelmed by their disassociation because they are constantly disjointed from their own reality, and it seems never ending. The survivor has contradictory emotions about the truth of what they are feeling, and the familiarity of confusion becomes a welcome relief from the clarity of their feelings. Confusion becomes a control structure the survivor uses to deflect the truth of their awareness of their own internal reality.

Many survivors cannot perceive the gravity of the impact of the abuse they suffered because they want to cling to the belief that their abuse is a normal part of childhood, adolescence and life, or they believe it does not matter and no one really cares. These survivors of abuse want to believe that the abuse does not affect the way they live life and their relationships with others. However, they do not feel secure in their own denial and this can cause them to be very controlling about all aspects of their life.

Non-believers

Some survivors' suppression of their history and unresolved emotions can create, what others may perceive as odd behaviours, and these may be used to question the sanity of the survivor. The survivor's fear of judgement causes them to either try to control the judgement or to rebel against it. This may cause their behaviours to escalate or to become a hidden behaviour. The survivor is conditioned by their experience of abuse, to create secret worlds. This leaves them perpetuating hidden habitual behaviours, fearing others will notice and judge them. They fear the shame of exposure. The survivor creates the belief that if they can hide aspects of their reality they can remain safe in their denial. They believe that if they can control their denial, then they can control their reality. The survivor uses their constructed beliefs to conceal their emotional reality from themselves, even though they are aware they have not escaped their unresolved emotions or their fear of their history. The survivors' mind chatter is relentless because while creating images to project to the world, they use their indifference to themselves to counteract any truth that may expose what they want to suppress. The survivor perceives the familiarity of their indifference as a way to control their denial of reality and to hide from the judgement they fear.

The judgement the survivor emotionally feels or fears from others is used by the survivor to doubt and undermine the seriousness of the emotional problems, caused by their inability to deal with the abuse. The survivor becomes obsessed with the judgement they have experienced or expect to experience, and their own judgement about this becomes an obsession. They can become obsessed with how to control others' judgement and how to use judgement to justify their own fears. This causes the survivor of abuse to become judgemental and reinforces their judgement, analysis and assessment of themselves, life, events and the image they believe they need to perform to keep their emotional turmoil hidden from the world.

Survivors who have experienced loved ones doubting their account of abuse, emotionally feel confused by the loved ones' inability to feel the truth of their pain. This causes them to fixate on how the loved one refutes their account of the abuse, and on their perception of the loved one's judgement of them. Some survivors become trapped in the habit of obsessively ruminating about the judgement being used to discount their integrity and their account of their experience and history. Survivors grieve when they feel the indifference within the denial of others, and this increases their denial of their own value, worth and significance, which causes the survivor to doubt the existence of love. The survivor's grief can manifest into a compulsion to prove they are being validated or victimised by everyone and everything they encounter. They use whoever and whatever is not pacifying their desire for control to become the source of their beliefs of being victimised. This causes some survivors to wallow in their own despair by identifying all indifference they encounter from others as a deliberate attack against them, even if it is not a personal affront. Every interaction the survivor has is taken as an opportunity to find the negative, to justify being angry and an excuse for being retributive. This causes them to fixate on negativity and to ascribe to the belief that nothing is 'good enough' to alleviate the pain, despair and disappointment they emotionally, energetically and physically feel. They deliberately separate from feeling their own soul truth and disassociate from the reality of abusing themselves with their own and others' indifference to truth. The survivor feels compelled to prove that they are a victim, and expresses their pain by creating more pain.

Some survivors obsessively anchor to the indifference they have experienced from others and themselves, which causes them to override their awareness of their soul's consciousness and the compassion they feel from others. The survivor fears the sorrow created from their own insecurity but continues to anchor to their emotional programming, conditioning and indoctrinations adopted from, or constructed in response to, the belief that no one will believe them. The survivor can transfer all the emotional angst they have from the abuse onto those who are unsympathetic or do not believe their account of their history. The non-believer becomes perceived as the source of all their emotional problems, which creates a fixation on having to prove in every situation that they are right and the non-believer is wrong.

Some survivors are so incensed by the non-believer's invalidation of their situation that they compulsively react with the desire to prove the non-believer is wrong about everything. This means the survivor starts nit picking with others to entice a competition and the survivor becomes a 'right fighter' compelled to be competitive in all their interactions. Every 'win' the survivor believes they have made within their competitive interactions is used to validate that they are right and justified in their emotional reactions. They have a very strong desire to avoid being truthful about how vulnerable they feel in their unresolved emotions, and this desire to avoid feeling drives them to constantly seek a competition to prove they are right. When the survivor believes they have not had a 'win', they believe that they are being victimised and plummet into their unresolved emotions, which incites the fear of vulnerability they were actually trying to avoid.

Some survivors compulsively align to their own indifference and rebel against the truth of who they are in an attempt to deny the reality of what they internally feel and to deny the truth of their emotional behaviours, believing denial is the easiest way to survive their own unresolved emotions and fears of indifference. Instead of seeking to resolve their stored emotional pain, the victim is trying to survive existing in their unresolved emotions, and anchors to opposing their awareness of themselves. This causes the survivor to compete against whatever or whoever exposes the truth of their emotional behaviour and stored unresolved emotions.

The survivor's self-rejection

The survivor's awareness of betraying the truth of who they are creates more confusion and emotional pain. These survivors engulf themselves in blame, guilt, shame and humiliation because they can feel their self-rejection as a betrayal of their own soul. Survivors use their perception of others' judgement of them, to compound their betrayal of themselves and to obliterate trust in their own integrity. The survivors adopt the doubt and indifference of others as an assessment of their significance in the world. Some survivors surmise their loved ones will judge that they are the problem and they fear setting themselves up for more indifference, which means they control themselves to keep the abuse a secret.

What the survivor surmises is often constructed from their fear of rejection. When the survivor defends what they surmise, even when there is evidence to the contrary, they are sustaining their own doubt of what they can and cannot cope with. This leaves them plagued with their own confusion.

Mind Chatter Activates Your Labyrinths Of Unresolved Emotions.

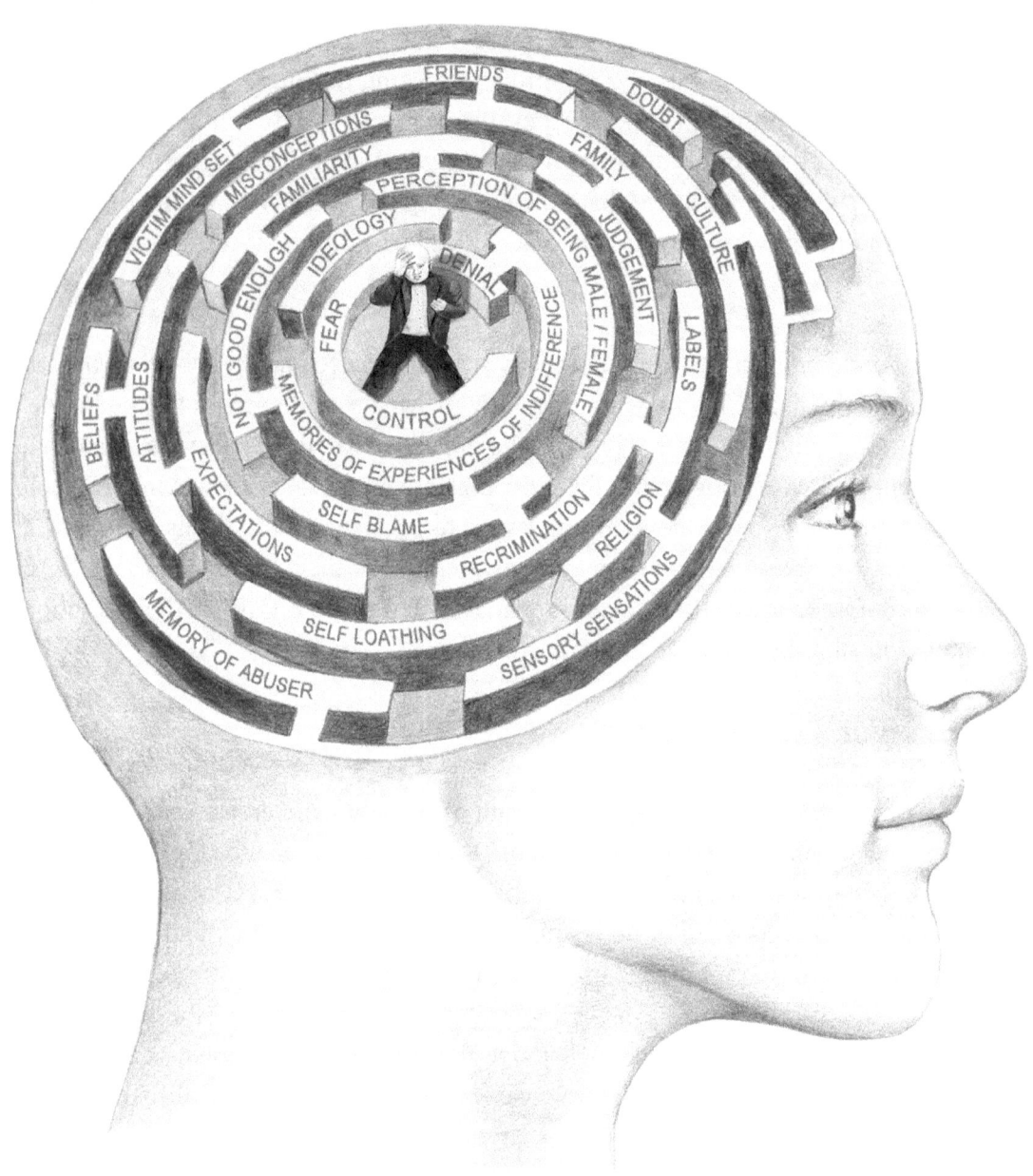

An abuse survivor's mind chatter of self-loathing creates emotional labyrinths, which causes more pain and despair. The survivor's attempts to control the suppression of their unresolved emotions causes them to be overwhelmed by their inability to manage their own emotional labyrinths. Some survivors become entrapped by, and remain in, the incessant nature of their own mind chatter.

Some survivors' predictions of their loved ones' possible reaction to the truth of their abuse is often totally fabricated, and at times not a true reflection of the care and compassion their loved ones would show if they were aware of the abuse. The survivors own desire to deny the reality of abuse, or their fear of the unknown responses of their loved ones, has them punishing themselves with what they believe the loved ones should think of them. Some survivors condition themselves to believe the loved ones should blame them for being abused. This belief is a direct result of the survivors willingness to inflict themselves with insults, self-loathing and hatred, as they convince themselves that their loved ones would have no option, but to agree with, and align to, the survivors own self-loathing and perception of themselves and the abuse. When the survivor keeps the abuse a secret, the secret eats away at the survivor's integrity and courage to acknowledge the truth of what they feel but try to deny.

The survivor's self-loathing and the mind chatter they generate by trying to keep the secret, creates emotional labyrinths of pain and despair. This leaves them entrapped in their own self-abuse. These emotional labyrinths incorporate memories of the abuse and misconceptions about the victim's part in the abuse, which are generally generated by self-blame, recrimination and doubt. The survivor obsessively and habitually ruminates about all their past experiences of indifference and judgement. These emotional labyrinths become the survivors filter for their perception of life, others, themselves and truth. The emotional labyrinths become a constant reference point for the survivors' analysis of how to interact with their life, others and themselves.

The survivor fears everybody's judgement, but adheres to their own harsh self-judgement, which they use to incite patterns of self-punishment. They relentlessly seek to inflict punishment on themselves to retaliatively reinforce their resentment for being an abuse victim. These survivors obsess with their patterns of self-punishment, seeking to have ultimate control over assaulting themselves. They are compelled to take themselves into an emotional abyss at the same time as attempting to perform an image of being functional. The survivor becomes reliant on their own disassociation from reality to resist, deny and avoid the truth of what they are feeling. Unfortunately, they use their own indifference to truth to undermine their ability to acknowledge the reality of what they are inflicting on themselves and how they have become their own abuser. As the survivor exacerbates their own self-abuse they become increasingly unable to conceal their own retaliative self-punishment. This causes the survivor to implode in their doubts and insecurities, and they get to the point of not being able to deny the reality of their own indifference. This emotional implosion creates the opportunity for the survivor to acknowledge that their denial of reality is an illusion of control that reinforces their own continuation of abuse, betrayal and indifference to their own soul.

When survivors feel the courage to be truthfully honest about themselves, they allow themselves to feel their soul's consciousness exposing their pathway to freedom through resolution and evolution. Their feelings are their soul's consciousness guiding them to truth, whereas their emotions are a by-product of their fears and embedded beliefs.

Truthful honesty is often the option a confused survivor of abuse disassociates from, as they seek to become reliant on their deception to hide from their own indifference. The survivor can fear being truthful, because they are scared they cannot cope. It is their own judgement that they cannot cope that often leaves them punishing themselves. The survivor attempts to use their indifference to conceal the truth of their soul. Indifference is not part of who they naturally are; indifference is an expression of being lost, lost in the unconsciousness of their soul.

The paedophile's mindset

One thing all paedophiles have in common is their indifference to the reality of their own actions and their indifference to the flow-on effect their abuse has on their victims. Some paedophiles experience guilt, shame and humiliation, and pretend they are remorseful for the abuse they inflict upon their victims and others. Some paedophiles' pretence of remorse becomes an internal conflict, because they have no intention of giving up any opportunity to abuse a child. As the paedophile's guilt, shame and humiliation becomes overwhelming, some seek sexual gratification of some sort, to quell being overwhelmed. Some paedophiles convince themselves that sexual gratification is going to alleviate the feeling of being emotionally overwhelmed, which perpetuates their willingness to be indifferent to their victims, and sustains their ability to be a predator who craves to be sexually abusive.

Some paedophiles focus on dissipating their own emotional upheaval and deliberately generate justifications for their vile actions at the expense of an innocent child. The sensation of sexual satisfaction is temporary, so as a way of quelling the unresolved emotions they obsess about, they attempt to secure the sensation of having ultimate control over whoever they have chosen as their prey. They use the thrill of their control to override any willingness to acknowledge the reality of the extent of the emotional, energetic and physical pain they inflict on those they abuse. The paedophile's desire to sexually satisfy their own craving for control can distort their perception of the reality and ramifications of paedophilia.

Some paedophiles use their narcissism to justify their desire to use children for sexual gratification. Paedophiles are all opportunists, but each individual paedophile has a different level of risk that they are willing to take. The more times the paedophile gets away with their attacks, the more confident and willing the paedophile is to take risks, and for some the increased danger enhances the thrill. These paedophiles use their narcissism to construct the belief that their ability to manipulate all those they encounter will ensure their secret world is safe from interference. This narcissistic belief is transferred to the victim and can often leave the victim believing that no one would accept their recount of the abuse, which is another way that the paedophile can silence them.

Some paedophiles are concerned by and consumed with their image, and go to great lengths to disguise the reality of their desire for sexual gratification at the expense of an innocent child. Some paedophiles use their ability to disguise the reality of being a paedophile to feed their illusion of control and superiority. The charade of their life is a constant source of thrill as they hone their manipulative skills. Some paedophiles revel in walking a tightrope between their image and reality.

The paedophile fears their own anxiety and fears having their secrets exposed, because it would prove their inability to control their image. Paedophiles perceive being exposed as proving that they are inferior to their own image of themselves. Paedophiles fear being caught by authorities because it means there will be an investigation exposing their secret perversion. These paedophiles fear having no control over being investigated, and fear having no ability to manipulate the authorities. Any exposure of their secret perversions would ruin their perceived control of their image and expose their secret world. This would interfere with their ability to justify what they are doing to innocent children.

When the discovery of abuse occurs without the authorities being involved, the paedophile often tries to manipulate the situation and the person who discovered their abuse. Some paedophiles will attempt to manipulate all involved by promising to change or offering to move away in order to save everyone from embarrassment. The paedophile will often pretend to be an advocate for the child's wellbeing and attempt to explain it is in the child's best interest if everyone remains quiet. The paedophile often attempts to convince the potential whistle-blower that exposure of the abuse will interfere with many aspects of the lives of all those involved. These paedophiles use their skilled slyness, deception and manipulation to constantly seek ways of protecting the secrecy of their sexual perversion and to counteract any ramifications of their sexual perversion being exposed.

Some paedophiles seek to create a reputation of being caring, honest and beyond repute and are often community minded; they manipulate all they come in contact with to believe the lies that hide their secret world. Often when paedophiles are exposed people are shocked and say, "but he/she was always so good with the children, I can't believe it" and are left confused about the reality of the paedophile.

The paedophile's behaviours

Some paedophiles are so vicious, sadistic, malicious and merciless, that they cannot control the physical evidence of abuse on their victims and seek avenues, such as child sex slaves, for this type of abuse. They pay for the opportunity to walk away from the damage they inflict with no fear of recourse. These paedophiles ooze indifference energy because they have no remorse for the pain they inflict or the market they support, and are indifferent to everything except their own desire to control and destroy. Some of these paedophiles keep their own children isolated from the world and prefer to live out of sight of others. These paedophiles prefer to keep close control of their secret world and train their victims to believe that there is no alternative to how they are living.

Some paedophiles who enslave their own children, attempt to limit their interaction with others and want the whole family to be left alone. These paedophiles believe with absolute conviction that they have the right and are entitled to regard children as play things for their sexual gratification, or slaves for their physical needs. They believe that children must be submissive to all their demands. These paedophiles will taunt their victims about their inability to look after themselves without the paedophile's presence. This is to create fear and doubt in the victim about their own ability to survive, which the paedophile uses to gratify their desire to inflict pain on another to secure their illusion of control. These paedophiles have little concern for an image or a charade and are often aloof, keeping themselves under the radar. They arrogantly believe they have nothing to be ashamed of because they believe they are entitled to own the soul of another and give little consideration to the odds of being caught.

There are a variety of methods of manipulation used by paedophiles. Some paedophiles use manipulative seduction, seeking to find what the victim is lacking and craving, such as attention, love or wanting to feel special. The victim's emotional cravings and needs become tools the seductive paedophile can use. Some paedophiles orchestrate for the victim to believe they are seducing the paedophile and are in control. The paedophile gives the impression that they are at the mercy of the victim. This incites a game for the paedophile to use their manipulative seduction skills to see how far they can go without being detected as a paedophile.

Some paedophiles manipulate the victim to be part of their conspiracy to conceal the truth of the insidious nature of the paedophile. The paedophile seeks to mentor the victim to be completely vulnerable to them. The paedophile's manipulation is callous and contrived and has the victim believing whatever the paedophile wants. The paedophile seeks to have power over the way the victim lives and emotionally feels righteous in deciding what is best for the victim and the so called 'relationship'. This is control, but the victim has been conditioned to accept this as care and love.

Some paedophiles use an illusion of love and admiration to coerce and control the victim into misunderstanding what is actually happening. The victim may remain unaware of the reality of the deception until the paedophile stops being attentive to them. Once the paedophile's desire to be seductive subsides, the victim becomes aware of the paedophile's indifference towards them and the illusion of love and care is exposed as manipulation and insidious control. This confuses the victim and inhibits their ability to acknowledge what they feel, know and want to deny. The victim often fights accepting the reality of the insidiousness of the paedophile and clings to the previous image that the paedophile projected. The paedophile uses the victim's torment as validation of their manipulative skills, and their thrill is heightened by the knowledge that they are affecting the victim's emotions even after they discard them. Victims become trophies paedophiles use, to enhance their own private image of themselves, and this heightens the paedophile's desire to find new conquests.

Some paedophiles may lose interest in their victim because the victim's body shape is changing and no longer suits their desires, or their ability to manipulate has become so easy that there is no thrill of the chase, or that the victim is exerting their own control over the paedophile and demanding their control be pacified. Some paedophiles may lose interest because their victim is no longer naïve and therefore not as appealing to the paedophile. Some victims have become so indoctrinated in the paedophile's ways of manipulation that they start to be manipulative against the paedophile. The paedophile has an adverse reaction to their own methods of manipulative seduction and control being used against them, and this leads to the paedophile no longer being interested in the victim.

Some victims who fall prey to the paedophile's manipulation, engulf themselves with blame, falsely believing they enticed the paedophile's attention. The paedophile manipulates the victims' self-blame as leverage to keep them silent. These paedophiles use their victims' silence to alleviate themselves from acknowledging their responsibility and to class their manipulation as extremely successful. The victims feel humiliated for not being able to see the manipulation as manipulation, and they berate themselves for not counteracting the manipulation with truth.

The victim may become obsessed with their abuser, wanting to prove that there really was a love affair and that the abuser will want them back when they return to their senses. The victim may pine for and crave to feel the manipulation, believing that means they are loved. They are willing to accept manipulation and abuse as love, because the victim believes that manipulation and abuse is the best they will get. This belief often propels them into entering another abusive relationship.

Some victims have been programmed, conditioned and indoctrinated into a false version of what love is and crave attention, becoming willing to subject themselves to abuse because they want to be wanted. This becomes a self-destructive merry-go-round as they have become unconsciously addicted, to attempting to control those who operate from indifference, to love them. Those who operate from indifference are willing to manipulate the victims' craving to be wanted for their own agenda, and are oppositional to the truth of who the victim is, which is a significant, unique, independent, individual soul of *True Source Divine Origin Consciousness*. This leaves the victim feeling insignificant, which can intensify their desire and desperation to be loved, perpetuating their own self-destructive emotional merry-go-round of soul oppression.

Some victims who refuse to acknowledge the truth of being abused carry guilt and shame, not realising the truth of being a victim. They often never truly contemplate that the guilt and shame should be carried by the paedophile, not by them. The victim may feel shame for not realising the seduction was the paedophile's manipulative control. Some victims may feel shame because they succumbed to the desire of wanting to be wanted, which makes the victim feel shameful about their own innocence and naivety. Victims naively believe they should have been able to control the situation they found themselves in. However, once they have been seduced or manipulated, victims believe they are partly to blame for the abuse. They can cease to acknowledge the truth of being victims to something they did not know how to control, and deny that they were in a situation that there was no way of controlling.

Some paedophiles hunt for opportunities to defy the truth within their own soul and seek to control another to the same nightmare of being disassociated from the love within their soul and disassociated from the love within truth. Some paedophiles want to control, command and have ownership of another's soul, but hide behind the shadows of sexual deception. Paedophiles distort the reality of themselves with images, and some paedophiles internally fight within themselves about what is right and wrong. Each individual paedophile will have their own set of rules about what is acceptable, which they may expand as they chase the sensation of their original thrill. Paedophiles use their own rules to justify the indecency of their actions and to regulate their own self-judgement.

Some paedophiles relish in the ability to supply themselves with a secret world, which they have created for their sexual desires. The secret world of some paedophiles is a replica of a world they have seen or experienced when they were innocent, and is the choice to become what they once despised. Paedophiles' desire to have ultimate control over another innocent soul, overrides their willingness to be honest about their awareness of becoming what they despised. Some paedophiles are perpetuations of their own abusive experiences as a child, acting out their emotional carnage on another. This is not an excuse, because they know and have experienced the carnage that abuse creates and yet they still choose to inflict it upon another defenceless child. This proves how debauched the paedophile is within their own indifference and the insidiousness of the choices they make.

The victim's confusion and fear

When they feel the control and indifference of the paedophile, the child is often scared to the point of being numb, because they instinctively know they are powerless against the experience of paedophilia. The child feels trapped by their inability to control the indifference they feel, and fears the paedophile's lack of boundaries. Their fear is exacerbated because they do not know how far the paedophile is willing to go, but are aware that the paedophile is capable of anything.

During the abuse, the child emotionally, energetically and physically feels powerless and they carry the fear of being powerless after the abuse. This can overwhelm the child and have them immersed in their own indifference. The experience of being rendered powerless and without the freedom to choose, leaves the child with the embedded belief that they are powerless. This is a constant fear that inhibits the development of their sense of self. Some children become programmed, conditioned and indoctrinated to pacify those who operate from indifference, believing if they always appease others it will quell the fear they feel. They fear what it feels like to be powerless and without freedom of choice, and choose to align to the pacification of indifference, believing that will allow them to escape the fear of what could happen, if they are not pacifying those who are indifferent to them. This creates an emotional, energetic and physical merry-go-round of appeasing and succumbing to indifference in an attempt to protect themselves from their own fear of powerlessness and their fear of being without freedom of choice.

The fear of being powerless and without freedom of choice creates an energetic shock, because it disengages their awareness of the flow of consciousness within. The victim's loss of awareness of their own flow of consciousness causes them to feel powerless and susceptible to aligning to any indifference energy being projected at them. The victim fears being at the mercy of those who are willing to be indifferent to their freedom of choice. The loss of freedom of choice creates an energetic shock that causes victims to attempt to use their denial of reality, to protect themselves from acknowledging and feeling the truth of another's indifference. This programmes, conditions and indoctrinates victims to be in denial of their emotional, energetic and physical reality. They focus on pacifying indifference energy, believing they will spare themselves from feeling the truth of their own unresolved emotions, carried victim energy and the guilt, shame and humiliation they have developed. Victims fear their own reactions and responses to the programming, conditioning and indoctrinations resulting from the abuse. The experience of indifference leaves them disassociated and oppositional to unconditionally loving themselves. Unfortunately, victims do not spare themselves and perpetuate their own indifference, sustaining the fear they desperately want to escape.

When the victim attempts to run from their own emotional tidal wave, they are already experiencing what they fear. They fear vulnerability but constantly feel vulnerable to their own and others' indifference. In spite of the victim's attempts to run from their own emotional tidal wave, they remain engulfed by their fear of their own unresolved emotions, reactions, responses and the results of their denial of reality.

Some paedophiles use the victim's lack of self-worth and insecurity, to manipulate them into believing they deserve abuse, and that if they had been of any worth the abuse would not be happening or have happened. These victims will use this manipulation to turn on themselves, inciting self-hatred, self-loathing, guilt, shame and humiliation. Victims carry the experience of abuse as evidence of their lack of value, worth and significance, and indoctrinate themselves to accept their indifference as a way of being. This is a misconception, created by manipulating themselves into believing their abuser is an authority over their worth.

Some paedophiles use what the victim seeks from others, such as wanting validation of worth, to feel loved and adored, as a weakness that is there to be exploited. The paedophile entices their victim by triggering the victim's desire for validation and then uses their desire to be validated as a weapon against them. The paedophile exploits the desire to be validated by invoking insecurity within the victim.

Some paedophiles programme, condition and indoctrinate their victims so that they will assess themselves as unworthy of the paedophile's validation and love. This type of insidious control is especially effective if the paedophile is a parent, relation or a figure of respect such as a coach, religious leader or teacher. The paedophile who is also a parent, uses beliefs of what a family should be or how the child should respond to the position they hold, to confuse the child. If the child cannot trust their own family or people with respected positions within society, what hope is there for their perceptions of the outside world? This insidious control traps the child into their own assessment of the world via their family's reality or the abuse they have suffered from someone who is respected within society, which ignites their fear and confusion about living in the world. The child's confusion is accelerated by their awareness of being coerced to maintain a family image or to uphold the charade of the one respected by society. This keeps the child in a fog, as they try to avoid feeling the truth of their reality, concretising their own indifference towards who they naturally are. To survive the indifference they feel and have experienced, children condition themselves with denial, believing they are unworthy to be loved and protected.

Some paedophiles create ways of determining if their control is working and use mind games to test the child's compliance. The paedophile plays with their victims' understanding of themselves and reality, seeking to impose their will and control upon their victims. The paedophile systematically works on altering the victim's perception of how others will perceive and judge them. The victim's understanding goes from believing that others will perceive them as just being a child, to believing that others will perceive them as not being good enough to be loved, acknowledged or accepted. The child's perception is that they are damaged goods and unworthy of compassion. They become unforgiving towards themselves and indifferent to the truth of being significant, and of worth and value to truth.

When any soul loses their awareness of the truth of naturally being of value, worth and significance, they align to the misconception of being 'not good enough' and become immersed in the abyss of their own soul denial. Truth is the origin of all souls. This lifetime is an experience and the foundation of truth is always there, regardless of the depths of our soul denial. The foundation of truth is that all souls are significant, unique, independent, individual strands of truth energy. Soul denial is the result of denying our awareness of truth and constructing embedded beliefs and fears that obliterate our sense of worth. When a child has had their foundation of worth ripped away at the hands of a paedophile, it leaves them doubting the significance of their soul.

The paedophile's manipulative games

Some children believe others have already typecast them as unworthy and they have no way of realising that this is part of the mind games created by the paedophile. The paedophile wants to have the child oppress the reality of who they are, which is a significant, unique, independent, individual soul of truth. The paedophile wants the victim to be immersed in the oppression they create and trapped in the insidiousness of their indifference. The paedophile wants to be the controller and seeks to inflict others with their indifference, believing they are entitled to their whims and depravities. The paedophile wants to control the level of indifference and how the indifference affects the victim, as a way of believing in their own illusion of control.

Some paedophiles toy with the child's emotions and at times validate and flatter their victim, which becomes a way to entice the child to do what they want. The paedophile bestows validation and flattery upon the child to gain more leverage and control. The paedophile is mindful of not wanting their victim to get completely lost in their own despair and wants to have an avenue of control that governs the victim's behaviour. The paedophile fears the child completely succumbing to their own despair in case others become concerned about the child's emotional condition. They also attempt to govern the child's reactions and responses fearing the child will emotionally explode and become a loose cannon that the paedophile is unable to control. The paedophile relies on being able to control their victim to crave their validation and flattery to secure their own illusion of control. The paedophile wants to control how the victim feels, thinks and acts. This has the paedophile using the victim's despair as an advantage for their control as they constantly try to coerce the victim to be indifferent against who they naturally are.

Some paedophiles manipulate the victim by giving them what they want, which is a moment where they hear or feel the paedophile giving value to their existence. The child may use these moments to enforce their own denial of reality and ignore the reality of what they are feeling. This causes the victim to chase and cling to moments where their denial works and overshadow the truth of what they feel about their own reality. The victim uses these moments as a reprieve from the confusion they feel, and are often more compliant because they are seeking validation for their existence from their abuser. The victim is programmed, conditioned and indoctrinated into denying the reality of abuse and to perceive the abuse as what they deserve or as a normal part of relationships. Victims are conditioned to believe having another's approval is compensation for the insidiousness of their abuse.

The more indifference victims feel towards themselves, the more they crave validation and acknowledgement for their existence, which secures their emotional, energetic and physical merry-go-round. The victim uses any type of validation as relief from feeling the reality of abuse, the reality of being an abuse victim and from their own beliefs of being unworthy and insignificant. This can make the victim more vulnerable because any attention may entice them to succumb to being manipulated. Attention becomes torturous because it is something they crave while expecting it to hurt them. This can cause the victim to become promiscuous. The victim's desire to feel validated and acknowledged blindsides their ability to acknowledge the truth of what they are feeling and the reality of their own actions. This can make them more vulnerable to manipulation and sexual abuse, reinforcing their belief that they are unworthy and insignificant. Victims become entrapped in their addictive patterns of self-manipulation, and this secures their own indifference towards themselves.

The paedophile wants to control their victims' perception of themselves and takes full advantage of their victims' desire for approval and validation. When the victim's perception of themselves is distorted by the paedophile, they succumb to using denial as a survival skill. The paedophile gives validation and approval, and then turns on the victim by withdrawing the validation and approval. This is part of the manipulation the paedophile uses which becomes a mind game, because the paedophile knows they can derive a lot of power by controlling their victim's insecurities.

Cycle of abuse

Some paedophiles try to overshadow their own history of abuse, by using their dominant control of another, to pacify the insecurities they feel within themselves. Some paedophiles use the dominance of their control over a child as an avenue to act out their rebellion against having once been a victim. The paedophile wants to be the controller because they fear being controlled. These paedophile's insecurities are so great, their compulsion to be in control of the indifference energy they feel drives them to want to oppress another into the same nightmare of indifference they have endured. These paedophiles are a product of their own loss of compassion. They are willing to inflict pain and trauma on an innocent child, because they refuse to deal with the truth of their own unresolved emotions. They prefer to stay separated from their awareness of the truth of their soul and are willing to be the insidiousness of indifference.

Some paedophiles believe they have the right to act out the damage they sustained during their own abuse, because their compulsion to abuse is created from the emotional, energetic and physical damage they sustained when they were abused. This is how they disassociate from the reality of their own choices and actions, succumbing to the compulsion to be an abuser whilst believing they are not responsible. These paedophiles get to a point where to acknowledge the truth of the abuse they inflict on innocent children, is to acknowledge the truth of the emotional, energetic and physical damage within themselves, which the paedophile will resist, deny and avoid at any cost. Acknowledging any truth about their own insidiousness shatters the paedophile's illusion of control and they perceive any loss of their illusion of control as being tantamount to being abused again.

Some paedophiles who are perpetuating the abuse they experienced have vowed to themselves that being abused will never happen again, so they anchor to being the abuser. These paedophiles believe that their sexual preference is an uncontrollable aspect of themselves that needs to be aligned to and perpetuated or it will destroy them. They become what they fear and attempt to control what they fear with more indifference. Once the paedophile believes they can control indifference energy, the illusory control of indifference becomes a compulsive addiction and obsession.

The paedophile who was once a victim of paedophilia, will try to escape their enslavement to fearing indifference. This causes them to create pathways of control by being indifferent. Instead of acknowledging the truth of their experiences and the opportunities to break the perpetual cycle of abuse, they seek to utilise indifference to secure a sense of control. Some modify how they abuse, to justify that they are not as sadistic as their abuser was, but their perpetuation of indifference and abuse of any type is them choosing to be the insidiousness of indifference. The paedophile willingly abandons their awareness of their own soul truth, and is willing to inflict pain and abuse on others as retaliation for not being loved and protected from their own experience of abuse. These paedophiles choose to immerse themselves in their own indifference to truth, because they fear not having control of their own storehouse of unresolved emotions and the energy they feel.

Some paedophiles rely on having an illusion of control and ferociously protect their indifference. They want to use their indifference to sustain their ability to deny responsibility or revel in being indifferent about the truth of their own actions. To deny responsibility for the abuse, they have to align to the belief that they do not have control over the indifference energy that affects them. If they are caught by authorities, they respond with the defence that it is an infliction stemming from them having been abused. When they revel in the abuse they believe they are in complete control. If they are with other paedophiles they brag about their conquests. They use their ability to be indifferent, to control their decision making, and to override the true ramifications of their choice to be a willing participant in the insidious nature of paedophilia.

Some paedophiles manipulate themselves into believing their own deception and equate being manipulative as power. They disregard how the emotional, energetic and physical stain they carry, from their childhood experiences of abuse, is affecting their perception of life, themselves and others. It is the paedophile's own denial of reality and denial of the truth of who they are, that perpetuates the cycle of abuse. These paedophiles choose to be at war with the truth of themselves and annihilate any feelings of and for themselves as a soul. Some of these paedophiles use the sexual abuse of children to annihilate any sense of being a soul and fixate on chasing the thrill of having ultimate control of another soul. Some of these paedophiles use sexual abuse of children to annihilate any sense of being a soul by using their own guilt, shame and humiliation to implode. They believe the only way to get a reprieve is when they become numb to their own unresolved emotions during the act of sexually abusing children, because they become consumed with the control energy of their sexual depravities.

Paedophiles who perpetuate their own history of abuse have chosen to perpetuate the energy of indifference. These paedophiles who believe they were deprived of their own childhood by another paedophile, seek to inflict indifference energy at another to sustain and reinforce the paedophile's indoctrinated belief that they are soulless and unaccountable for their own actions. Some paedophiles believe that if they perpetuate indifference they will rid themselves of the energy they cannot stand feeling. However, this is a misconception that actually immerses the paedophile in exactly what they are trying to rid themselves of. These paedophiles control themselves to be the insidious energy they once wanted to escape from, by being willing to perpetuate indifference energy. These paedophiles have become the monsters they once despised and have chosen to willingly abandon feeling the truth of who they are.

The survivor's pain, and their buffers to reality

Some survivors of child abuse abandon their natural ability to feel their own soul and become an expression of their unresolved emotions, such as pain, hurt, frustration, rage, denial, anxiety, fear and heresy against the truth of themselves. They become indoctrinated into controlling how they feel by using heresy energy, which means they immerse themselves in indifference, resentment, shame and humiliation, allowing themselves to be oppositional to the essence of their soul, becoming anti-the truth of who they naturally are. They become disassociated from the truth within their soul and oppose what they feel of their own core essences, becoming judgemental of themselves, others and reality. This reinforces the indifference they have experienced and felt on a soul level.

The indifference energy survivors have felt from their childhood abuse, encapsulates their understanding of themselves. The survivor's desire to control how they feel can become insatiable, which internally frustrates them because they cannot work out how to pacify their own control. It is actually their desire for control of their own feelings and emotions that becomes what they believe is an uncontrollable force within them. The survivor's unresolved emotions cannot be controlled with denial, indifference or more control. Their desire to control what they feel becomes a source of anxiety within them and the survivor generates a fear of acknowledging the truth of their own feelings. Some survivors attempt to control their unresolved emotions, because they fear being truthful. They fear being truthful because they fear losing their illusory control of their ability to suppress and override what haunts them, which often causes them to lie to themselves about their constant battle to suppress the unresolved emotions that haunt their day-to-day existence. Their fear perpetuates the emotional cycles that haunt them and these emotional cycles become as damaging as the initial experience or experiences of abuse.

Unresolved emotions can only be resolved by being truthful. When someone is truthful about their feelings, they expose the truth of their unresolved emotions. When they attempt to control the suppression of what is unresolved within, they are choosing to abandon truth, to separate from their awareness of their soul and to disassociate from feeling the truth of reality. Their belief in the misconception that they can fix their unresolved emotions, by concealing the truth, with superficial images and illusions of reality, means electing to exist within their own indifference to truth.

When survivors of abuse attempt to seek a solution to their emotional upheaval without acknowledging the truth of being enslaved to their own indifference to themselves, truth and others, they create an emotional bond with their victim mentality and use their carried victim energy as an identity. Some survivors of abuse will try to escape their reality by enslaving themselves to indifference energy, without acknowledging the truth of what they are enslaved to. These survivors believe by being indifferent to themselves they will create emotional, energetic or physical buffer zones between themselves and reality.

There are a wide variety of emotional, energetic and physical buffer zones, which are as varied as individuals.

Emotional buffer zones:

- Creating an emotional wall in an attempt to defend yourself from getting hurt or feeling vulnerable, which means you are constantly defensive.
- Emotionally distancing yourself from others and the truth of your relationships.
- Allowing yourself to just go through the motions of being in a relationship, by being aloof and insipid in your interaction with others.
- Creating a charade to perform, while not letting yourself be honest about how you feel or refusing to be present in what is occurring.
- Only responding to life with negativity and opposition.
- Using emotional labyrinths to complicate your awareness of reality, activated by your programmed responses to the different energies you feel. The end result of the emotional labyrinths is to spiral into despair and confusion, becoming drawn into the repetitiveness of your fears and embedded beliefs.
- Creating a domino effect with your own emotions, seeking the despair.
- Only perceiving yourself as a victim, seeking opportunities to be a victim or allowing yourself to be victimised, in order to prove you are right in your assessment of being a victim.

Energetic buffer zones:

- Projecting heresy energy and judgement at anyone or anything that interferes with your illusion of being in control of your reality and suppression of your unresolved emotions.
- Constantly inciting the activation of your own unconscious energy produced by your unresolved emotions, while addictively ruminating.
- Fuelling your own unresolved emotions and relentless mind chatter as you assess potential threats and possible fears, while attempting to be in control of all probabilities.
- Seeking to emotionally feel in control of life, yourself, others, relationships and truth by projecting indifference energy in an attempt to have others oppress their awareness of truth.
- Constantly seeking to incite indifference in others in an attempt to prove you have no choice but to be indifferent, in order to defend yourself from their indifference, while denying you are the inciter of indifference in others.
- Wanting another to feel worthless by deliberately projecting at them what made you feel worthless when another had emotionally and energetically projected that at you.
- Disengaging yourself from feeling the truth of your present moment.
- Disassociating from the energetic reality, to ensure you can deny responsibility and accountability for your own energy.
- Assessing your present moment via your fears of repeating your history of being overpowered by an abuser's control or indifference.
- Attempting to be the one in control, often not realising that your control is sabotaging friendships, trust and the opportunity to experience the purity of love.
- Using control energy within your sexual experiences in an attempt to prove you can control any sexual experience.

Physical buffer zones:

- Becoming overweight, in an attempt to become safe from anyone's physical interest in you.
- Hiding your figure under uncomplimentary clothes.
- Using your addiction to drugs and alcohol to numb you to the emotional upheaval within.

- Becoming a hermit and isolating yourself from others and social interactions.
- Using sex to manipulate others to succumb to the demands you inflict on them to prove you have control.
- Using sex as self-punishment.

Created emotional, energetic and physical buffer zones intermingle, and may be hard to identify as just purely emotional, energetic or physical. What starts as emotional becomes energetic, which creates a physical reaction. Truthful honesty is required to identify the entirety of the truth of the created buffer zones. Survivors of abuse use their emotional, energetic and physical reactions to oppose resolving the buffer zones they have in place to hide the truth from themselves. Created buffer zones are perceived as a way to secure the survivor's resistance to, and denial and avoidance of the truth of their emotional, energetic and physical reality. They become what the survivor is codependent on, to oppress their awareness of their soul's consciousness and truth. These survivors become addicted to their own ability and willingness to oppress the truth within themselves, both the truth of their soul's consciousness and the unresolved emotions of their soul's unconsciousness.

The survivor's emotional, energetic and physical buffer zones are the choice to abandon any opportunity to resolve the unresolved emotions that haunt them. Some survivors deny their indifference towards the truth of who they are, continuing the emotional haunting created by their experience of abuse and remain immersed in their own indifference to themselves.

Emotional overload

In an attempt to minimise how hurt they feel, some survivors use the false belief that they deserved to be abused. They attempt to protect themselves from feeling the true extent of their emotional, energetic and physical damage. They fear feeling the emotional, energetic and physical hurt they carry, and contrive justifications and labels to enforce the belief that they deserve to be abused and should not expect to be treated with anything but indifference. Some survivors believe that if they expect love and do not get love, it is worse for them than if they expect abuse and get what they expected. They fear expecting anything better than abuse, believing that the disappointment of not feeling loved and cherished will be harder to deal with than the trauma of waiting on high alert for the next round of abuse. Survivors fear creating more pain for themselves, because they are already suffering from the burden of being emotionally o verloaded.

Some survivors of abuse try to control themselves with their victim mentality and various ways of being indifferent. They use whatever they believe will distract or deflect them from their awareness of their own reactions and emotional state. These survivors use their avenues of indifference to try and escape their emotional reality. However, their use of indifference towards themselves has them immersed in the carried victim energy that stems from their experiences of abuse. These survivors struggle to perceive themselves without the sense of powerlessness, helplessness and hopelessness they felt during their abuse. Unfortunately, they become stuck in the abuse experience constantly trying to define who they are. They become swamped by their own negative self-judgement and anchor to the misconceptions they adopted during and after the abuse.

Within the horror of the abuse, the victim tries to make sense of the reality of having been chosen to be abused and they misconstrue their own answers as to why the abuser chose them, believing they are unworthy of respect. Victims do not realise they are trying to comprehend something from within their own confused state and the shock of the abuse is what is altering their perception of themselves. They feel dirty, damaged and like a second-class citizen, and instead of this remaining as a feeling, they take it on as their identity. Victims use their own negative beliefs about themselves to justify why the abuser chose them, and can use the abuse experience to expand their own self-negativity.

Some victims watch the charade the abuser acts out to conceal their paedophilic tendencies from others, and wonder why they were picked out to be abused rather than left to be one of the non-abused recipients of the charade. They watch the effort the paedophile puts into acting out their charade and come to the false conclusion that all the recipients of the charade are more worthy than themselves. The victim may use this misconception to believe the paedophile had insight into their worth and decided that they were insignificant. The paedophile seeks to use any insecurity within the victim to hone the victim's belief that they are unworthy, and manipulates the victim into believing that no one is watching or cares, which leaves them more vulnerable for abuse. This is reinforced if no one notices the change in the victim after the abuse, which the victim uses as further evidence that no one cares, and they become helpless within the paedophile's charade. If others do notice a behavioural change in the victim, and do not realise it is the result of being abused, they may become judgemental and critical of the victim, which reinforces the victim's belief of being unworthy. The victim acts out their emotions, which alters their behaviour and often creates fear reactions, because they are unable to explain and deal with their emotional turmoil.

Some victims want to be acknowledged and wait to see if someone will notice their emotional state. They want to ascertain if others realise they are being abused or if they are isolated in their experience of abuse. When others do not notice, they can interpret this as evidence that they deserved to be abused and will victimise themselves about their own vulnerability. This causes the victim to be emotionally swamped by their negative self-judgement and despair of feeling alone. Some victims anchor to their judgement of themselves believing this is all they have, unable to feel or acknowledge their innocence and natural significance. Victims can adopt the indifference, complacency and lack of awareness in those around them as testament to their lack of value, worth and significance. Victims' judgement of themselves can leave them feeling desolate and isolated in the world, lost in the misconception of having been abandoned by whatever they classify as the divine higher power.

Some victims get to the point where they do not want others to notice them, and expect to be ignored, even welcoming it because they have worn themselves down by devaluing themselves and losing their own sense of worth. This is a direct result of routinely blaming themselves and falsely assessing that they are the problem, which consequently causes them to falsely believe they deserved or caused the abuse. The victim's shame and insecurity about the reality of the abuse has caused them to emotionally deconstruct their ability to feel their truth and their true value, worth and significance. This leads the victim to elect to abandon the unconditional love truth has for them and that they had for themselves. These victims judge themselves as unworthy, because they believe they are damaged and have the misconception they are irreparable. These victims attempt to deny the exposure of their own unresolved emotions and deny that they have an opportunity to deal with their unresolved emotions honestly. The victim implodes within their own victimhood. Unfortunately, for children in this situation, they are at the mercy of the adults that surround them. If the adults deny reality or are complacent about the gravity of what is occurring, the child is inflicted with even more indifference.

The adults that surround the child need to acknowledge the reality of the confusion the child feels and, explain the opportunistic nature of the paedophile and that the abuse is not a reflection of the child's value, worth or significance. The adults have the responsibility to guide the child to acknowledge the truth and to surround the child with compassion, love and grace. The child needs to feel the unconditional love and support of those around them, without judgement or indifference, because the child has been indoctrinated into the reality of indifference and seeks to feel the reality of unconditional love.

Some survivors use their victim mentality to be indifferent to the reality of being a significant soul of truth and reject any unconditional love they feel. The carried energetic shock of their childhood experiences of abuse, means the survivors anchor to their own denial of their natural value, worth and significance, conditioning themselves to rely on denial as a survival skill, regardless of what they create with their denial. The survivors become accustomed to using their own denial, indifference and desire for control as survival skills and avoidance techniques. They ascertain what they believe works for them, are reluctant to reassess their own methods of survival, and miss the ramification that their avoidance builds the momentum of their emotional angst. Their survival skills are created from their confusion and they become entrapped in their own denial of reality, because they simply do not know what else to do. These survivors congest their awareness of truth, and become trapped and stagnant within the energy of their own soul's unconsciousness, while denying being a significant soul. They unconsciously trap themselves in their own indifference to the reality of their soul and become embattled in their harsh self-judgement.

Some survivor's childhood abuse encapsulates their understanding of themselves. Their childhood experiences of abuse leave them struggling within emotional quicksand, constantly in fear of feeling the reality of not being able to control the indifference they feel, have felt and have experienced. The survivor's fear of indifference becomes a radar for identifying indifference within any other experience, which they use to prove the validity of their fear and that their struggle against others' indifference is ongoing. Unfortunately, the survivor can class anyone who is not appeasing their control as being indifferent to them, which they use to validate their continuing identification as a victim.

Some survivors seek a solution to their emotional upheaval without acknowledging the truth of being enslaved to their own indifference and self-manipulation. This causes survivors to create emotional labyrinths that reinforce their embedded beliefs and fears, and they inherently continue to inflict themselves with indifference via their own unresolved emotions and the unresolved emotions of others. These survivors manipulate themselves to use their past as permission to justify their abuse towards themselves and become addicted to abusing themselves by denying reality. The survivors may be unconscious to the reality of being addicted to reacting from and to indifference, and fuelling their own negative judgement of themselves, others and reality.

The victim's misconceptions

Some victims feel the indifference of the paedophile's manipulation and interpret it as being desired. The paedophile will use the victim's desire for validation and craving for love as a way to manipulate them into being completely compliant to their demands. However, validation is a lure, which the paedophile has no intention of allowing the victim to become secure in. Victims can become addicted to the chase for validation and pursue what they think will create a sensation of love, at the same time as conditioning themselves to believe that they are unlovable and that validation is a prize for appeasing another's control through sexual acts. The victim is conditioned to chase emulations of what they really want to feel but they settle for far less. They want to feel the truth of love but are scared to be hurt, so they settle for being controlled by sexual energy. Sexual energy becomes an emulation of love they seek and crave, which leaves them susceptible to manipulation by the paedophile and reinforces their own misconceptions and embedded belief of 'not being good enough'.

Some paedophiles use the victim's misconceptions that devalue the truth of who they are, to inundate the victim with criticism that triggers more self-loathing. The victim fear being judged and assessed as unworthy, unlovable and damaged, and become defeated by their own self-judgement and self-manipulation, which makes them more pliable to the paedophile's control and demands. The victim never feels secure because they fear experiencing the paedophile's criticism, and their own barrage of self-judgement. They fear the paedophile's criticism because they are already in emotional overload and extremely sensitive to any negativity directed at them. The combination of their fear and being emotionally overloaded makes the victim susceptible to reluctantly comply with the paedophile's control. This is because they have been conditioned to believe compliance will mean they endure less emotional, energetic or physical pain.

Some victims who have been conditioned to believe compliance is their only choice become extremely confused about their own internal contradictions. Some victims fear and loathe being sexually abused, at the same time as craving the attention of the paedophile. These confusing contradictions within the victim cause them to anchor to their misconceptions about the paedophile and their own significance, self-worth and love. These misconceptions become misguided self-judgement that plagues the victim's understanding of reality and causes them to be immersed in internal conflicts, battling against their own emotional contradictions. The victim becomes consumed with their internal battle and self-loathing, which overshadows how the paedophile has orchestrated immersing the victim in the conflict of their internal contradictions. The paedophile sidelines the hideousness of what they are doing, by conditioning the victim to concentrate on their own guilt, shame and humiliation. This leaves the victim focusing on their internal angst and is how the paedophile keeps them compliant and silent.

Some victims align to their misconception of being damaged and use their embedded beliefs of being of no value, insignificant and unlovable to accept their own indifference towards the truth of themselves. The victim opposes their own natural value, worth and significance, and believes that their experience of abuse was caused by their insignificance. This is a fallacy that they have been manipulated into believing which causes the victim to deny the truth of who they are. The victim will seek an image to align to, that causes them to feel superficial and hollow, because they are losing their awareness of the essence of their soul. These kinds of misconceptions cause the victim to give up on their self-worth, often turning to drugs, alcohol or a promiscuous lifestyle. They can put themselves in haphazard and tenuous situations, indiscriminately causing themselves more harm and grief to contend with, because they have become addicted to retaliative self-punishment and self-confusion. This means they exist in a constant state of self-loathing and denial of their own significance.

Some victims' indifference towards themselves has them constantly feeling insecure and they obsess about anything which can be turned into a negative connotation. This may cause the victim to anchor to their desire to control another, in an attempt to emotionally feel secure in their illusion of control. Unfortunately, some victims oppose feeling the core essences of their soul, such as unconditional love, integrity, compassion, trust and grace, and have been conditioned by their own indifference to perceive these feelings as a weakness. They fear feeling truth because they have controlled themselves to survive in indifference, and fear that the exposure of truth will unhinge their ability to anchor to their illusion of control. Victims indifference towards themselves creates behaviours that they use as a self-definition. When the victim believes there is power and control in their indifference, it allows them to secure their denial of reality and continue to be indifferent.

Some victims become accustomed to their own indifference within themselves and have created a false sense of security out of the familiarity of their indifference. The victim anchors to their indifference, which has been developed through experiences of abuse. This enables their self-judgement to flourish. The victim anchors to addictive avenues of indifference and continues to deny their own natural value, worth and significance. The enormity of what they have experienced and felt is beyond their comprehension, which leaves them reeling in their own misconceptions. Victims can become addicted to securing their own struggle with themselves, life and others, often remaining trapped in a self-punishing mentality.

The paedophile's abuse of innocence

Paedophiles contribute to the insidiousness of the energetic collective of mankind's indifference to truth, and are parasites that prey on the innocence and naivety of our most vulnerable: our children. Paedophiles seek to obliterate awareness of the truth of what they are doing and operate with a complete disregard for what they create for their victims to endure. Many paedophiles seek to sever from their own internal knowing of the truth of their soul and disregard the reality they create for their victims. They want to bypass the importance of truth and be a law unto themselves with no interference from truth. However, truth is always present, regardless of the paedophile's denial and others' inability to acknowledge the truth. The insidiousness of paedophilia is a scourge on humanity.

Some paedophiles want to indoctrinate another to experience the same indifference to truth that they feel. The knowledge of causing another to be indifferent to truth creates a power surge of control for the paedophile. Some paedophiles get a thrill from knowing they are the creators of pain and despair. They also surge in the mercilessness and malice of their elation of being able to attack the purity of truth via the innocence of another soul. They class the innocence and purity within a child as a representation of truth, which they seek to be the destroyer of. Paedophiles seek to destroy the innocence of a child to prove to themselves the prowess of their control. The paedophile wants to possess the innocence of the child and to be the reason why a soul withdraws from their own soul knowing. The paedophile wants to corrupt a child's innocence, believing this corruption is the pinnacle experience of wanting ultimate control of another soul.

The paedophile knows truth does not interfere with mankind's freewill and uses this as false justification that they can do whatever they desire. They attempt to deprive the child of their awareness of their freedom of choice and is willing to swamp the child with their control and dominance. The paedophile wants to become the orchestrator of the child's perception of their identity. Paedophilia is an attack on the child's flow of consciousness, which is the child's awareness of their unique and independent relationship with the truth of who they are and with their origins; labelled here as *True Source Divine Origin Consciousness*. They attempt to annihilate the child's awareness of truth and of their own soul's consciousness, abusing not only the child but *True Source Divine Origin*

Consciousness' unconditional love for mankind. This is an abuse of the opportunity life presents to all souls.

Some paedophiles seek to fulfil their own desire to have ultimate control over their intent to judge the worth of another soul. Paedophiles judge the usefulness of a child based only on their rating of how they suit the paedophile's sexual preferences, and completely disregard everything else about the child including that they are a soul. Paedophiles judge children as prey whose only use is to satisfy their indifference and gratify the sexual deviousness that haunts the paedophile. Some paedophiles seek to be numb and to disassociate from the truth of their own soul, and fear not being able to oppress their awareness of their soul truth. Some paedophiles construct an inflated ego around the supremacy of being able to take what they want and disregard the reality of their actions. The paedophile judges the value of their prey on their ability to contribute to the fulfilment of their role in satisfying the paedophile's depraved sexual desires.

Some paedophiles disassociate from the longevity of the pain, hurt and trauma they create for their victim to endure, and other paedophiles revel in the knowledge of the longevity. The disassociation or the revelling is how the paedophile sustains their capacity to abuse again. When the paedophile is hunting opportunities to abuse, the paedophile believes they are the rulers of their own and others' destiny. Some paedophiles' egos are so great that they delude themselves into believing that the innocent children, who they perceive as prey, are offerings to satisfy their sexual desires.

Paedophiles interpret trust as permission to do as they want. Paedophiles interpret naivety as an opportunity to control. Paedophiles interpret freewill as a licence to inflict their internal pain on another and permission to give their sexual depravities free rein. Paedophiles class innocence as a trophy. Paedophiles utilise others' indifference and complacency to take advantage of the child as a controllable commodity. Paedophiles interpret any indifference to the child, or self-absorption of the child's carers, such as parents, extended family, guardians or officials, as permission to descend into the entirety of their depravity. The paedophile has a compulsion to interpret the complacency or trust of others as permission to abuse, and to turn every opportunity to their advantage. They have a total disregard for the ramifications of their actions to the child and to all those associated with the child. They also derive a thrill out of being able to seize an opportunity to abuse, when others believe the child is being cared for.

A person's willingness to be a paedophile entraps them in the cesspit of their own indifference to truth. They deliberately reject their consciousness and allow their own indifference to parasitically consume their awareness of truth and the natural value, worth and significance of their victim. A paedophile uses their indifference to truth to create the insidious belief of being justified in their perversion. This is how the paedophile willingly inflicts the cesspit of their indifference on another. They knowingly make the choice to interrupt another's awareness of the worth of their own soul. Paedophiles knowingly deprive themselves of resolution and evolution, and also attempt to deprive their victims of resolution and evolution. The paedophile conceals the truth of being the instigator of another's severe soul oppression, and is attempting to limit the victim's potential in this lifetime. When the paedophilic experience is assessed as just sexual, the abuse to the soul is omitted from the reality of what has occurred. Some paedophiles attempt to deny how abusive they are to their victim's soul by fixating on their own sexual cravings. They derive smug satisfaction by temporarily inducing a sensation of control from being completely indifferent to another. Paedophilia is menacing soul abuse.

Paedophilic networks

While some paedophiles attempt to hide their secrets, some delight in sharing their conquests with others. They share their conquest anonymously on the internet or with others that approve and partake in the same paedophilic behaviours, or with someone they have personally corrupted to either accept their depravities or to be inflicted with the same abhorrent addiction. Some paedophiles train others to be abusers, indoctrinating them into believing they are making a lifestyle choice, that children are of no real importance and just fodder for their desires. They use comradery to overshadow the abhorrence of being willing and able to control a naïve child to be sexually, emotionally, energetically and physically at their mercy.

Some paedophiles delight in indoctrinating others to believe in the superiority they construct from having ultimate control over a defenceless, innocent child. They orientate to their perceived righteousness of being able and entitled to govern over a vulnerable child, and relish in the exploitation of the child's innocence and powerlessness. The controlling paedophile can also revel in training others to align with their deceptive justifications, to expand the network of those that are willing to exploit children in the same way as they do. These paedophiles seek to control others to apprentice to them in an attempt to franchise their own type of sexual depravity. These paedophiles derive pleasure from watching their behaviours being emulated by another, who may or may not realise they are being manipulated by the paedophile, to feed the paedophile's thirst for control. The apprentice is willingly under the control of the deviousness of the paedophile's manipulation and is enslaved by their own and the more experienced paedophile's thirst and compulsion for ultimate control of another soul.

The internet has contributed to the ability of the paedophile to seek and find other paedophiles with ease and with minimal fear of recrimination. Some paedophiles celebrate the internet as a way of sharing their conquests and make a business out of exploiting and damaging the innocence of children. When paedophiles band together, they use the belief that they are the victim who is being dehumanised for being a paedophile, and seek the company, support and approval of other paedophiles. The energetic collective of paedophilia easily builds momentum with the use of the internet. The internet has become an educational tool that paedophiles use to enhance their skills and to enforce the superiority, righteousness and justification of their indifference to the victim and to others. Some paedophiles use the internet to share tips and their so-called tricks of the trade.

For example:

- How to avoid detection
- How the laws work
- How to camouflage their reality
- How to groom victims
- How to conceal physical damage
- How to find others with exactly the same taste in victims and sexual depravities

When a paedophile is celebrated and supported to believe they have the right to sexually abuse children, the paedophile uses that support to remain indifferent to their own indifference, as their loyalty is to the protection of their sexual depravities. The sexual abuse of any child is an emotional and energetic abuse not only of the child, but also of anyone who cares about the child and society as a whole. Paedophiles fight their own internal mechanism that questions their indifference to the reality of their actions and the ramifications they create for their victim.

Some paedophiles do not want to be involved in typical everyday life and just want to be immersed in paedophilia all the time. Their total focus is on having their sexual depravities satisfied. They choose to be surrounded by like-minded paedophiles and organised rings, and are even willing to share their victims or the recordings of their exploits. Some paedophiles use the support of other paedophiles to quell their own insecurities and their internal fear about how depraved they are, seeking solace in the validation that others are involved in the same repugnant exploitation of children. It is paradoxical that they seek solace and mercy for themselves, but offer none to their victim.

Some paedophiles use the support of other paedophiles to justify forsaking their own internal knowledge of the harm and carnage they are causing to satisfy their desires and gratify any compulsion within them. These paedophiles use the support and accolades of other paedophiles to reinforce their ability to abuse the innocence of another soul with a total disregard for the soul carnage they are creating. Some paedophiles anchor to their own sadistic narcissism, so they can utilise the full force of their indifference to truth as a weapon against the innocence of a child.

The internet has become a highway that paedophiles can cruise, as they seek to create random opportunities to satisfy their sexual depravities by either finding a victim or another paedophile to share information with. Paedophiles use the internet as an educational tool where information is being pooled, which is creating an ever expanding resource. The fact that this resource is continually expanding is used by paedophiles to justify their own indifference, and as justification to continue their exploitative and abusive behaviours.

Some paedophiles use the internet to train each other, attempting to perfect the insidious nature of indifference and their ability to remain under the radar of society. We as a society have to ask if we are indifferent to the reality of paedophilia.

- Do our laws protect the innocence of children?
- Do our laws represent how we as a society feel about paedophilia?
- Do we as a society acknowledge the cost of paedophilia to the victim?
- Do we as a society acknowledge the cost of paedophilia to society as a whole?
- Do we turn a blind eye to the sexual, emotional, energetic and physical reality of paedophilia?
- Do we deny that the internet is allowing the perpetuation of the paedophiles' secret world to expand?
- Do we as society support law enforcement's ability to eradicate opportunities for paedophilia?
- Do we hide from the reality of paedophilia because it makes us uncomfortable?
- Do we as a society protect our own denial?

Silencing the victim

Paedophiles manipulate our fears because paedophiles know we do not know how to react or respond to paedophilia. Paedophiles know our first reaction may be disbelief and denial, often followed by attempts to downgrade the severity of the impact of sexual abuse, to protect ourselves from the insidiousness of the sexual, emotional, energetic and physical abuse. We are uncomfortable with our inability to control paedophiles because we want to deny the magnitude of the experience of abuse and the generational effect abuse can have on all those connected to the paedophile and the victim. Our fear of truly acknowledging the truth of paedophilia means we respond to the energy of indifference with avoidance and denial. Unless we are honestly dealing with the effects of the reality of abuse, our indifference perpetuates opportunities for more abuse.

Some paedophiles use the victim's fear to manipulate them, creating the belief in the victim that their survival is at the mercy of the paedophile. Some victims are very aware that their abuser is someone who has no boundaries and are never sure how indifferent to them and their safety the paedophile will be. Some victims are aware of the paedophile's disassociation from reality, and are therefore very fearful of what state they will be in after each abuse experience. Some paedophiles will ignore the risk to the life of the child if they believe it will enhance their sexual thrill; the child victim may fear for their life many times.

Some victims are manipulated into believing they should carry the guilt, shame and humiliation of the abuse, and that they will be safer if they keep the truth a secret. Even if threats were not made verbally, the victim believes they have to keep quiet, because they can feel the energetic intimidation being projected at them and respond with a fear reaction of freezing and silencing themselves. The paedophile uses the victim's fear of being vulnerable to create the belief that their denial and silence equates to survival.

Some paedophiles can use the child's love for another, such as a sibling, as insurance for compliance and silence, often threatening to abuse the one they love if they create problems for the paedophile. The fear of triggering another to be harmed, keeps the child under the paedophile's control. It is not uncommon for children to strive to protect each other, not realising the one they believe they are protecting is suffering the same abuse. Each child the paedophile is able to silence, ensures the paedophile's ability to manipulate another with the same threats. These paedophiles orchestrate ways of perpetuating the silence, that enables them to continue the manipulation of innocent children.

Some paedophiles know the abuse may cause victims to give up on themselves to the point where their opposition is uncontrollable. In order to bring the victim back into being submissive, the paedophile threatens to harm another. This ensures the diminishing care victims have for themselves and life will not affect the paedophile's ability to control the victim and the victim's silence. The child's choice to strive to protect another while enduring an emotional, energetic and physical hell, shows how compassionate and naturally loving the child is. The paedophile's decision to invert the child's unconditional love and compassion into a weapon the paedophile can use against the child, proves how heartless the paedophile is.

Some victims will separate from feeling the truth of their own soul, weakening their ability to enjoy life, until their life becomes just an experience they endure. Victims control themselves to anchor to their survival tactics and attempt to train themselves to survive their own separation from their awareness of their soul and disassociation from feeling truth. The paedophile relies on the victim's sense of hopelessness to create a numbness in them to the reality of the abuse, which leaves the victim aligning to the mindset of having to endure life. This mindset has them willingly withdrawing from their own sense of value, worth and significance, which the paedophile perceives as insurance for the victim's silence. The paedophile uses the victim's silence as an essential component for their own protection.

Some victims become consumed with attempting to orchestrate ways of surviving their own silence in the belief that they are protecting themselves, by actively seeking to disassociate from the torture of their emotional, energetic and physical reality. This leaves them in a state of numbness within their own indifference; the numbness protects their indifference and their indifference protects the numbness. This cyclic pattern eventually exacerbates the pain they fear acknowledging. The strategies they use to annihilate what they are feeling, in an attempt to survive their own silence, become cyclic patterns of self-torture. The victim's fear of exposing the truth and their desire to hide from their own reality inadvertently exacerbates the paedophile's ability to abuse again. The victim does not intend to protect the paedophile however, silenced truth keeps the paedophile protected.

Some victims are bombarded with the paedophile's indifference and separate from their awareness of their own soul in an attempt to resist, deny and avoid feeling the truth of the projected indifference. Some victims separate from their awareness of their soul to protect the inner sanctum of whatever they fear feeling and acknowledging. However, while separated from their awareness of their soul, the victim adopts the belief of being unworthy, because they have felt the paedophile's willingness to be completely indifferent to their natural value, worth and significance. The victim becomes enmeshed in the indifference they have felt inflicted on them by the paedophile. The victim becomes confused by what they feel and by how the paedophile has affected them. Due to the emotional and energetic shock of the insidiousness of the indifference felt during the sexual abuse, the victim loses their ability to differentiate their own energy from the paedophile's or any other indifference energy they may experience. This can trigger automatic reactions of guilt, shame and humiliation. The guilt, shame and humiliation for the sexual abuse belongs to the paedophile, however, it becomes part of how victims define themselves and remains a heresy energy within their soul's unconsciousness they are left to contend with. The guilt, shame and humiliation the victim carries becomes a stain they fear they will never escape from.

No victim deserves to carry any guilt, shame or humiliation and yet the majority of victims do, due to their own harsh self-judgement and distorted view of what they should have done. The victim overrides accepting that there was little they could have done and discounts the magnitude of control the paedophile had over them and their circumstances. The innocent child was made to experience something no one should ever have to endure. Sadly, because they have been made to experience the epitome of someone's indifference, they develop the belief of being insignificant. It is their belief of being insignificant that has fuelled their guilt, shame and humiliation.

Guilt, shame and humiliation become unresolved emotions the victim believes they have to survive and control. This all becomes a cyclic trap that back feeds the victim into the despair of feeling totally used and abused. Their memories of abuse, unexpected flashbacks and the stain they feel leave them stuck pulling veils of denial over their awareness of their own soul system. Unfortunately, guilt, shame and humiliation becomes their default emotional position.

The victim can take distorted comfort from the emotional familiarity, which entraps them in the false belief that they can hide from the truth of their feelings as long as they endure the guilt, shame and humiliation they carry. Unfortunately, they can hide from nothing. The despair, pain and hurt are always within the trepidation they feel, and they know they cannot sustain suppressing their feelings. Often, they endure the guilt, shame and humiliation in silence. Some victims never realise that they do not deserve the guilt, for they are not to blame. Shame belongs to the abuser, not the victim, as there is nothing wrong with who they are. However, the responsibility for the return of dignity rests on the victim. They are the only ones who can bring themselves out of the guilt, shame and humiliation. Others can support, be insightful and loving, but recovery and peace within is dependent on victims' willingness to value themselves. Victims' withdraw from the truth of themselves, because they are overwhelmed by their fear of being unable to escape the emotional traps resulting from their history of abuse.

Some victims attempt to survive their experience of abuse while disassociating from the reality of the emotions they have adopted and carried, and are unable to establish any clear understanding of the reality of the guilt, shame and humiliation they feel. Victims can become fixated on controlling themselves to attempt to suppress the truth of the emotions they are contending with. The paedophile relies on this fear reaction of suppression to ensure the safety of the secret, knowing the victim will ultimately seek to protect the secret to avoid being confronted with exposure of the guilt, shame and humiliation they feel and carry because they have been sexually abused. The victim can become obsessed with the fear of not knowing who is aware of the abuse and in what context the abuse has been portrayed.

Some victims' hopes and dreams for themselves become diminished due to their fear of exposing their internalised humiliation, shame and guilt. The victim's insecurities increase and they downplay the truth and significance of who they are. This means the victim will remain silenced and continue to cripple their true potential. Their attempts to suppress their memories of abuse cause the victim to create control structures that inhibit them from feeling their own natural value, worth and significance. This is an attempt to avoid the truth of what they feel about themselves as an abuse victim, the abuse and the paedophile. These victims use their desire for control to play mind games with themselves that disassociate them from their own clarity. Victims seek ways to hide the reality of the abuse from themselves. Some victims anchor to anything they believe will keep their mind too busy for their memories of abuse to creep in, others anchor to physical exhaustion working themselves to the point of being too tired to think. Others seek to be oblivious to everything and become addicted to drugs, alcohol, overeating, sex or gambling. Some become obsessed with anorexia or bulimia. The victim becomes consumed with battling their own suppression and the addictions they have created to suppress feeling their unresolved emotions.

Incestuous abuse

Incest is sexual activity between people who are closely related, linked by blood and are forbidden by law to marry. Incest is a form of rape when there is a non-consenting or underage person involved. Incestuous abuse can be extremely confusing for the victim if the perpetrator is not of an adult age. If the perpetrator is an adolescent or classed as another minor, the victim can struggle to comprehend that what is occurring is actually sexual abuse, as the abuse is often portrayed as a game. These incestuous abusers distort their family bonds warping the victim's perception and their experience of relationships and childhood fun.

Often the one who initiates the incestuous abuse uses manipulation to have the victim collude with them in their sexual game. This means the victim is trained to participate in sustaining the game. By making the sexual abuse seem like a game, they coerce victims into unknowingly entangling themselves in a distorted version of childhood interactions, where victims can be an active contributor even though they are unaware of the reality of the distortion. If the abuser believes they have convinced the victim that this is a game, they promote it as secret fun just between them to ensure the victim stays silenced. Regardless of the age of the instigator, they seem to know they need to coerce the victim into keeping it a secret. The abuser ends up believing they have ownership of their victim and are entitled to coerce them into doing what they want. The abuser, regardless of their age, believes they can hide what they are doing from the people surrounding the victim and control the environment to facilitate their secret sexual games.

In cases where the abuser is underage themselves the family may seek to protect the abuser by aligning to denial and silence, believing the abuse is just a childhood game that accidently went too far because of their naivety.

When the abuser is an adult and the family is aware of the abuse, often because it is a generational systemic problem, the family is expected to remain silent about what is occurring in their midst. The family is conditioned to perpetuate everyone's denial of reality about the true ramifications of the abuse and to continue the systemic interactions of abuse within the family. Incestuous abuse is the choice by the abuser to oppose the natural value, worth and significance of the child, for the purpose of dominating the child's world with their sexual depravity. Incestuous abuse destroys the child's awareness of their uniqueness, independence and individuality, and leaves them ensnared in the abuser's control of their life situation.

Incestuous abuse is a direct attack on the gift of life and family relations, because the victim is born into the abuser's control. This means they are entrapped by and enslaved to the abuser's sexual depravities. Incestuous abuse is the choice by the abuser to use the sacredness of family as the arena for the insidiousness of sexual abuse.

The victims of incestuous abuse are often conditioned to not question the actions of the abusers and to respect the role of the abuser in the family such as father, grandfather, uncle, brother, mother, aunt, grandmother, sister or cousin. The victim is programmed to accept the abuser's family role as an authority over how they should perceive their own purpose in life. The victim and all members of the family may anchor to their roles within the family, in an attempt to protect everyone's denial of reality. These roles within the family become anchor points for everyone to control themselves to and provide family members with a charade they can hide behind to pretend to be unaware of the family reality. Some family members may suspect abuse but fear knowing about it, so they pretend to be unaware. The family collective that is aware of the abuse becomes dominated by the abuser's desire to control everyone's denial and silence to create complacency.

Some survivors are conditioned to accept forced submission to abuse and silence, and this seeps into, and has ramifications for, all avenues of their life. They have been trained to be submissive, which means they inhibit their natural integrity and disassociates from feeling the importance of their own freewill (freedom to choose). Their enforced compliance and submission leaves them devaluing the truth of who they really are. The paedophile has taught the victim to be quietly engulfed by their own unresolved emotions and to deny truth. The victim inhibits their sense of self within this enforced silence, by torturing themselves with mind games. The secret world of self-abuse begins, which means they repel any ability to feel the significance of who they are with their indifference, confusion and self-judgement.

Some victims are conditioned to accept abuse from anyone who they believe is in a position of authority over them and will continually feel at their mercy. These victims believe they have to be submissive to those in positions of authority, and struggle with the power they believe someone else has or could potentially have over them. The victims' history of abuse confuses them over what is acceptable behaviour and what they have the right to complain about or protect themselves from. These victims perpetuate their own internal shame and fear of being humiliated, because they believe they do not have the right to use their freedom of choice to be an equal in most situations. Their fear of abuse and of confrontation often leaves them susceptible to silently enduring many forms of abuse. People who are willing to be abusive and are in positions of authority will identify the nervousness and vulnerability of an abuse victim as an easy target, sensing the victim has been programmed, conditioned and indoctrinated to be silent about abuse and submissive to authority.

Some paedophiles believe they have the right to be an authority over the child, demanding and expecting the protocol they set up to be upheld by the victim, which includes the victim remaining silent about the abuse. Many survivors fear speaking out even when they are older because humiliation, shame and a distorted sense of guilt have become so ingrained in their sense of themselves. They have also been conditioned to believe they have no entitlement to self-efficacy. These survivors use their distorted beliefs about themselves to anchor to the familiarity of their own denial and indifference, which becomes a secret illusory world hidden within their mind. The survivors' perception of themselves is plagued with insecurities that the survivor is constantly fighting. Some survivors can be relieved if another takes authority over their life. At times they become willing participants in abusive relationships, because they have been conditioned into believing they have to be reactive to others. They deny themselves the ability to freely express the truth of who they are and to be proactive in their choices. The abuse within the relationship gives the survivor something tangible to fight, and becomes justification for the familiarity of indifference they feel towards themselves and for the indifference they feel from others. The acceptance of abuse has conditioned them to live embattling many forms of indifference, constantly embroiled in a struggle with life. The familiarity of indifference creates an avenue for the survivor's denial to keep manifesting their stagnation produced from their patterns of soul oppression.

As they mature, the victim may begin to comprehend the truth of the abuse they were subjected to, and this can turn into a debilitating fear causing them to be plagued by a constant undercurrent of confusion. The confusion arises from the belief that they were not forced or coerced, which is a ramification of being unaware of the manipulation they have experienced. Some victims may never disclose the abuse and other family members may be perplexed by the tension between the abused and the abuser. The victim's desire to uphold the family image means they remain silent about their abuse, which often incurs a cost to their own emotional well being. To protect the family image they may coerce themselves to deny the potential continuation of abuse within their family. The victim's confusion can cloud their own assessment of the risk and the possibilities of the perpetuation of abuse. Some victims may even turn a blind eye to the abuse of their own child in an attempt to protect their own denial of reality.

In some families, where the abuser is a child, the victim as well as the family may shield the underage abuser in an attempt to protect the image of the family. They shield the abuser because they believe they are doing the right thing for the family and their children. Their desire to protect the family and the family image has them competing against what they know to be true. They manipulate themselves to believe their silence and compliance is protecting the family, and that they are capable of preventing further abuse. The programming and conditioning of the family can be so strong that years later the victim may expose their own child to their former abuser, denying the reality of their past abuse, and instead anchor to the image of family and family obligations. The victim may deny there is a threat to the next generation, believing they can keep their children safe while not really knowing if the former abuser is still interested in the incestuous abuse of children. The victim is confused and unsure about the abuser because they do not know if they are still a threat or if the abuse was just a childhood game. The fact that they do not even question whether it is appropriate for the abuser to be around their children shows the level of protection they have for the family image and the level of confusion they have about the reality of their history of incestuous abuse.

When some families discover the reality of incestuous abuse, each member of the family reels as their foundation of life rips apart. When the reality of how they perceived their life is ripped apart and they discover something they thought could never occur in their own family, they become traumatised. It is a tortuous path to navigate between disbelief at what has occurred and the reality of what has occurred. Each family member feels torn about how they used to perceive the abuser before they knew of the abuse and how they now relate to them becomes riddled with confusion. Many feel they get to the brink of madness unable to reconcile with the truth of the abuse within their family and the reality of the abuser. This sense of being at a complete loss festers as they start to assess why they did not know and this contributes to their confusion about how this could have happened without them realising.

If the abuser is denying the abuse and the victim is visibly disturbed the family struggles to comprehend what is occurring. An unfathomable shift occurs when the family start to fear that the one they love (such as: father, mother, grandfather, grandmother, son, daughter, brother, sister, uncle, aunt, nephew or niece) has been capable of the insidiousness of sexual abuse. Those who seek the truth, can also fear knowing the truth. They know that the reality of what has occurred will forever destroy what they thought their family was, how their family should be, and any predications they had for their family's future.

In some cases, the fundamental question as to why the abuser became abusive may never have an answer. This can leave family members blaming themselves for missing the reality that there was an abuser in their midst, and the complexities of loving someone who has caused so much pain, suffering and upheaval becomes an internal battle they fear they may never reconcile.

The victim can identify the abuser with two different filters. One filter is that the abuser is caring and easy to spend time with during normal family interactions. This means the victim has to try to pretend the other part of the abuser is non-existent in these family times. The victim's disassociation from reality is a survival mechanism, which allows them to operate in the family dynamics seemingly oblivious to their experience of the abuse. They desperately try to retain a sense of normality. The other filter is that the abuser is dangerous and indifferent to them, which leaves them fearing the middle of the night or being alone as these are the danger times. Victims can feel the disclosure of abuse is the reason their family is falling apart and distort the blame onto themselves. This can cause great harm as they beat themselves up for not being able to remain silent, and it is often the exposure of the victims' internal chaos that alerts others that there is even a problem. The victim struggles to contain their emotional upheaval, which can be the first indication that there is something untoward going on or has been going on in the past. Victims can torture themselves about the emotional fallout unable to reconcile the pain they feel and often mistakenly believe they have caused the destruction of the family.

The survivor's mind chatter

The incessant way the survivor creates mind games with their constant self-questioning is part of the self-abuse that plagues and impales them with indifference, judgement, guilt, shame and humiliation. Survivors have been conditioned either by their abuser or themselves to reinforce their own disassociation from feeling truth, self-love and compassion, which leaves them confused and disorientated about their own natural value, worth and significance. Their mind chatter can become relentless as they feel they are an enigma, unable to find a solution to how they feel about themselves. Survivors' mind chatter become cyclic questions that they struggle to answer. They can become consumed with so many misconceptions, that their perception of themselves and what they have experienced is distorted.

A victim can become trapped by their constant questioning, such as:

- Why me?
- Does it show?
- Where is God?
- Did I want this?
- Did I create this?
- Did I deserve this?
- Is it because I'm ugly?
- Is it because I'm pretty?
- When will this stop being my first waking thought?
- Why was I born?
- Am I going to die?
- Does anyone care?
- When will I be free?
- When will this ever stop?
- When will this happen again?
- Is it because I'm worth nothing?
- Did I deserve this because of karma?
- Are my parents/brothers/sisters/ safe?

These questions within their mind chatter reinforce their own indifference towards themselves, distorting any truth they might realise. Their mind chatter chips away at any recognition of their own value, worth and significance. This leaves them crippled in their distorted understanding of their own significance, unwilling to be honest about reality and avoiding the truth of their unresolved emotions. They settle into the perception of themselves of being a victim and compare themselves to the world via their victim mentality. This leaves some victims stuck in the belief that others are entitled to be an authority over them, whereas some victims fight any authority. This can be problematic to holding down employment and working with others with dominating personalities.

Some survivors can become addicted to their mind games, which results in them being contrary in how they interact with themselves and others. They constantly protect their own misconceptions and negative perceptions of themselves, others and their false reasoning for why they became an abuse victim. This has them constantly anticipating potential affects on what they are trying to protect. These survivors use mind games as calculated mental processes that become tactics to manipulate themselves and others, for the purpose of creating confusion or intimidation. The survivor is plagued by many mind games, which results in the perpetuation of their emotional despair and creates an arena where they constantly feel emotionally embattled by their history of abuse. This can be a hidden internal world, orchestrating sly interactions with others or an explosive external way of interacting with others. Survivor can become unaware of how manipulative, to themselves and others, their mind games are and how entrapped they are in their own self-abusive tactics. Unfortunately, because the survivor is consumed with mind games, they can slip easily into the narcissism of believing they are the smartest person in the room, willing to exploit every situation to enact their fears or to become entwined in a power play. Either way the result is indifference to the significance and value of being honest with and about themselves.

Some survivors fear they are worthless, powerless and insignificant, and continue to feel as helpless as they felt within the experience of abuse. These survivors fear the way they emotionally feel about themselves is true; this is a misconception that has them denying the value of their own soul. These survivors have been conditioned to attack themselves with their denial of their own value, worth and significance, and to devalue any recognition of truth. This allows the paedophile to secure their position of authority over the silence of the abused. Survivors torture themselves about the authority they believe the paedophile has to silence them. Survivors fear not having the stamina to stand alone in truth and to expose the insidious nature of the abuse and the abuser, because they have become compliant to what was forced upon them, surreptitiously aligning to the indifference energy that surrounds them.

Some survivors are reluctant to acknowledge the truth of what their denial or mind games are doing to their understanding of themselves, because they fear accepting their own contribution to oppressing themselves. When survivors remain indifferent to their victim mentality, they stagnate their own ability to participate in the resolution of the unresolved emotions caused by their experience of being abused. They cling to a victim mentality, believing it keeps them emotionally, energetically and physically safer, because they fear confronting what they have experienced and the ramifications they are enduring. Resolving the emotions caused by the experience of abuse is complex and requires a willingness to be completely honest, which can be very daunting.

Some survivors believe they can hide from the reality of themselves. However, they are not hiding from their unresolved emotions, they are immersed in their unresolved emotions, seeking to justify and pacify their emotional, energetic and physical reality with the label of victim. The label of victim limits their perception of themselves and causes them to be stagnated in their unresolved emotions, unable to resolve beyond their own perception of being a victim. Some survivors become too frightened to challenge their own perception of themselves, incarcerating themselves in an emotional prison. To hide from the reality of their soul some survivors create floods of emotions, which are used to sustain and validate their own indifference. The survivor uses their mind chatter to create decoys to resist, deny and avoid acknowledging the true effect their denial and victimhood is having on the way they live life.

Silence causes the survivor of abuse to anchor to denial and to inadvertently protect the familiarity of struggling against the truth of being a significant soul. When indifference to truth is protected we give permission for our denial to silence truth. When a victim is flanked by silence, created from the willingness to be indifferent to truth, they use their internal mind chatter to oppose the silence while they render themselves unable to clearly communicate what they have felt, experienced and endured. The trauma the survivor has experienced causes them to deny the significance of how they feel and that their feelings are signposts exposing the truth of their own reality. The survivor struggles to oppress the significance of their own uniqueness, independence and individuality as a soul and the value of their soul journey.

When a survivor is immersed in their unresolved emotions and in denial of their own significance, any evidence of their natural value, worth and significance can be met with distrust and they become willing to sabotage their own awareness of truth. Their experience of abuse and indifference has the survivor devaluing the essence of truth and devaluing that they have the key to feeling freedom from their own oppression. The key to resolution is their realisation that regardless of the abuse they have experienced, they are of value, worth and significance.

The victim wants to believe that their freedom comes from not physically seeing or being at the mercy of the paedophile, but there are other aspects to freedom which cannot be discounted, such as being free from their own silent torture. Silence empowers the control the hunter has over the hunted. Part of victims' resolution is to know what is haunting them and to trust themselves to acknowledge their own unresolved emotions, such as denial, resentment, indifference, internal rage and self-judgement, so they can give themselves permission to value their own ability to evolve beyond their limited perception of themselves.

The paedophile's depravities

Some paedophiles emotionally feel like they are persistently gunned by their own compulsions, sexual depravities and unresolved emotions. These paedophiles feel their own indifference towards themselves goading them to abandon the truth of their soul for the familiarity of their own indifference. They become seduced by their desire for control and their prevailing disposition to be indifferent. They become addicted to the secrecy, believing they can control the outcome of their sexual depravities and the emotional carnage they cause and inflict on another soul. These paedophiles fear the exposure of the secret world of their sexual deviance because they do not want to be confronted with their own weakness, and want to protect themselves from acknowledging the truth of their own struggle within themselves. Some paedophiles want to secure their indifference to feeling the reality of their own disassociation from truth and to ensure their own willingness to be silent about what they despise.

Some paedophiles have an awareness of how insidious their sexual depravities are but refuse to acknowledge their own freedom of choice, clinging to the image of being a victim to their own sexual depravities and compulsions. These paedophiles refuse to be honest about the reality of what they have become and the ramifications of their quest to control their ability to satisfy their selfish desires. Some paedophiles believe their compulsions cause their actions and separate themselves from the reality of making the choice to abuse a child. Some paedophiles separate themselves from the reality of the emotional carnage caused by their sexual depravities and compulsions. They have conditioned themselves to dwell in their own mind space, manipulating themselves to believe they are innocent and that they are controlled by their own sexual desire or circumstance. Some paedophiles choose to believe they are a victim, in an attempt to justify their own lack of self-control and willingness to harm a child.

Some paedophiles blame the child for igniting their sexual desires. They use this mindset to justify their own willingness to abuse, and to be indifferent to the emotional carnage they are creating for the child to carry and endure. Some paedophiles justify their addiction to sexually abusing children, because they deny they are the problem and instead blame the opportunity to be alone with a child as the problem. They often use manipulation and deception to overshadow the reality that they created the opportunity to be alone with the child. Paedophiles are very dangerous; especially those who delude themselves into being separated and disassociated from the reality of their own behaviour, manipulation, deception, indifference and denial, because they set no boundaries for themselves. Some paedophiles are constantly attempting to shift the blame for their desire and compulsion to abuse and to be indifferent to what they are doing, by saying that it is something outside themselves that is making them do it, like the devil. This is in an attempt to deny responsibility and suppress their own fear of internally knowing there will be a day of reckoning.

Some paedophiles have created the perfect scenario for their sexual depravities by controlling the environment the victim lives in. These paedophiles control those around their victim to be financially reliant on them for their survival or to supply the lifestyle they want. Some paedophiles will deliberately control the parent or carer of the child to be emotionally attached to the lifestyle they supply, knowing that the lifestyle is what the parent or carer of the child want to sustain for themselves. When the paedophile knows the parent or carer do not want to be alone and seek to feel loved and valued, they manipulate the parent or carer to turn a blind eye to what is happening to the child. The paedophile will use the parent's or carer's fear of being alone as leverage for more control. Paedophiles know that by inserting themselves as an integral part of the family unit, they will have more liberty to disguise their intentions.

The code of silence

Individuals within the family can feel cornered into being fooled by the paedophile's control and image, and adopt a code of silence around the truth of what they can really feel about the predatory nature of the paedophile. They feel cornered because to follow through with the truth of what they feel, means they will have to confront what is incomprehensible to them and because it is a feeling, they are unsure how to substantiate if it is a reality. Individuals who feel the predatory nature in spite of the paedophile's charade, may become confused about what they are feeling, and will anchor to the image being portrayed, especially if it quells their fear of having to confront the truth of what they feel. Individuals within the family may override their own concerns about feeling uneasy and that something is off or not quite right, because they believe they cannot do anything about what they are feeling. When an individual is unsure about what they are feeling, they align to the family's collective behaviour towards the paedophile. When the paedophile is a family member or an integral part of supplying a lifestyle for the family, the concerned individual often denies and overrides the uneasiness they feel for fear of creating conflict and rocking the boat.

Individuals who are suspicious of the paedophile, can be reluctant to trust their own awareness and baulk at articulating the truth of what they feel. We can all be reluctant to acknowledge the significance of what we feel and have been conditioned to discount the importance of our awareness. In the arena constructed by the paedophile we are made to distrust what we feel even more, and for such a big accusation we think we need substantial, tangible evidence to support what would be exposed. The fear of being wrong and of falsely accusing another of paedophilia can cause us to retreat into a code of silence. Individuals can retreat into a code of silence, because they have been conditioned by their fear of judgement to believe their feelings will be easily discredited and dismissed as nonsense. Individuals can be reluctant to express the truth of what they feel, because they fear being ridiculed, or that they will be the cause of trouble. We are programmed, conditioned and indoctrinated by our fear of judgement to assess the situation as treacherous for our own reputation, knowing that the focus of others will most probably be diverted from the reality of the situation, and become about the validity of the whistleblower.

When an individual becomes concerned about possible sexual abuse and is aware that others will protect their own denial at any cost, they can begin to fear that those within the collective denial surrounding the sexual abuse might ferociously turn on them. They fear being accused of dispelling the images and illusions of those who want to retain their own denial of reality. For their own reasons all parties connected to the paedophile and victim may align to the code of silence, fearing their inability to cope with the truth and reality of exposing sexual abuse. Those concerned individuals who feel tortured by their awareness of abuse or suspected abuse, energetically feel the collective energy of denial, but are often unable to explain to themselves what they are feeling. Some automatically withdraw and implode within their own self-judgement, while fearing they are contributing to the abuse by being silent. Some concerned individuals can feel controlled by those who want to hide from the truth, such as families who form a collective of denial and are willingly protecting the paedophile. The potential whistleblower can feel controlled and coerced to remain silent and to uphold the images and illusions of those they feel are hiding behind a charade.

Individuals who sense the presence of abuse or the presence of a paedophile, but have no physical evidence, can either allow themselves to doubt to what they feel, be tortured by the belief that it would be inappropriate to judge someone without proof, or feel the angst of not knowing what to do. Individuals can be confused by their own reactions to what they feel and may retreat to their own mistrust of what they can sense, and judge themselves for being unable to know for sure. The paedophile knows that, "if there is no proof then the accuser can be judged as being paranoid, a trouble maker or a vindictive attention seeker" and they use this to hide behind. Some individuals who feel the energy of the paedophile relinquish their awareness because they do not know what to do. They anchor to the image being projected by the paedophile or the victim, and use that as a means to discount what they feel.

Paedophiles use the fear of judgement as a buffer zone to protect themselves, knowing that even if someone is suspicious they would have to negate their own fear of being judged to verbalise their concerns. If the paedophile is aware of another's suspicion they may manipulate others to be suspicious of the prospective whistleblower's integrity. The whistleblower can end up being classed as the insidious one if others succumb to the paedophile's manipulation. The whistleblower ends up being accused of creating carnage and being the problem as the paedophile manipulates others to believe that their reputation is being viciously attacked and that all accusations are false.

Some paedophiles may use another's suspicion as an indicator that it is time to move on, and instigate a search for their next victim, contriving a new plan to protect themselves from being exposed. Unfortunately, the potential whistleblower's concerns can be quelled when paedophiles remove themselves from the situation. The individual who felt uneasy with the predatory energy of the paedophile may never fully understand the feeling, and as soon as the predatory energy is removed from their presence, the individual's awareness of the paedophilic energy may subside. This is why many paedophiles who cannot control an image to conceal the truth of their sexual depravity will create opportunities to constantly move locations, or be in a situation where they have continual access to different potential victims.

Potential whistleblowers who retreat from articulating their concerns, generally implode on themselves, if their concerns turn out to be true. They may blame themselves, fearing their silence contributed to the continuation of the abuse. They judge themselves harshly for being a bystander and ignoring their own internal reaction to the paedophile. What the potential whistleblower is reluctant to admit is that they too are a victim of the manipulation of the paedophile. The potential whistleblower reassesses, judges and emotionally relives the memories of sensing something was not quite right. They berate themselves about being able to acknowledge that they could feel something but were unable to prove the reality of what they were feeling. They cruel themselves on their own previous justification for ignoring what they felt. However, flanked with others' denial, they had nowhere to go to expose the suspected truth. Denial creates insecurity and potential whistleblowers may be unforgiving towards themselves and feel overcome with guilt and shame, which causes them to wallow in their inability to control reality.

Unlike the controlled persona of the paedophile, the victim's inability to cope with truth can cause them to emotionally act out. This can make them an easy target for critical judgement. Often the abused can become the accused, and the reality of the paedophile and sexual abuse is omitted out of the equation. The most vulnerable become targeted with indifference by those who seek to secure their denial and pacify their own illusion of control. This becomes another layer of indifference that the victim, the supporters of the victim and those seeking truth have to contend with. Each individual who becomes involved in the ramifications of the abuse brings their own opinion and agenda to the situation. This broadens what the victim has to contend with, which can be even more overwhelming for them. Each individual who becomes involved may righteously fight and defend their own judgement and assessment of reality. They make their involvement about being right in their judgement, even if it means being to the detriment of the abused and overriding any evidence that contradicts their judgement. The victim may feel others' willingness to protect their own judgement as another attack on their worth, causing them to plummet further into the despair of believing they are insignificant.

At times, the loved ones of the victim become overwhelmed with their inability to cope with reality, and become shocked at the enormity of the fall-out created by the abuse. The loved ones become lost in their inability to know what to do to fix the situation and emotionally reel in the realisation that they are, and were, unable to control reality to suit their own illusion of control. The loved ones struggle to overcome their fears for the victim and themselves, which can leave them immersed in their own negative beliefs of being useless and not good enough. This causes them to become shell-shocked and overwhelmed by their harsh self-judgement.

When people involved in the aftermath of abuse come from their own agenda, they can inhibit the exploration of the truth of the situation. Individuals or organisations who are inhibitors to the discovery of truth can be connected either to the victim or the paedophile. Individuals and organisations who want to fight the reality of exposing the truth of the abuse, can become a collective force of denial and indifference to reality via their judgement of the abused, the abuser or the whistleblower. They will use their ability to manipulate the perception of reality, to discredit any exposed truth that counteracts or interferes with their assessment of how reality should be perceived. If someone challenges their judgement of reality they will seek to assassinate the credibility of the challenger. The ones who want to protect their own denial of reality will omit asking themselves what their motivation for denial is, and without understanding their own motivation may become as insidious as the abuser. This indifference to reality can cause the individuals or organisation to be venomous in their appraisal of reality and of those they believe are opposing their version of how reality should be perceived.

Those who inhibit revealing the truth about the abuse or the paedophile will want to secure their own indifference to reality and will attempt to protect themselves from acknowledging the reality of what they are contributing to. If an individual or an organisation is opposing the uncovering of the truth, they will align to protecting their own denial for the purpose of trying to control their image or to avoid any inconvenience they believe the truth will cause. This is the choice to be manipulative, deceptive and indifferent to truth. Some organisations put a lot of resources into sustaining their own indifference to the abuse that has occurred under their banner. They try to hide the reality of their own indifference to protect the organisations' image. This stems from a belief that the organisations' image is more important than truth and the victim's wellbeing. If an individual or an organisation wants to dictate what the truth is, they will align to any denial that enables them to remain fiercely protective of their own indifference to truth.

The victim feels emotionally violated by the silence of the bystanders, and the individuals and organisations who inhibit uncovering the truth. Bystanders are not physically involved but are aware and choose to do nothing. The victim will resent all those who knew of the abuse but chose to deny their own awareness and will be disgusted by how indifferent others have had to be in order to ignore the victim's emotional pain, fear and vulnerability. The victim's recognition of others' indifference can be used to reinforce their belief of not being worthy enough to acknowledge the abuse. When others do not face up to the truth of their abuse, the victim perceives this as vindication that they are insignificant.

Public opinion within society is a form of mankind judgement. This becomes multi-layers of emotional, energetic and physical energy, which compounds the abuse experience. Different factions of mankind judgement join together to form energetic collectives of the same opinions. Those within the collective judge and assess the validity of the victim and the paedophile, while potentially ignoring the reality of their own indifference to truth and reality. Once the collective force of opinion aligns to what they want reality to be or what they think reality is, truth is sacrificed to public opinion. Those in control of the collective force want to protect their version of reality and will systemically try to control the judgement of others to reinforce their opinion. The ones who want to protect their own denial of reality align to the public opinion that most suits the energy of their own unresolved emotions. Some people will align to a public opinion, even when they have no knowledge of the entirety of the situation they are judging. Some people will anchor to their own 'I know' beliefs and will be very dismissive of the reality of the abused, the abuser and the abuse.

When a collective of people deny the abuse, they will attempt to steer and build a momentum of public opinion to create a witch-hunt against the abused or the whistleblower, because they want to shift the focus away from the paedophile and the reality of the sexual abuse. This becomes another experience of indifference that the victim feels and has to contend with. Those wanting to protect their denial will want to remain indifferent to the reality of the paedophile and indifferent to the experience the abused has endured. The members within the collective of denial are there to protect their own interests and are content for the abused to be ostracised and left to fester in their own unresolved emotions. Those wanting to protect their denial retaliate against any exposure of their own insidious nature and can be relentless in their pursuit for control. Those wanting to protect their denial do not take being interfered with lightly, and the desire to control the denial becomes an insatiable source of indifference that is constantly injected into the situation.

People protecting their unresolved emotions can easily become willing to remain unconscious to truth. They will oppose what interferes with their denial and fight whatever and whomever exposes their indifference to truth and reality, regardless of any evidence that contradicts their opinions about reality. Those wanting to protect their denial of truth and reality attempt to impose a code of silence. If an individual breaks from the collective denial of reality and refuses to conform to the code of silence, the individual will have to withstand the scrutiny of others' judgement, indifference and the energetic wrath of those protecting their denial.

We have all been programmed, conditioned and indoctrinated to believe we will be emotionally assassinated by judgement generated from others' vindictive disregard for truth. This perpetuates our willingness to withdraw and hide from the reality of abuse. The victim should be commended and supported for holding to the value of truth, especially in the face of vindictive judgement.

A paedophile's cult leadership and domination

When the paedophile controls the environment, such as a family or a cult situation, and believes there is no need to hide the reality of their own paedophilic nature, they will command others to accept their sexual depravities as their entitled right. They train others to be indifferent and compliant to the reality of their sexual desires, abusive actions, invasive demands and obscene justifications for their outrageous behaviour. The paedophile's sadistic presence causes uneasiness in the collective of people living within their control. There is a constant undercurrent of tension as others try to anticipate what is going to happen next and who the paedophile is going to focus on. The paedophile may use different methods to subjugate or subdue each of the individuals living under their control. The paedophile will target some individuals for their sexual gratification and will use physical or verbal abuse to keep others subdued. Individuals in this environment have to separate from their awareness of truth and lose their compassion for themselves and others to survive with any sense of security or control. This leads them to align to an illusion which only results in emotional and physical pain for all involved, creating an insidious merry-go-round of denial, corruption and abuse.

As those worshipping the paedophile deny or justify the pain caused by their paedophilic leader, they secure the paedophile's ability to have free rein to be the master of their domain. This means they are complicit in helping to orchestrate a supply of victims for the paedophile. The paedophile uses outrageous lies and shows complete disregard for the ramifications of their abusive behaviours, beliefs and desires that sustain their own insidious agenda. They are also reliant on those surrounding them to be obedient and devoted to their web of deception as they scheme to have ultimate control, and have everyone aligning to their constructed charade.

Individuals within this paedophilic environment try to keep the paedophile calm and in control, fearing a backlash toward themselves and others they care about. They are often aware that if the paedophile chooses to harm someone they care about, they will be powerless to intervene. Everyone within the paedophile's environment has been programmed, conditioned and indoctrinated to pacify and be submissive to the sadistic nature of the paedophile, turning a blind eye to reality and accepting the paedophile's demands. They have been conditioned to deny the reality they feel and to accept the paedophile's will as the status quo. They fight the truth of their own feelings with indifference towards themselves, reality and truth, which causes them to become a willing or unwilling co-conspirator with the paedophilic leader.

When children are born into the paedophile's control, the children are programmed, conditioned and indoctrinated to believe they have no right to oppose what is occurring, and they can become unwilling co-conspirators with the paedophile's illusion of control. These children have to be compliant, silent about their feelings and reality, and be an enabler of the ego of the paedophile, to actually survive their own internal and external nightmare. The child's confusion has them anchoring to whatever they believe will alleviate their fear and insecurity created from being abused, which may consist of denial, illusions, anger or depression. Some children are conditioned to compete with other children to be on top of the paedophile's pecking order. This has the paedophile securing their position of power over the children by having them compete, and this divides and crushes the children's loyalty and compassion for each other. This infighting among the children, is orchestrated by the paedophile to distract the children and others involved from realising the power they could have if they unified and sought outside help. The children's fighting takes the focus off what is really going on, and the children often become identified as the problem.

Within cults or a family dominated by an unabashed paedophile, the paedophile will use brainwashing methods which programme, condition and indoctrinate the members to believe the paedophile is a supreme being with elite knowledge. The paedophile projects an image of having the exclusive privilege of a direct line of communication with their god. The god the paedophile refers to is actually their own ego and desire to control. To gain control over the member's thought process, the paedophile manipulates the member's insecurities and desire to be special. The paedophile manipulates the members to override their internal doubts and to conform to the paedophile's control. To prove their devotion to the paedophile's imaginary version of god, they must be willing to please the paedophile's every whim and sexual desire, under the guise that this is acceding to their god's decree.

The members of the cult are expected to give the paedophile authority over their children as proof of their loyalty to the cult and communal lifestyle. The paedophile exerts their illusion of control as the authority of truth in every aspect of the member's life. Unfortunately, by aligning to the paedophile, the members separate from feeling their own soul integrity and become willing to conform to and believe in the authority of the paedophile. Members of the cult become obsessed with securing a sense of belonging and significance within the insanity of the cult structure, which means they forsake the truth of who they are and ignore the value of their own independence and integrity. This allows the paedophile to programme the members into trusting the paedophile in spite of being able to observe and feel the madness.

The cult members forsake feeling the reality of being unique, independent, individual souls of truth who are naturally significant, to be puppets of the paedophile's manipulation. The paedophile has the members believing the pacification of the paedophile's demands, sexual depravities and desire to be revered is the path to god and redemption. The adherence by members of the cult to the paedophile's insanity, means they deny the reality that all souls are of origin truth and that each individual soul has their own direct line to truth. Only insidious narcissistic people who are separated from their awareness of their soul and disassociated from feeling the truth of themselves and the insanity of their actions, would use the concept of being of truth to manipulate, abuse, rape and attempt to destroy others' souls for their sexual depravities and desire to control. Truth communicates truth; the paedophile communicates deception, lies and their own insanity.

When people separate from their awareness of their soul and truth, they become immersed in their own unresolved emotions, which makes them susceptible to the manipulation of the paedophile. It is the paedophile's ability to manipulate the unresolved emotions of others that creates the charade of elitism. The paedophile wants to keep the members reliant and does this by deliberately identifying the members' unresolved emotions, using their insecurities as a weapon to control them. The paedophile uses their reliance to govern the members' beliefs, thoughts and behaviours. Worshiping the paedophile is construed as essential for the members' development within the cult. The members' willingness to be reliant on the paedophile sustains the arena for the paedophile to continue deluding them.

The paedophile seeks to gain ultimate control of the cult members' life experiences and dictates how the members should perceive themselves, so the more favourably the paedophile acknowledges the member, the deeper the member's devotion becomes to the paedophile. The paedophile knows how to use the member's ego and fears to nullify any doubts and questions they may have about the reality of the cult and the reality of the paedophile's insidious nature. This can cause a cluster of paedophiles to take up senior positions within the cult, creating a cesspit of different types of debauchery and abuse under the guise of being ordained by their god, or by the leading paedophile.

The members' internal confusion has them constantly manipulating themselves to align to the cult's perception of reality. They seek to use the cult to fulfil their desire to be validated, elite and to create a sense of belonging. The paedophile becomes who the members desire to be validated by, in the belief that the paedophile is superior to all other beings. Individuals become members because they are seeking a replacement for their own reality and align to the paedophile's illusions and plans for the future. They become mesmerised by the paedophile's image and illusions, while denying the reality they are experiencing within the cult. The paedophilic cult leader seeks to isolate the members from society, to ensure the paedophile has ultimate control over the way they perceive the world.

Children who are born into the cult are even more isolated and susceptible to the paedophiles' image and illusions, because they have no knowledge of the outside world and nothing to compare their reality to. Regardless of how brainwashed they are, sexual abuse leaves a stain on the victim, which produces an internal pressure and ignites an internal knowing that abuse is not respectful, caring or pre-ordained. Some victims align to the survival mechanism of suppressing their own awareness of the insidiousness of the paedophile with denial of their own awareness of the truth. This causes victims to take the paedophile's outrageous claims and lies, and regurgitate them as their own commentary, in an attempt to shield themselves from the insanity of what is occurring. Sexual abuse, regardless of the denial, leaves an innate bewilderment and awareness of insanity.

Often the paedophile creates fear within the cult members that the outside world will interfere with their purity and seek to destroy their relationship with their god. This fear breeds paranoia about the influence of the outside world, so the cult members isolate themselves and do not question the truth of the cult. The secrecy the cult aligns to enables the paedophile even more uninterrupted control over the cult. The members of the cult can become suspicious of anyone who displays any doubt, or questions the validity of the paedophile's directives, which means they will be met with collective judgement from within the cult as it attempts to rein in any disruption to the paedophile's control or potential exposure of the truth of the cult.

The paedophile manipulates the cult with the illusion of being wise and selects words of wisdom that appeal to the members' insecurities and fears. The words they select to use are not a true reflection of the paedophile and are part of their manipulation for control of the members. To create an illusion of security for the members to anchor to, the paedophile often promises the members rewards for their loyalty in this life, in heaven or their next life. These promises secure the paedophile's ability to manipulate and challenge the member's emotional, energetic and physical boundaries, which causes the members to accept the orchestration of the paedophile with little resistance. The paedophile arrogantly believes no one should question their ability to fulfil their promises and expects blind faith.

The paedophile is indifferent to the soul carnage created by their lies, deception and manipulation, and only seeks to pacify their own desire for ultimate control of others and to control a safe environment for their own sexual depravities. Paedophile use their interpretation of the concept of god and the word 'god' as a weapon against the truth of all souls being significant, imposing themselves as an authority over truth, reality and god. The paedophile uses the word 'god' to hide the reality of their own manipulation, deception, indifference and desire for ultimate control. The paedophile controls the members' concept of god to ensure that they allow the paedophile's insidious nature free rein. The paedophile uses the word 'god' to manipulate the members into believing that god had a destiny plan for them all to appease the paedophiles' sexual depravities and desire for control.

Sadly, the children of the cult members become the innocent offerings to the paedophile; these children have no ability to reject any proposal of abuse, because they are flanked by everyone's denial of reality within the cult. These children are at the mercy of those who are brainwashed into believing they have the entitled right to impose their illusions and sexual desires onto the children. The children have been programmed, conditioned and indoctrinated into the ultimate control of the paedophile and fear being ostracised and abandoned by their families, inflicted with physical pain or the punishment of being delivered to the paedophile for opposing the cult's rules. The children fear verbalising the reality they feel and instinctively know how vulnerable they are within all the layers of deception.

The cult members who want to secure their position within the pecking order of the cult, indoctrinate their children to be compliant to their desire to be validated by the cult and the paedophilic leader. They reinforce the programming, conditioning and indoctrinations of the cult to their own children because they fear being judged. The members use their own children to appease the paedophile seeking to validate their positioning within the hierarchical system of the cult. These members use their children to appease their own ego and justify their actions because they are lost in their unresolved emotions, disassociated from feeling the truth of their own reality and seek validation for their worth from the paedophile.

The confusion created by sexual abuse conditions the victim to always feel vulnerable to their oppressors. The impact of the confusion is greater when the victim feels and recognises the insidiousness of the abuse, because they realise that what is being spruiked by the paedophilic cult leader and conspirators is actually fraudulent, faulty concepts and blatant contradictions designed to enhance the paedophile's power and control. When the victim can acknowledge the self-interest of the co-conspirators that support and conform to the paedophilic leader, they uncover the insanity fuelling the cult. This intensifies the vulnerability they feel and they become entrapped in fear, uncertainty and their own awareness of the lunacy and betrayal perpetuated by the paedophilic leader and the cult members.

Paedophiles are always oppressors and operate from the desire to make their victims puppets for their sexual depravities. Some will even get their victims to become a co-conspirator to find other victims, as they seek continuity for their opportunities to abuse. When the victim is unable to escape everyone's lunacy, they may feel compelled to conform to the paedophile's control and demands, even after they have been discarded. It is a travesty of the abuse they have endured and the indifference they have suffered, that they succumb to the brainwashing that enables them to condemn another soul, or generations of souls, to the paedophile's demands and desires.

Betrayal of trust

Some victims experience more indifference when they seek help from others but are ignored, ridiculed or told to accept the sexual abuse as normal and to remain silent. It takes an inordinate amount of courage to reveal the truth, because the victims are exposing themselves and could incur the paedophile's wrath. When the victim risks breaking the code of silence by trusting someone enough to tell the truth of their abuse, they feel very violated if they are ignored, ridiculed or told to accept the sexual abuse. When this trust is betrayed it has a devastating effect on the victim. The victim uses the violation by the one they trusted, to concretise their belief of being worthless and insignificant. This leaves them generating self-destructive pathways which they emotionally implode in.

Some paedophiles groom the family of their victims to continue the secret world of abuse and encourage infighting within the family. The internal family conflict becomes classed as normal behaviour and allows the paedophile to govern over the dysfunction as either the patriarch or matriarch. These paedophiles programme, condition and indoctrinate all their victims to act out their emotional angst on each other. The paedophile trains their victims to attack, judge and compete against each other. The victims seek a place to vent out the suppressed anger, rage, resentment and defiance that they have about their own experience of sexual abuse, and often become willing participants in the family conflict. This can cause a family of victims to judge and compete against each other and violently attack each other with their own suppressed unresolved emotions.

In some cases of perpetuated sexual abuse within families, the progression of victims can be trained to be violent and indifferent towards the current victim of the paedophile. The current victim is more vulnerable within the family because there is a myriad of abuse being hurled their way as they become the scapegoat that everyone inflicts their own frustration and denial upon. The family has been tainted by the paedophile's control and conditioned to be sadistic as they are unable to contain their inability to cope with the reality of the abuse within their family. Victims can turn against another victim who is experiencing or has experienced the same emotional pain and indifference as themselves, because the victim reminds them of their own experience of being controlled by the paedophile and feeling powerless and insignificant. Some victims want to emotionally feel empowered over something and are willing to be indifferent and abusive towards another victim to emotionally feel in control of someone else. These disturbed victims act out their resentment or rage on someone who is as vulnerable as themselves. When the victim abuses another, being abusive adds to their internal torment, because they feel shame and guilt for hurting another. Their willingness to be abusive inhibits them from being compassionate towards others and themselves. Everyone involved is left with emotional scars.

In some perpetuated cases of abuse the competition between the paedophile's victims can become violent as they become indifferent to the reality of each other's emotional pain. Jealousy overrides each of the victim's ability to be compassionate for one another, even though they have all experienced the same abuse. Their jealousy causes them to compete in every aspect of their lives, such as:

- Physical appearance
- Who has been able to control their life to be better than their childhood
- Who is superior and more righteous within the family
- Who has the ability to cope with their history of abuse
- Who has the clearest recollection of their abuse
- Who has been the most devoted to and protective of their abuser
- Who has protected the family image
- Who has made the greatest sacrifice for the family
- Who is controlling their own life
- Who is the best at denial
- Who has suffered the most
- Who has been able to perpetuate abuse undetected
- Who did or did not make the mistake of living with another paedophile or another type of abuser

The judgement and competition with each other can be relentless and is a way of distracting themselves from how they feel about their history of abuse. Unfortunately, for some victims they have been conditioned to compete for the attention of the paedophile and have a very misguided perspective of their own emotional reality. This can sustain family upheaval.

Some victims act out their suppressed unresolved emotions via verbal abuse. Their verbal abuse becomes an intoxicating way of trying to control their environment. They use their rants, raves and insidious nastiness to verbally abuse those around them. They want to use the unpredictability of their emotional reactions to life to make others feel vulnerable in their presence. The victim seeks to gain ultimate control of the ones they love, fearing if they are not in control they may get hurt. They use their ability to verbally abuse as a weapon against the ones they love. They want those they love to be submissive to them, and use fear to control them to be compliant to their needs and desire to be in control.

They want their loved ones to be a willing dumping ground for their unresolved emotions. These victims want to control the love of others to be vulnerable to their demands and to support their illusion of control. They have become a version of what they despised, they may not sexually interfere with children but they are willing to verbally attack another to gain an illusion of control. They want to be able to dictate how their loved ones feel about themselves, believing that the worse they feel about themselves the easier they are to control.

Some survivors of abuse become immersed in their own indifference and this causes them to seek avenues for having ultimate control over others. While they are aligned to their own indifference, they regurgitate the energy they have experienced and utilise it manipulatively against others. Some survivors do not use the sexual component of their abuse but willingly anchor to being emotionally, energetically, mentally and physically abusive. They use their history of being a victim to manipulatively justify emotionally, energetically, mentally and physically abusing those they want ultimate control over. Their judgement causes them to be bitter and resentful towards those they believe are living an easier life, and this may even include their own children. Unfortunately, the survivor has become the indifference they despised and they are using their denial of reality to protect and defend their belief of being entitled to be controlling and abusive.

Some victims become disassociated from reality and truth, immersed in their own unresolved emotions. This can cause the victim to become sadistic in the way they interact with others, even their own children. These victims use their internal rage to fuel and retain their unresolved emotions related to the abuse and use this to justify their own indifference to the truth and reality of becoming a perpetrator of indifference. These victims will arrogantly ignore all evidence of themselves being abusive, which may not include sexual abuse, but could be prolific verbal, physical, emotional or energetic abuse. They ignore or adamantly deny their knowledge of how the abuse has affected them, and may even deny the potential threat if a paedophile is still involved in their life. Victims cling to their denial to protect themselves from experiencing or feeling their own reality. The victim's protection of their own denial causes them to implode and to feel demoralised, leaving them to believe they are a shell of a person. They lose themselves to the oppression which is a ramification of the abuse and their abuser. They can choose to create an illusion to exist in, that enables them to deny their own reality.

Some victims use denial to create an illusion of security while anchoring to the familiarity of being oppressed, and oppressing themselves with emotional pain. They want to deny the existence of their own indifference and pretend it does not affect others. The truth is, the use of denial is their indifference to truth, which allows them to align to the role of being an unwilling or willing perpetuator of abuse of another. These victims become what they despised; someone who ignores cries for help and pretends to be in denial of the reality of abuse. When you become what you once despised, you harden to the reality of abuse and downgrade the impact of your own indifference.

False entitlement

Some paedophiles programme, condition and indoctrinate their victim to be devoid of feelings, removing their sense of self. It is this ability to be devoid of feelings which contributes to the denial of reality. They believe the paedophile does in fact have ownership over them and can dictate the way they live. Paedophile's beliefs of ownership via bloodline creates generations of souls being affected by the insidiousness of paedophilia. Victims within this scenario have a twofold experience of indifference to contend with; the indifference of the paedophile who is abusing them and the indifference they observe in others ignoring the reality of the abuse. The innocence of the child is violated by both the paedophile's abuse and by those who ignore the reality of abuse. All within this scenario are participating in the continuing cycle of indifference to the value, worth and significance of everyone being a unique, independent, individual soul. The innocence of a child is abused not because they lack value, worth or significance, but because the child is in a position of powerlessness. A child is powerless over the paedophile and those who turn a blind eye to abuse. Unfortunately, the child believes the abuse is because of their lack of value, worth and significance, and this is a misconception that haunts them. Abuse of children is an abuse of innocence, unconditional love, compassion and naivety.

Some parents of abused children can be jealous of the attention the child receives from their paedophilic partner, former abuser or potential partner. They blame the child for the abuse and the interference to their plans of how life and their relationships should be. Some even use their child as a bargaining chip to get what they want from the paedophile and allow themselves to ignore the reality of abuse or the warning signals of the potential of abuse. Some parents perceive the child as an enemy or competitor, and are willing to constantly compete with the child to get the attention of the paedophile.

The child becomes the scapegoat for everyone's indifference to truth. The parent uses the child as the scapegoat for all the problems within the relationship and seeks to destroy the child's confidence and understanding of who they are. The parent blames the child for ruining their security within the relationship, and inflicts mental abuse to coincide with the physical and sexual abuse already being inflicted on the child. When the child realises the parent is deliberately ignoring reality, the child experiences an added torture of being aware of the extent of the indifference flanking their existence. The parent uses their denial to conceal the reality they feel or are aware of. They have become indifferent to their own reality and fear acknowledging that their paedophilic partner is only with them to have access to a child. The parent believes they are a victim of the child's betrayal because they want to anchor to an illusory relationship, regardless of the fact that it is with a paedophile.

Some paedophiles can be extremely jealous and fearful of any other attention their victim receives. If the victim is receiving attention from the outside world, (such as teachers, boyfriends, girlfriends, parents of friends, friends of the family), the paedophile may feel the vulnerability of their own illusion of control, knowing someone else is observing the child and the child's behaviour. The paedophile fears not being able to control the victim to be compliant to the code of silence or to uphold the charade the paedophile wants to portray. The jealousy the paedophile feels exposes to them the vulnerability of their control. The greatest fear of a paedophile is to lose belief in their own control. The paedophile fears losing control of their ownership of the victim, having another interfere with their illusion of control, or having to contend with competition for control of the victim. The paedophile creates a territorial war with anyone who is seen as interfering with their believed ownership and control of the victim.

The paedophile becomes more manipulative as their victims mature, and struggles to maintain the veneer of control. Maturity of the victim naturally brings different elements that cannot be completely controlled by the paedophile, this includes the possibility of pregnancy or the victim becoming more autonomous.

The paedophile's fear of exposure intensifies with the maturity of the victim, as they become unable to conceal the cause and effect of what they have been doing. This can manifest as victims becoming indifferent towards themselves, which can lead to:

- Promiscuity
- Entertaining suicidal thoughts and tendencies
- Self-mutilating
- Suffering from anorexia or bulimia
- Overeating
- Indulging in drugs and alcohol
- Wallowing in emotional depression
- Raging at the paedophile or others

The victim can become uncontrollable and the paedophile focuses on how to subdue the victim's emotions or the situations created by the victim's emotions. The paedophile will become either a part of the concerned chorus for the victim covertly letting the victim know that the paedophile is still in control, or pretend to be an advocate who advertises the victim's mental instability creating stories that the victim has always been difficult even from a young age. The paedophile wants to influence how others perceive the victim and the potential truth that the victim may expose.

In an attempt to undermine the credibility of the victim, the paedophile expands their manipulative skills to encompass all those observing the victim. Some victims surrender to the belief that the paedophile can control others to believe whatever they want them to. These victims are conditioned to believe the paedophile can control any situation or person to their advantage. The victim uses this conditioning to believe the abuse will never end, even though the physical act of sexual abuse may have ended. Some victims become trapped in the belief that the paedophile will be able to permanently impact the victim's experience of life and their mental health status. Some victims surrender to their own indifference towards themselves and use the paedophile's indifference as a catalyst for denying their value, worth and significance. This can often lead to a lifetime of depression, and even suicide can seem like an option when the victim believes there is no way they can escape from the influence of the paedophile.

Reactions to abuse

Some victims struggle to comprehend their own fear of exposing the truth of the paedophile and their abuse experience. These victims are in constant fear that others will believe and judge them as inferior, mad or untrustworthy. Unfortunately, due to the impact of their own suppressed unresolved emotions, when the victim emotionally explodes or implodes, others feel the energy of their unresolved emotions and can interpret it as a type of emotional madness. Some people negatively judge the victim for their inability to control their unresolved emotions. These people fear being in the presence of another's uncontrollable emotions because it brings up their own vulnerabilities and so they demand that the victim contains their emotions. This can cause victims to believe they are inferior because they cannot contain their emotions, or be consistent in aligning to a charade that conceals the emotional hurt and trauma they feel. Unfortunately, these victims struggle to trust anyone, anything or themselves, and this may be interpreted by others as the victim being judgemental and untrustworthy. Victims can use others' reactions as verification of 'not being good enough' to have others love them, and being too damaged to find peace within themselves. These victims believe they need to protect themselves from exposing their assessment of their own mental state, and try to control themselves to be able to hide from society, intimacy and the truth of themselves.

When a survivor of abuse acknowledges the full extent of their own abuse and how it affects their life, they realise they have been trapped within their own unresolved emotions and may emotionally feel even more demoralised. Due to their own denial, fear and their compulsion to suppress their unresolved emotions, the realisation of the full extent of their abuse may not occur until years or even decades later. The victim takes a big leap of faith to break the code of silence and some do that in the belief that it will free them from their emotional pain and all their problems will be fixed. However, if they do not have an ensuing feeling of freedom from their emotional pain, their disappointment can intensify their emotions. The reality is the survivor needs to resolve their indifference to the truth of who they are, before they can find freedom from their own emotional entrapment.

When family members, friends, authorities or even partners hear of the history of sexual abuse or about current abuse, their reactions may confuse the victim. The news will feel surreal if people have no inkling of this reality, especially if the victim has completely hidden their experience from those who they are close to. Partners can be extremely shocked at never having had an inkling of the abuse. Family members will assess their own history, searching for evidence of what the new insight into the reality of sexual abuse may explain. The disclosure of sexual abuse causes an influx of confusion and emotional reactions that are unprecedented for both the victim and the ones receiving the news. Emotions can overwhelm all involved and first reactions can be reactions to the shock they feel, which may not be a true expression of the feelings the one receiving the news has for the victim.

The survivors of abuse may have an expectation of how others should respond and if their expectations are not met they can class this as another violation. The survivor may judge others' responses as an indictment of their value, worth and significance, without giving the receiver of the news time to come to terms with the reality of sexual abuse. The survivor may underestimate the emotional shock caused by the news and seek to emotionally manipulate the receiver to respond the way they want them to. The survivor may pin all their hopes of feeling free from oppression on the reaction of others, falsely believing that others should be able to fix how they feel.

The survivor may attempt to control others with their victimhood and this can confuse the receiver of the news. Instead of being able to respond from how they feel, they fear offending the survivor and become trapped by not knowing what to do. The receiver of the news may feel extremely confused by what they are emotionally feeling from the survivor and their own response to the survivor. Disbelief may be their first reaction because they are overwhelmed by the reality of the abuse, and the survivor may interpret this as indifference, believing they are being accused of lying. The survivor may use this to spiral further into their own despair. The survivor seeks to feel the sincerity of others. If the person is responding from their own unresolved emotions the survivor may take this as insincerity and react with angst and resentment.

The receiver of the news of sexual abuse may be reacting from their own unresolved emotions, and seek to protect their illusion of control and denial of reality. They may in fact discount the survivor within the scenario and assess the reality of sexual abuse in terms of how it affects their own image. Their first reaction may be to assess how they believe others will perceive the news of abuse. They may become overly concerned with what they believe they will be judged on. Many will reject the truth of the survivor's experience because they refuse to accept the part they played, which may just have been being oblivious to the reality happening in their own home. They fear conceding to the reality that they did not know what was happening. If they fear they contributed to the paedophile having opportunities to abuse, they may respond to the survivor's disclosure with denial.

Some receivers of the news of sexual abuse may zone out from what they are hearing, because it triggers their own suppressed memories of a personal experience of abuse. This may cause them to appear apathetic as they struggle to contain their own emotional unrest.

The receiver of the news may want to avoid public exposure of the abuse, fearing there could be repercussions from their connection to someone who has been sexually abused. The protection of their own image overrides the gravity of what they are actually dealing with. They extend this protection of their own image to include the family image and reputation. They have an image of the victim they do not want to break because it may reflect upon their own image. Their denial of the importance they place on their own image may have them automatically responding to the victim with indifference. They may not even realise that they have not considered how their reactions affect the victim's sense of value, worth or significance. The receiver of the news may want the victim to align to the protection of the family image, and may be arrogantly dismissive of the reality of abuse.

The receiver's desire to protect their own image has them being incapable of giving full attention to the victim and supporting them with unconditional love, compassion and honesty. They may encourage the victim to reassess their version of truth and attempt to downgrade the severity of the abuse, expecting the victim to conceal and dilute their reality by anchoring to denial. They may blatantly accuse the victim of being a trouble maker and oppose every part of the victim's account of reality. They may prefer to believe the victim is wrong or insane, as they would rather accept the belief of insanity than acknowledge and deal with the reality of sexual abuse.

Those who want to protect their own image and illusion of themselves, their family and reality will attack and discredit the victim's account of the abuse. They may in fact bombard them with counteractions, arguing about dates, locations and other elements of their recount of abuse. This bombardment may leave the victim swirling within their emotional reaction to another's denial. Victims may emotionally anchor to the confrontation between themselves and their perceived new oppressor, becoming obsessed about the angst that stems from their sexual abuse being denied.

The traumatic impact of abuse causes some survivors to become confused and disorientated about specific details. Whether the abuse has been consistent over a period of time or sporadic events, their recollection can become a blur because of their constant state of being disassociated from feeling the truth of their reality. Their disassociation is a protective mechanism that creates an emotional and energetic filter, enabling them to exist in a surreal state. The survivor is actually immersed in their own emotional shock, which can become their normal or create voids in their memory. Some survivors become transfixed in their own emotional shock, which creates a cyclic emotional loop the survivor attempts to deny or control the suppression of. In order to expose the truth of the abuse, survivors have to negotiate their own disassociation and confront the reality of their emotional shock and the voids they are aware of but cannot explain.

Some family members want to deny or conceal the abuse, and put pressure on the survivor to conform to their dismissal of the impact of the sexual abuse. This can create factions within the family that debate the best course of action for all involved with complete disregard for the victim. This transpires into the victim feeling like they have no voice and are just a renovation project for the family as no one is considering them or what they believe will enable their own recovery. Some victims believe they have to conform to what suits everyone else within the family and this can make them feel helpless and silenced.

Expectations of recovery

Supporting the victim requires everyone to use care and complete honesty, as it is a delicate process. When you completely take over and start dictating to the victim how they should recover, the victim who is now a survivor feels controlled and overpowered again. This just leaves them retreating into their fear. You cannot control the survivor of abuse to adhere to your expectations. When you pander to the survivor's victim mentality, you become an enabler, prolonging the fear and can accidently encourage the survivor's oppression of recovery. When you deny truth, you can become an abusive opponent the victim has to contend with. Compassion is the ability to be truthful about all aspects of the abuse and the aftermath, which enables you to support the survivor. Support may mean at times simply being a witness to what is occurring and waiting until the survivor is ready to deal with their own reality. Support may mean you ask if the survivor wants to hear what you can observe they are doing to themselves. You support when you can walk beside the survivor, unconditionally loving them and reminding them of their natural value, worth and significance. Recovery is complex and difficult for all involved, but support and unconditional love are always a blessing.

The survivor may feel they are always defending their state of being and become very defensive of their victim mentality. This can cause them to want to incite guilt in those who deny the reality of abuse or who do not align to appeasing their victim mentality. This causes the victim to manipulate their own unresolved emotions and intensify the conflict within the family to find out who is on their side. The survivor's emotional state becomes indisputable; however, different members of the family may interpret the behaviour to suit their own judgement and assessment of the reality of the survivor of abuse. Those who want to deny the reality of sexual abuse will use the survivor's behaviour as evidence to prove their beliefs that the survivor is delusional and unstable. The survivor may feel they have to be manipulative in an attempt to get others to believe them. Those who want to protect their denial use the evidence of the survivor's manipulation to discredit the victim's account of their abuse. This causes the survivor to feel frustrated and violated again. Often the survivor becomes willing to use others' denial to reinforce their own harsh self-judgement, loathing and beliefs of being insignificant.

Those in denial may make it their mission to undermine the survivor in order to discredit their account of reality and justify their own judgement of the survivor. This can create a battle for control between the survivor and different family members. The battle for control and others' loyalty becomes either a covert undercurrent or an all-out brawl within the family. The ones in conflict will constantly try to recruit others to validate their judgement. The survivor will be in conflict with the ones they want to feel loved by and may try to control them to be remorseful or sympathetic. However, as soon as others feel the victim's manipulation and attempts for control of sympathy they reject them as manipulative and controlling. This leaves the survivor feeling rejected and abandoned, and this increases their own hold on their victim mentality.

Other family members may align to those who deny the sexual abuse, because it is easier than facing the reality of their own family history, and some may even have something they want to hide. After witnessing the reactions of those who deny, others may be more determined to hide their own history of abuse. The battle by those in denial to control the survivor, and at times the survivor's desire to control those in denial, can become a war within the family. This battle means any search for truth becomes obsolete and instead the focus is on right-fighting. The control battle for both the survivor and those in denial becomes about trying to outsmart each other, and the focus is diverted from the reality of abuse, to attempting to prove each other wrong.

The family may expect the survivor to recant their disclosure of abuse and to exist in a state of denial, with the expectation that the survivor will align to a charade that appeases the family image. This may cause the survivor to either rebel against or align back to the code of silence. The survivor may feel obligated to uphold the family image and seek to pretend they never exposed the truth of the abuse. This will internally eat away at the survivor's sense of self and they will either become robotic or resentful. In these cases survivors either isolate themselves from the family or the family may ostracise them, because any denial is unachievable while they are present.

Some individuals within families where sexual abuse is being exposed can use the sexual abuse as an anchor to vindicate all the emotional problems within the family. They discount and disregard all other aspects from the family's history of interactions with each other, and blame the experience or exposure of sexual abuse for all of the family's dysfunction. Those who use the sexual abuse as an excuse for all other family dysfunction disregard the truth of their own reactions, behaviours and beliefs, which results in them being indifferent to the survivor of abuse. They blame having to deal with the sexual abuse within the family for everything that does not suit or comply with their illusory control. These individuals deny the reality of their own domineering control and manipulation. They try to use their domineering control and manipulation to fix the family, the survivor of sexual abuse and the emotionally charged environment in which they all live. These domineering controllers create rules on how to deal with the abuse, arrogantly ignoring the complexities of all the emotions involved. They want the survivor to adhere to their expectations and believe they can set up a plan for the survivor to follow, which entails suppressing the reality of their abuse.

In some families the paedophile may still be a part of their lives and the survivor of abuse may be expected to continue the charade of happy families even though the paedophile is present. The code of silence may be broken in one part of the family but kept intact in another part of the family. The paedophile may be unaware that the code of silence has been broken by the survivor. However, there will be an uneasiness within the family which the paedophile may notice, regardless of whether the family supports or denies the survivor's account of sexual abuse.

Some survivors do not feel they have the right to expose the truth of the paedophile because of their indoctrinated beliefs about family loyalty. Some survivors desire to retain the family image may keep them indifferent to their own abuse and willing to uphold the family charade even while they endure the presence of the paedophile. Some survivors may fear the exposure of abuse could ruin their own denial of reality, which motivates them to protect their own codependency on the illusion of the family. The survivor may feel obliged to attend family functions and gatherings with their children, in spite of the paedophile's presence, to protect and sustain the illusion of family. The survivor has been conditioned to keep the abuse a secret and to protect the illusion of family, which means they become willing to condition their children to exist in the orchestrated family charade. The survivor can down play the potential risk to their own children in order to protect the family's denial.

Some paedophiles may believe the survivor cannot remember the abuse and feel very secure acting out the charade of family life. Some paedophiles may constantly try to assess if the survivor is aware of the abuse. They will attempt to ascertain if the survivor is unaware, in denial or playing the charade with a full awareness of the paedophile, the abuse and the history of how the paedophile covered up their sexual preference for children. The presence of the survivor may cause the paedophile to feel their own guilt, shame and humiliation, creating an anxiety triggered by their fear of being exposed as a paedophile. Some survivors are aware of the anxiety their presence causes the paedophile when they cross paths later in life, because the paedophile no longer has complete control of them or their environment. The survivor can have mixed emotions, in one moment they can feel their delight in watching the paedophile's unease due to their presence, and then they can feel their own unease due to the paedophile's presence. They may feel a mild satisfaction that their presence affects the paedophile's ability to perform their charade, but become consumed with resentment because there has been no retribution or remorse for their abuse.

The generational impact of abuse

Some survivors of abuse obsess about protecting their children from sexual abuse but are unaware that they are inflicting excessive control and fear, and deny the effect their over protection has on their children. Some survivors parent with the belief that they have honourable intentions, and having absolute control equates to safety. However, their obsession about what they fear and their obsessive desire to have control can become an abuse of the child's uniqueness, independence and individuality. The child is expected to live within the parent's perceptions and fears of reality, and the only way the parent feels secure with reality is by believing they have control. This causes the child to become immersed and entrapped in the parent's desire for control. The child may be oblivious to the parent's history of sexual abuse which is influencing their behaviour, perception of reality and beliefs. The child may be unaware of the cause of the parent's obsessive desire to control the child and their fear for the child's safety. The child of the survivor of abuse believes their parent's obsession, with control and their fears, is a sign of their indifference towards them. This can cause a rift between the parent and the child that neither one knows how to resolve. The only way to resolve the misconceptions and fears which created the emotional rift is for both parties to be honest and compassionate.

Some children of survivors are programmed to perpetuate their parents fear and desire for control into their way of being. This often occurs without the child understanding that their parent's history of sexual abuse is why their desire to control all aspects of reality is so strong. Some children of survivors are indoctrinated into perpetuating the parent's fear, which can distort their perception of themselves. Some children of survivors can come to the belief that when they are old enough, they too will have the right to inflict their control onto their children and others. They can become indifferent to the reality they create with their control and indifference to truth.

Some children of survivors of abuse grow up in the energetic residue of indifference and sexual abuse, and are bewildered by their parent's reactions to life, relationships and the child's presence. The child may be unaware of the parent's history and confused by what they feel from the parent. The child may fear the unpredictable volatility of their parent's desire for control, or fear the parent's withdrawal and internal implosion of depression.

The child may in fact feel like a victim to their parent's emotional carnage. The child may wonder why the parent is domineering, or distant and aloof towards them, not realising the parent has a fear of feeling and expressing the truth of their feelings, because they are trapped in an emotional hell created from their history of sexual abuse. The child may be very aware of the denial that is employed by the parent to conceal the reality of the parent and child relationship, but unable to explain why there is an emotional rift in the relationship.

Some survivors' inability to cope with the reality of being abused can create a residue of indifference that conditions the next generation to be affected by sexual abuse, even though they have not directly experienced being sexually abused. Some survivor's unwillingness to acknowledge and comprehend how they are inflicting their children with their fears, indifference and denial sustains living in emotional upheaval. This creates an undercurrent of insecurity within the family which can develop into fractured relationships, leaving everyone confused about the reality they are living in. The children of the survivor may perceive their reality differently than their parent. They may be fully aware of the parent's fear but not fearful themselves, which leaves them perplexed by the some of their parent's behaviours and beliefs.

Parents may attempt to conceal their emotional reality from themselves with the charade of a happy family and the belief that they are doing the right thing, not realising the complexities of their own behaviours, fears and beliefs. This causes them to defiantly and compulsively discount the emotional effect their unresolved emotions are having on their child's day-to-day experience of life. The parent often believes that their children harbour the belief that they are 'not good enough', which incites the demand for their children to adhere to all their commands as a sign of respect.

Some parents project their own beliefs of insignificance at their children, and create a control battle they believe is only won when the children are completely submissive to them. This creates conflict within the relationship that the survivor, parenting from fear and insecurity, uses to reinforce their own beliefs of being discarded and constantly betrayed. This builds the momentum of the survivor's bitterness, resentment and desire to control, which can leave all involved with the survivor perplexed about what is truly going on. The child of the survivor may feel victimised by the enormity of the parent's unresolved emotions and negative beliefs, with some children believing they are 'not good enough' for the parent. The ramifications of denying the cause and effect of sexual abuse, means that the parent indoctrinates their own children into perpetuating negative beliefs about themselves. Paedophilia can have a generational effect and children of the survivor can experience a confusing upbringing, often without realising that their parent is a victim of paedophilia.

The survivor of abuse feels relieved that the children have not had to deal with sexual abuse, but can be complacent about the reality of what the children experience under their guidance. Some children of survivors have to navigate a huge array of unresolved emotions that could include explosions of rage to debilitating depression, all of which have an effect on the child. The survivor may intend to keep their children safe but deny that they are externalising their own indifference onto their children, partner and life in general. They can be in denial about their inability to be truthful with themselves and the enormity of the impact their unresolved emotions, fears and negative beliefs have had on how they interact with others. The survivor fears exposing the truth of their abuse because they have no way of knowing what to do with the fear, confusion and emotional pain that may be dredged up to the surface. The parent may believe the only way to quell their fear is to secure control over all they are involved with, which can become suffocating for the family.

Some survivors have a belief that the sexual abuse was the starting point of their indifference towards themselves and others. Everything prior to the abuse becomes obsolete as their experience of sexual abuse consumes them. The child of the survivor has no way of comprehending the undercurrent of their parent's behaviour, and has nothing to use to explain the indifference displayed and felt within the way their parent keeps interacting with them. They may never know of their parent's experience of sexual abuse and have no understanding that this is what drives their parent's indifference to themselves and others.

Some children are exposed to a variety of unresolved emotions that their parent is unable to contain and are conditioned to ignore what they feel, observe and experience in order to align to the family image, which is used to secure the denial of reality. This means the child is indoctrinated to deny reality and to uphold an image. The child may be constantly exposed to a mismatch of image versus reality, and come to the conclusion that denial is the method of survival that will allow them to withdraw from the emotional reality they feel. This means they align to their own indifference to themselves, others and life.

Some children of survivors of abuse live in an emotionally charged environment experiencing a volatile explosion of unresolved emotions or feeling an undercurrent of oppressive energy, such as resentment, defensiveness and envy. The common denominator they feel within the energy is indifference. Some children may assume the emotional explosions and the indifference they feel are an expression of their parent not wanting them and blame themselves for their parent's reaction to life. These children have trouble differentiating between their own emotions and what is being inflicted upon them, and they become enmeshed in the emotional chaos of their environment. They feel confused and often disillusioned by the emotionally charged environment, unable to explain to themselves why they feel the way they do. The child's reality is plagued by the parent's inability to deal with their own history and unresolved emotions. Survivors feel confused about themselves because of their experience of abuse, and this becomes part of the emotional environment endured by all members within the family collective. The undercurrent of unresolved emotions causes the child to be confused about their own value, worth and significance. The survivor may not intend to confuse their children about their value, worth and significance to the family, however the survivor's unwillingness to be honest about their own emotional reality produces an environment that perpetuates indifference.

Some children of survivors of abuse carry their childhood experiences into their parenting, relationships and life. They are indoctrinated into being indifferent about how they treat others and may even go to deeper levels of indifference beyond their own experience. They may parent and interact with others from indifference that perpetuates more indifference, continuing their denial of the reality of the emotions being passed on from generation to generation. It is only our truthful honesty about how we interact within our own reality and how honest we are about the truth, that will alter what we perpetuate.

Some survivors may use their sexual abuse as a smokescreen to excuse the reality of their own reactions, habitual behaviours, desire to control and the way they have parented. They want to use their history of sexual abuse as permission to demand to be appeased and to not be held accountable for their actions. These survivors use their sexual abuse as an excuse to justify trying to control and manipulate others to pacify all their insecurities. These survivors can become demanding and judgemental, and are constantly denying the reality of their own desire for control. They can be obsessed with their scrutiny of others' behaviours and reactions towards them. Some survivors look for and use any indifference towards them to justify being indifferent to themselves. When the survivor's attempts to control fail to deliver the results they want, they automatically blame being a victim of sexual abuse as the reason why they cannot get life or relationships to pacify their demands to be in control. Their failure to control everything fuels their indifference towards truth and reinforces their obsession with control. They obsess about control because they fear what could happen if they are not in control. Those who grew up in an abusive family may hold onto having to be in control of others, because they fear the alternative is they will be controlled and open to being abused in some way. Their fears override the opportunity to be honest about their own reality and to trust themselves to freely express their feelings, which secures their own indifference to truth.

The survivor's fear

Some survivors of abuse are very aware of paedophilic energy, and because this energy is so familiar to them they have developed an internal radar for paedophiles. Some survivors freeze in the presence of a paedophile or to anything they believe reverberates with paedophilic energy, they are reacting to the fear of being powerless. They can be so fearful of experiencing abuse again or that their children could be in possible harm that they try to eliminate potential risk, living in isolation and afraid of life. This fear can be transferred to their children, creating anxiety, insecurity, fear and inferiority as the norm.

Some survivors of abuse have no intention or capacity to sexually abuse their children or any other child, but emotionally fear that their experience of abuse could turn them into what they despise. This fear becomes a tortuous self-judgement and a vigilant fear of hidden deviancy which leaves them feeling vulnerable. They associate vulnerability with abuse, because that is what they have experienced. The confusion they have felt, carried and denied causes these survivors to fear feeling vulnerable. This fear can develop into a misinterpretation that vulnerability is something to attack, or being vulnerable makes you a target that can be attacked. They can feel the vulnerability of a child and interpret this as knowing there is an opportunity to abuse; in fact they have no intention to harm the child but torture themselves for even being aware that there is an opportunity. Survivors can misinterpret themselves as a potential abuser, creating a debilitating fear within themselves. They can become obsessed with judging everything they think and feel with the fear of either being abused again or becoming an abuser. Unfortunately, their own fear of acknowledging what they feel, and their fear of turning into an abuser, has them analysing every thought that can be potentially misinterpreted as sexual or abusive. The survivor's fear of being a potential abuser does not allow them to relax and accept that they have no desire to sexually abuse a child and that their self-judgement is the result of unfounded fear. This inhibits them from accepting the truth of who they are and can create separation from their ability to love and enjoy being with their children.

The survivor can constantly relive their own confusion and the unresolved emotions they have felt, carried and denied, overwhelming their awareness of their present reality. Survivors can trigger themselves to emotionally relive the confusion and their vulnerability connected to their own abuse. This leads to the survivor replaying and reliving their own emotional labyrinths created from their history of abuse. This can cause survivors to faze out and to become unaware of themselves within their present moment reality.

The survivor of abuse may be unaware of how vulnerable and naïve they were at the time of their abuse and, can become confused as to why feeling vulnerable and naïve triggers unexplainable or inappropriate thoughts. Some survivors will unsuccessfully seek to suppress any type of vulnerability they feel. However, by constantly trying to assess what or who will make them feel vulnerable, they make themselves emotionally feel more vulnerable. This causes the survivor to panic about their own state of being and ability to control their fear of vulnerability. Some survivors debilitate themselves with the fear of being unable to control their own emotional reactions and responses to their own thoughts.

Some survivors fear their thoughts represent who they really are, but their thoughts can be generated from the unresolved emotions suppressed within and are often irrational, distracting them from the truth of who they are. They use their unresolved emotions to torment and torture themselves, fuelling their denial of the reality of who they are. The survivor may attempt to create an image to suppress and conceal the truth of them ever having been abused. The effort required to secure their image, causes them to feel vulnerable as they are constantly assessing whether their image is being believed. Unfortunately, the presence of a child's vulnerability can be a trigger for their own insecurities, and this creates a fear reaction which leaves them being indifferent towards the truth of who they really are.

When the survivor observes the vulnerability and innocence of a child it can trigger emotional and energetic memories of feeling the paedophile's conniving reactions to their vulnerability, innocence, gullibility and naivety. Some survivors of abuse feel the vulnerability of children, and this can trigger an emotional reaction that has them regurgitating what they felt when they were vulnerable and susceptible to abuse. Their reaction is not because they have paedophilic thoughts, it is because they intensely fear being vulnerable. Some paedophiles were themselves once a victim but not all victims become paedophiles. Many survivors live in fear that they will become one of the statistics of sexual abuse and turn into a paedophile themselves. These beliefs about the statistics can become a fear for the survivor to endure, even when they have no desire or compulsion to abuse children.

Some survivors of abuse are emotionally confused by the constant re-surfacing of their memories about how the paedophile reacted to them. These are memories which can disturb the survivor, because they expose the enormity of what they have experienced when they were too young, naïve and confused to comprehend what they were experiencing and feeling. The survivor has a delayed reaction to the truth of paedophilia, which can induce an emotional shock at how impacted they were by the paedophile. Feelings, smells, sounds, awareness of energy, environments and the time of day or year can create emotional flashbacks. These flashbacks incite an energetic and emotional shock, which the survivor may not be able to explain, especially if they are attempting to secure their denial of the impact of the abuse experience. The survivor may interpret these emotional flashbacks as proof of their own instability and inability to cope with their present moment reality.

During these flashbacks, the survivor may relive the energy that was present at the time they were being abused, such as another's desire for ultimate control, unbridled rage, narcissistic indifference and manipulation. They may not realise the flashbacks they are feeling are their history being relived and evidence of their unresolved emotions. They can become fearful of what they feel within the flashback, such as extreme fear, powerlessness, hopelessness and helplessness. This causes the survivor to remain confused and frightened by their own emotional reactions, responses, thoughts and fears, often not realising they are stuck because they are unable to acknowledge their present moment unencumbered by their past.

Some survivors may observe a child who is of a similar age to when they were abused and become shocked at how young, innocent and naïve a child is at that age. Their perception of themselves at that age is totally different to the truth of that age and they may feel traumatised by the realisation of how young they were and how distorted their perception of themselves was and is. This can cause the survivor to become immersed in their resentment of how the experience of sexual abuse deprived them of a 'normal' childhood and impacted their life, which leaves them with a grave sense of loss.

Some survivors of abuse may fear any type of sexual energy because it induces a fear of being vulnerable and gullible to another's control. These survivors fear experiencing their feelings and have become addicted to attempting to govern what they feel by being in control of all aspects of their life, or by numbing themselves from feeling anything. They can fixate on their beliefs about how reality should be which includes themselves, others, sexual relationships and life. This may also include dogmatic views on other areas such as their finances, real estate or clothing. If they believe they are in control, they believe this means they are secure and not vulnerable. However, if they feel their control is being overridden or discounted, they can become retaliative towards themselves and others, causing themselves a lot of conflict in their life. They may fear sexual energy because they believe it upsets their illusion of control. They may fear they cannot control the sexual energy and they will be unable to dictate to themselves what to feel or become unable to assess what to control for. When the survivor reacts to their history of abuse they become frightened by their own reactions, which is why they seek to have control over their sexual desires, either by withdrawing from all sexual experiences or being the controller of their sexual experiences.

Some survivors of abuse feel disgusted and humiliated when they become sexually aroused while hearing stories of others' indifference and sexual abuse. Their arousal is a body memory response to someone having ultimate control over another, which is what they were sexualised into by their abuse. The survivor is aware of how being indifferent can equate to being in control and has a physical reaction to the control within the story. Some survivors' history of abuse has left them programmed, conditioned and indoctrinated into associating control and indifference with sexual energy. They cannot understand their own reaction and response to stories of sexual abuse. This may cause survivors to assess themselves as suppressed sexual deviants, which leaves them fearing what they might be capable of.

The survivor's fear of intimacy

Some survivors of abuse have been conditioned to believe that their sexual experiences will always be coloured with indifference. These survivors struggle to differentiate between love and control using sexual energy. This causes them to think having control of another is love, and if their partner is willing to accept their control they believe they have a shared love. The trouble with this way of relating is that the partner will tire of always having to appease the survivor's control, because they will not be able to feel any love underneath the control, even though the survivor may in fact love them.

Some survivors of abuse may use their sexual desires to control others, because they want to secure their own illusion of being able to control. Some survivors use their sexual desires to oppose feeling their real feelings. They overshadow what they feel and use their sexual energy to coerce others to be submissive. Their sexual experiences become an exercise in trying to control their thoughts, feelings and unresolved emotions. The emotional upheaval created by trying to control all aspects of themselves, while trying to create an image of intimacy, causes survivors to be overwhelmed by their inability to control themselves to be neutral and non-reactive to their own or another's sexual feelings. Their sexual feelings either becomes something they attempt to embrace with their control or something they avoid because they fear not being able to feel in control. Survivors often feel shallow because they are scared to allow themselves to feel at ease with being intimate.

Some survivors of abuse use their sexual energy to covertly transfer their indifference onto another, and create an illusion of control by denying another the ability to feel valued, loved or significant during the sexual experience. These survivors use their present sexual experiences as an excuse to externalise their own insidious desire to oppose being intimate. Some survivors avoid intimacy in the sexual experience, preferring indifference, manipulation and arrogant control as they seek to undermine their partner's confidence in themselves. These survivors desire to inflict the same debilitating indifference on their partner that plagues their understanding of themselves, life, sex, love and relationships. The survivor wants to inflict their partner with sexual insecurity in an attempt to control their partner so they will avoid and discontinue their desire for intimacy.

Some survivors of abuse use their sexual experiences to immerse themselves in guilt, shame and humiliation. These survivors will seek and manifest sexual experiences that emphasise their own opposition to themselves. They seek to emotionally, energetically or physically hurt themselves through sexual experiences to reiterate their own denial of being of value, worth and significance. This causes some survivors to imprison themselves in their indifference to the reality of who they are. These survivors immerse themselves in the emotional, energetic and physical pain that they have become addicted to, because they do not know how to resolve the internal pain they carry. The survivor stays in the emotional, energetic and physical pain, which is how they buffer themselves from accepting that they can feel their own soul's consciousness. Their non-acceptance of the truth of who they are causes them to miss the opportunity to be honest with themselves that they are significant, worthy of love and are of value.

Hangover of degradation

Some survivors of abuse deny how their victim mentality and denial of how they interact with reality has become debilitating. Their denial of the way they interact with life and others can cause them to believe they are a victim to everything and everyone, because they always feel immersed in their own victimhood. These survivors totally disregard the reality of their self-manipulation, how their victim mentality affects others and how others respond to their victimhood. These survivors automatically lie to themselves about their ability to be honest about reality, because they fear being unable to control an outcome and fear being unable to respond to life from the position of a victim. Their victimhood becomes an identity they use to create barriers to the truth of their emotional, energetic and physical reality. They want to use their victim mentality to secure a sense of control, but it causes a desperation in them, which they struggle to appease.

The self-annihilating behaviours of some survivors of abuse are the result of their own indifference towards the truth of being a unique, independent, individual soul who is significant to truth. The survivor's inability to deal with the indifference they have endured at the hands of their abuser, results in them being indifferent to themselves. This triggers their fears and embedded beliefs that engulf their awareness of their natural flow of conscious energy, which causes them to discredit the uniqueness of who they are.

The survivor can be haunted by their own disgust at what the paedophile has left them immersed in. Unfortunately, they identify this as part of who they are, because they cannot escape feeling the residue of indifference they carry. The survivor is immersed in the belief that indifference is all there is. What they are feeling overshadows who they naturally are and the enormity of that means they struggle to understand their own natural value, worth and significance. Their experience of abuse becomes the anchor point and point of reference for the survivor's own indifference towards themselves. These survivors become their own humiliator, seeking every opportunity to emotionally, energetically and physically downgrade their own value, worth and significance. They condition themselves to be their own emotional attacker and set themselves up to recreate and relive what emotionally plagues them.

Soul carnage

Some paedophiles react with compulsion when they identify an opportunity to abuse; others respond methodically and systematically create a conducive environment for their preferred type of abuse. Often seeking to secure longevity for the opportunity to be abusive. Paedophiles ignore the true extent of their indifference to truth because they narcissistically focus on their own desires while inflicting their depravities on an innocent child. They are not satisfied until they externalise their torment and actually revel in diminishing the value of another. They seek to humiliate their victims because they innately know that humiliation makes the victim more susceptible to their control. The paedophile seeks to contaminate the innocence within another's soul, deriving a sense of power from being able to contaminate someone else with self-loathing and fear.

The experience of being abused by a paedophile contaminates the purity of the victims' understanding of themselves, life, trust, sex, relationships and love. Everything becomes tainted and corrupted into avenues of internal emotional torture as victims become conditioned to deprive themselves of the joy of life, sex, relationships and love. The emotional torment activated through their life experiences conditions survivors to obliterate their ability to trust themselves as a soul, or to care and love themselves unconditionally. Some paedophiles delight in being the instigator of the victim's own willingness to eradicate any ability to love or feel the truth of who they naturally are. They want the victim to exist in the same dirtiness of indifference that they initiated. Any experience the survivor of abuse believes could become a potential trigger for feeling that dirtiness of indifference they were unwillingly initiated into, activates a fear of feeling. This causes them to become consumed with trying to avoid feeling and keeps them running from the potential of their life experiences. Their desire to avoid engulfs the survivor in the fears and embedded beliefs that resulted from their experience of abuse. Some paedophiles want to ensure there is longevity to the abuse they are inflicting and delight in the knowledge that their victims will self-impose their own indifference, extinguishing their ability to feel at peace with the truth of themselves.

Indifference to truth creates emotional and physical carnage. Being indifferent to truth is what needs to be resolved, whether they are the victim of abuse or the perpetrator of abuse. Victims are inducted into the severity of indifference and their recognition of how this indifference has affected their definition of themselves enables them to find what needs to be resolved. If souls identify themselves only as a victims, they embroil themselves into the chaos of their past experiences of indifference. Victims can become trapped, defining themselves by the indifference that has been inflicted on them or how indifferent they feel about themselves.

The victim can become trapped in their denial of their freedom of choice, which inhibits their honesty about their own internal reality and the dynamics within their soul. The travesty of this is that they become stuck being their own source of indifference. Their dishonesty and unwillingness to resolve causes them to be immersed in what emotionally, energetically and physically hurts them, and is what takes them further from the truth of their own soul. Some survivors of abuse struggle to be truthfully honest with themselves, because they believe they are broken beyond repair, and feel as if their soul is shattered. To resolve they must hurdle their fears and confront the truth of their own indifference and the truth of what they have experienced. When souls believe they are broken beyond repair and can feel the dirtiness of indifference, they struggle to be truthfully honest with themselves, because they fear feeling the enormity of their own distress.

The perpetrators of abuse define themselves by how willing they are to inflict indifference, and by the satisfaction they derive from having ultimate control over the vulnerability of an innocent child. They prey on the weak, deriving a thrill from getting away with the unspeakable. They also define themselves by how far they will allow themselves to be indifferent and then commend themselves for holding back on the degree of severity they could have inflicted. This means the perpetrator of abuse has to be remorseful to comprehend the entirety of their depravities and if they remain indifferent to the truth of their actions, they will remain a threat to any child they encounter. When a paedophile is unrepentant, any opportunity to abuse ignites their indifference.

Some paedophiles struggle to reconcile their compulsion to shatter another soul and struggle with the harm they have done to an innocent child. To escape feeling their own internal struggle to reconcile what they have done to another, they start defining their abusive actions as conquests and distort their reality with even more indifference to truth. They fear taking responsibility, acknowledging the truth of their actions and confronting the insidiousness of their history of being the abuser. Their lack of compassion for their victims becomes what the paedophile uses as a catalyst to ignore the truth of their depravity and the level of carnage and damage that results from the insidiousness of their indifference to another. The paedophile minimises the depths of their own indifference, and distorts the gravity of what they have initiated because they are attempting to deny responsibility for the soul carnage they created by their choice to be indifferent to the child they victimise.

Society's struggle

We, as society struggle to be honest about how to deal with the reality that there are some individuals who are so depraved that they are capable of abusing an innocent child. When we turn a blind eye, we become part of the problem. We are prone to ignore what is unfathomable because we struggle to understand the reality of paedophilia. The problem of paedophilia becomes exacerbated because we do not talk about it, and this leaves us caught in the dishonesty and avoidance of how insidious paedophilia is. Our willingness to confront the reality of paedophilia will enable all of us to learn from societal mistakes, which have perpetuated systems that allow paedophilia to flourish. Our dishonesty has a real impact on how reality unfolds. When we struggle to address our fears, denial and avoidance of abuse and paedophilia, we can become complacent about the cause and harmful effects of hiding from the reality of paedophilia.

Mankind has a history of being indifferent to the truth of souls and of seeking ultimate control over the exposure of truth. This has perpetuated many forms of indifference, which is evident in the way that paedophiles and the ramifications of paedophilia have been dealt with throughout history. When societies are indifferent to paedophilia, and are reluctant to hold those who turn a blind eye to the reality of abuse accountable for knowingly leaving children vulnerable, we become part of a collective problem. As a society, we collectively choose what is important, through our laws and how we conduct ourselves, and there is nothing more important than protecting those who are most vulnerable.

Societal indifference in the aftermath of paedophilia is the choice to override the significance of truth, which creates ongoing collateral damage for any soul involved. This includes those who have been silenced about their own observations because they were flanked by indifference. The only way to deal with the reality of a paedophile and paedophilic abuse is for the truth to be valued and exposed, because denial and indifference perpetuates the opportunity for the abuse to continue. When those who raise concerns about the truth of what is occurring are asked to condone the indifference, they are placed in an untenable position because they know there will be no change to the situation. Our fear of responding, or fear that there will be no response can mean we override our ability to be sensitive to truth and conform to the indifference. When we choose to be indifferent by ignoring what is occurring, we enable paedophiles to secure their position and everyone is left in a fog of indecision and inaction, which condemns the victim to further harm.

Throughout history, society's complacency about the plight of the vulnerable has left emotional scars, because we have used indifference to develop ways of hiding, covertly and overtly, from the truth of paedophilia and what it means to be a soul. When we shield ourselves from the reality of paedophilia with our ignorance, avoidance and dishonesty, we inhibit the possibility to discuss it truthfully. We often seek to avoid the truth, because we fear feeling the enormity of what has occurred. We vent our concerns and then we hide from reality, fearing there is no way of coming to terms with the truth of paedophilia. We do not know how to stop it, we do not know how to control it, we do not know what to do about it and we do not know how to cope with the ramifications of paedophilia. This results in us retreating into indifference, becoming complacent about the impact of paedophilia on our society. Acknowledging the truth of paedophilia broadens our understanding of the true impact abuse has on our society and the victims. The victims are the experts and the more we listen, the more can be learned and understood.

Anything to do with paedophilia is difficult to resolve and reconcile. It is an ongoing process to discover the best ways to assist and support the victims of paedophilia and to deal with the reality of paedophiles in our society. If we remain trapped in our indifference to paedophilia, we continue to enable paedophiles by leaving them with an arena to prey in.

We, as mankind, perpetuate indifference by trying to control indifference with denial. It is our indifference to truth that causes us to devalue the significance of all souls and it this denial that has us constantly inflicting various types of indifference on each other. Paedophilia is at the extreme end of the scale of mankind's use of indifference for the purpose of seeking ultimate control of another soul. People with paedophilic tendencies are willing to go to the extremes of indifference and will often deny the truth of their own actions.

Perpetuation

The victims of paedophilia have suffered unimaginable indifference and it becomes extremely difficult for them to deal with their experience. When they are unable to deal with their experience, they can fall into a spiral of being indifferent to themselves. This can cause some to become very abusive in the way they interact with others and cause some to epitomise the perpetuation of indifference, because in spite of what they have suffered they choose to become a paedophile themselves. The perpetuation of indifference is the result of being unable or unwilling to resolve the indifference they have felt towards themselves. We become perplexed and our compassion wanes when we have to confront the reality of a victim morphing into a paedophile.

When a victim becomes a paedophile, they forgo their innocence and we lose our compassion for them because they are choosing to perpetuate the insidiousness of indifference. A victim is innocent when they are abused. Victims can believe their innocence is lost and they are damaged beyond repair; they hold themselves in a false perception that they are no longer innocent, but they are innocent. However, those victims who choose to become a paedophile know exactly what they are inflicting on another soul because they have already lived with the stain of paedophilia as a victim. The victim is an innocent party; however, they are not coming from innocence if they choose to be a paedophile and abuse another.

In order to be honest and compassionate about the reality of how abuse is perpetuated, we have to understand the enormity of indifference, manipulation and the desire to control.

If we, as society gloss over the perpetuation of abuse, we reinforce the normality of oppressing another soul. Perpetuating a history of abuse is not an excuse, although it is a contributing factor.

A victim who chooses to perpetuate paedophilia is stuck in all aspects of abuse such as indifference, manipulation and the desire to control. A paedophile oppresses their own soul and often revels in being the starting point for another's extreme indifference towards their own soul. Paedophilia is the choice to be the insidiousness of indifference. Paedophilia is the choice to be willing to manipulate and physically overpower a child who is innocent and vulnerable, to appease their own desire for ultimate control. The paedophile believes they can appease their desire to have ultimate control by making a child their victim. Paedophilia is the choice to be the emotional, energetic and physical stain for another soul to carry.

A paedophile is a fractured soul who is abusive and seeks to fracture another soul. Paedophiles are willing to continue deceiving themselves about the truth of what they inflict on their victim and how their sexual depravity is infesting another with indifference. Some delight in being the starting point for others to be indifferent towards themselves. These paedophiles smugly contrive whatever story they want to tell themselves to justify their sense of entitlement to be soul abusive to another, and their denial of reality perpetuates their indifference to truth.

Some paedophiles carry memories of their victims like a trophy they are entitled to, which is an indication of how insidious their indifference is. These paedophiles revel in defiling an innocent child, believing this makes them superior to society as a whole, because they got away with tarnishing the most precious members of our society. If the victim is aware of being a paedophile's trophy it leaves a continuous undercurrent of abuse, that can infest victims' understanding of themselves. Prosecution may alleviate some of the angst victims feel, as they can see themselves as the instigator of justice and the victor.

Trapped in victim mentality

Paedophilia is one form of indifference we fear; however, being stuck in the victim mentality is something to fear as well. When victims are unable to see themselves beyond their own victim mentality, they become immersed in debilitating and destructive self-annihilation, which is how they manifest indifference to the truth of their soul. This causes victims to be trapped in their own fear of their unresolved emotions and imprisoned by their own indifference to themselves. The collective acknowledgement of the insidiousness of paedophilia, and the ensuing compassion and respect for the emotional, energetic and physical harm a victim has endured, assists survivors to feel supported as they endeavour to resolve the ramifications of being abused.

When survivors live from a victim mentality and are trapped by their own indifference to themselves, they have a harsh existence. From their victim mentality, resolution can seem like an unachievable goal. Paradoxically, they can feel offended when confronted with the reality that resolving how they feel about the abuse experience and their own victim mentality is what will free them from the oppression they feel. Resolution does not discount the horror of being victimised; resolution is the choice to not remain in the oppression another has indifferently inflicted, which leaves survivors with a corrupted perception of themselves. Having a victim mentality can cause them to cling to the belief that they have to wait for a sincere apology from their oppressor before they will be free. Some survivors may want the truth of the damage acknowledged by the perpetrator. However, anyone who operates from indifference, to the degree of being able to abuse an innocent soul, is often incapable of sincerity and is unwilling to take full responsibility for their own actions. This means the survivor is stuck in their past, and misses living their present moment; they are waiting for something that will most probably never arrive, which means they inadvertently become indifferent to the truth of their soul and life.

When survivors of abuse are unable to acknowledge the truth of their own natural value, worth and significance, they become trapped defining themselves by how the paedophile treated them. The strength of this self-definition is a terrible entrapment that leads to the perpetuation of indifference in one form or another. The survivor remains haunted by the paedophile's ability to treat them as insignificant.

Some survivors of abuse get caught in a cycle of abusing themselves and what they put themselves through is emotionally, energetically and physically painful, and soul-destroying torture. These survivors can become unwilling to understand the truth of their own significance. Their lack of acknowledgement of their own significance disables their compassion for themselves and distorts their understanding of the reality of their circumstances. Some survivors seek a fresh start and believe that suppressing and hiding their awareness of the abuse they have experienced will mean they can create a new beginning, but this is a misconception. The survivor is constantly in battle with their own denial as they forgo the reality of being a naturally significant, unique, independent, individual soul of truth. They want to believe they can control their own emotional, energetic and physical reality with denial, but their battle with denial wears them down, leaving them extremely disappointed in themselves. The experience of abuse becomes how survivors perceive themselves, and this binds them to their indifference to themselves, which becomes their constant unwelcome companion. These survivors will struggle to trust themselves to be without the familiarity of the emotional pain they feel, and will inadvertently create a struggle to perpetuate their own victim mentality. Some victims' emotional pain is so overwhelming that it keeps them entrapped and they stay stuck in the emotional, energetic and physical effects of the abuse and indifference towards the uniqueness of their own soul.

Some survivors of abuse enter relationships with others who are predominantly indifferent, because they believe they deserve nothing better. They have conditioned themselves to gloss over the reality of how it feels when someone is indifferent towards them, which is how they perpetuate their own oppression. Some survivors manipulate themselves to accept the familiarity of indifference as reasonable, because they are conditioned to expect oppression as their normal. The survivor may acknowledge their perpetuation of oppression but continue to be indifferent to their own reality, because they have a false belief that oppression is all they deserve. Survivors' unwillingness to trust themselves causes them to avoid seeking the truth of who they are. Their own indifference towards themselves has them cycling in self-annihilating patterns of behaviour, either allowing themselves to be abused or by becoming a self-abuser. These survivors believe life without abuse or without the anxiety the abuse has created is an unattainable dream and is not possible for them. This belief has them aligning to the acceptance of abuse as normal and is a catalyst for the perpetuation of their indifference to how they oppress their own soul.

When a victim is trapped by the stain they feel from their experience of being abused, they can continue to wear the victim mentality like a cloak. Continuing to carry the victim mentality separates them from feeling the significance of their soul. Unfortunately, victims can constantly manipulate themselves to deny the magnitude of their own consciousness. Carried victim energy means remaining stuck perpetuating many aspects of the abuse. Their indifference to themselves, self-manipulation and desire to be in control become a concretised emotional, energetic and physical barrier to the truth of who they are. When a survivor is trapped by their carried victim energy they keep regurgitating their unresolved emotions, which is how they perpetuate staying oppressed. When victims feel trapped by their history of abuse, they bind themselves to their fear of never escaping their experience of abuse. They fear how the abuse experience has left them feeling shattered and compelled to annihilate any sense of self-worth. This fear becomes an inhibitor to resolution, which is why it is imperative that a victim feels and experiences being unconditionally loved and supported by those who become privy to their current experience of abuse or history of abuse.

The survivor who is trapped by their carried victim energy can become consumed by their fears and embedded beliefs, which inhibits their awareness of the free flow of their own soul's consciousness. The survivor develops misconceptions from their victim mentality that fuels their emotional, energetic and physical merry-go-round, depriving the survivor of the opportunity to resolve and evolve beyond their abuse experience. Carrying victim energy leaves survivors succumbing to being dishonest with themselves. This means they automatically reject their own significance, uniqueness, independence and individuality, and become oppositional to acknowledging they are a soul of *True Source Divine Origin Consciousness*. Resolution of carried victim energy means the survivor can realise they are more than just what another has done to them, and that the experience of the insidiousness of indifference that the paedophile has inflicted upon them does not define who they are. There is more to the survivor than the abuse they have experienced.

The survivor of abuse struggles to acknowledge they have a choice to resolve beyond the infestation of indifference and their automatic reaction to secure the perpetuation of their own emotional, energetic and physical pain. The abuse experience has caused the survivor to be separated from their awareness of the truth of their soul. When this occurs at a very young age the survivor struggles to feel any sense of self and often exists in an emotional void they struggle to comprehend. This causes them to be immersed in a state of emotional upheaval, which can be internalised or externalised. The victim struggles to feel the truth of who they are and often exists on their emotional merry-go-round, which continues to manifest and perpetuate the beliefs that oppresses their ability to feel the truth of who they are. Being truthfully honest is the choice to break the cycle of perpetuating soul oppression via a victim mentality. Unfortunately, survivors can deny themselves the freedom of choice to acknowledge their ability and opportunity to resolve beyond their own emotional, energetic and physical pain. Victims who refuse to be honest about the truth of who they are, can be overwhelmed by the soul abuse they have experienced, and sadly wallow in their own indifference towards themselves.

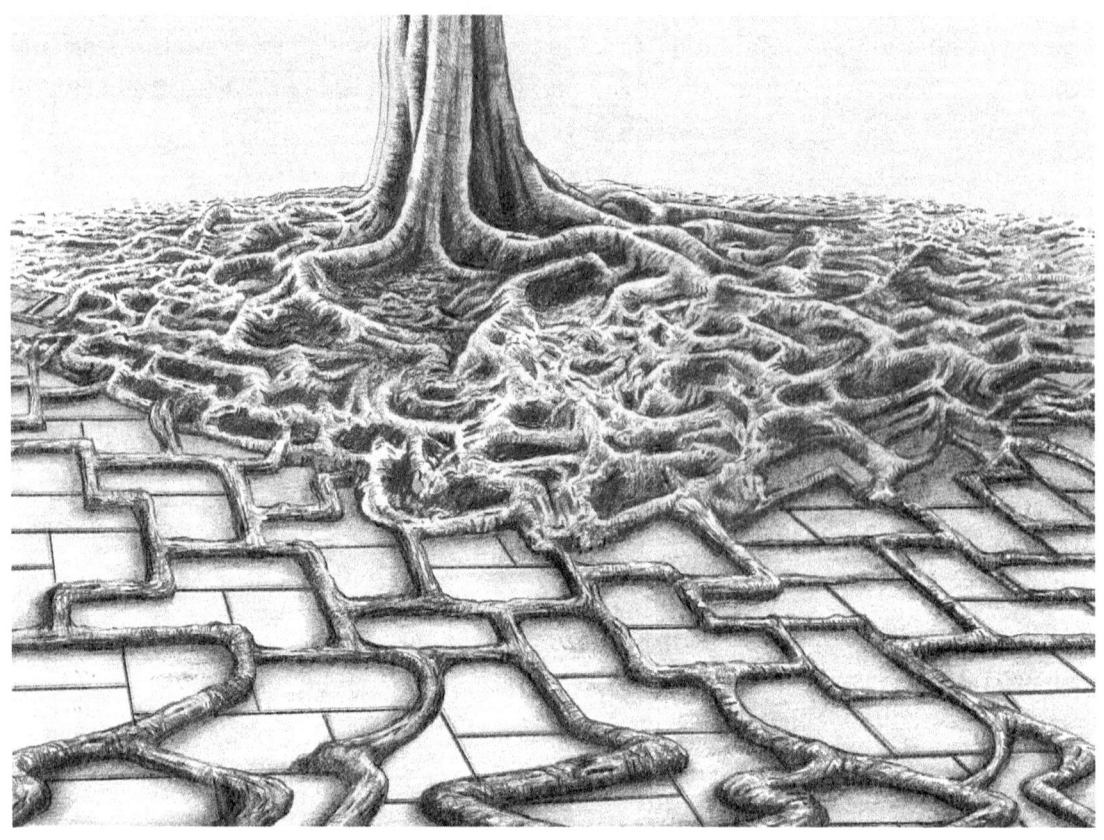

Sexual abuse alters the natural development of a child. The sexual abuse becomes part of who they believe they are, leaving them to exist in a mass of confusion. They can believe they are predestined to exist being indifferent to their own true value, and to remain stuck following the unresolved emotions created from the trauma.

The stain the experience of abuse leaves on the victim taints their ability to realise they have a choice in the aftermath of the experience. When the survivor is unable to realise they have a choice about how they respond to what has happened, they become lost in their victim mentality and believe they are entrapped by their experience of abuse. The victim endures the injustice of being left reverberating in the stain of the abuse even when the physical component of the abuse experience has ended. It is important for the victim to realise that the stain they feel is not a natural part of who they are, but is the residue of feeling the paedophile's indifference and the absolute unfathomableness of their abuse experience. This stain changes how they perceive themselves and it is their acceptance of the reality of the abuse that can allow them to shift to a different perspective about themselves and reality. When they choose to unconditionally love their own natural value, worth and significance, they no longer feel the stain that limits how they define and describe themselves. This is not easy but every survivor of abuse is worth the effort required for resolution. Resolution is dependent on the process of evolving truthfulness, which enables the victim to feel their own natural value, worth and significance.

Societal fears

The perpetuation of indifference can take many forms and continues for many reasons. It is not unheard of for victims to be bullied when their abuse becomes known, and for the harassment to be ignored or glossed over. If we as a society do not acknowledge the gravity of abuse, we send a covert message to victims that we do not care. This also sends a message to the paedophile that we continue to be inept in dealing with the reality of abuse.

We, as a society have been reluctant to be honest about sexual abuse, because we are horrified by how inept we are at dealing with and accepting the reality of the damage sexual abuse does to the soul. We attempt to gloss over the reality of the abuse to the soul and the ensuing indifference to their reality. This leaves us floundering in the void created by our separation from our awareness of our soul and truth. We ignore the magnitude of the reverberating affects sexual abuse has on all involved. We can become rigidly stuck in wanting to ascertain the rights and wrongs of what occurred and often override the enormity of the emotional and physical pain sexual abuse inflicts. We often want to disengage from the ramifications of abuse, which can allow us to continue to deny the depth of damage to the soul who has been abused.

We have conditioned ourselves to class sexual abuse as a taboo subject, and this means we have programmed ourselves to gloss over how prolific sexual abuse is within society. We do not know how to respond to the victim or the perpetrator of paedophilia, and so we often react automatically with fearful avoidance. We fear not being able to control, conceal or heal the emotional pain the victim carries, and we fear the emotional damage indifference creates within the victim. This causes us to feel overwhelmed and means we, as a society, respond ineptly.

Our collective fear of how some people can be completely indifferent to others causes us to fear being unable to stop the perpetuation of abuse, and the denial and avoidance of truth. We especially fear being unable to protect the innocence of children who are the most vulnerable within society. Collectively as a society, this fear of paedophiles has caused us to encroach on the natural freedoms of childhood and we constantly put limits on how we allow our children to interact with the world outside their family home.

This fear can morph into the belief that we are inept at protecting our children, which perpetuates and indoctrinates our children to be limited by fear.

When we are unable to confront the truth of our fear, being indifferent becomes how we attempt to protect ourselves from acknowledging the truth of paedophilia, sexual abuse and the ramifications for each soul. The perpetuation of the denial and avoidance of truth and indifference becomes an expected and accepted normality, and we all get lost in the void indifference and denial creates. When we fear something may affect our illusion of control, we forget how to be compassionate and present in the truth of what is emotionally, energetically and physically occurring. When we are willing to deny reality, we create emotional labyrinths to justify our indifference to and fear of acknowledging how paedophiles have already affected our paranoia about risks to our children. We all use denial to hide from what we believe we cannot fix, which leaves us indifferent to truth and stuck in the reverberations of fear.

When the perpetuation of denial becomes familiar, we allow the insidiousness of indifference to manifest within us all. We are horrified to hear stories of sexual abuse but unless it has a direct effect on our personal reality, we easily become complacent to the flow-on effect sexual abuse has on our society. When we have conditioned ourselves to feel compassion for only a moment and then ignore the reality of what we feel, we become willing to gloss over the impact and align to being indifferent to truth. Sometimes it is not knowing the answers but being willing to question the stagnation of our denial and our own indifference that will create change.

- How do we break the cycle of perpetuated abuse, if we do not have compassion for all involved?
- Can we afford to continue to be dismissive about the carnage left in the wake of sexual abuse?
- How long are we going to be complacent and in denial of the indifference required to abuse an innocent child?
- Do we withdraw our compassion from the paedophile because of the choices they are knowingly making?
- Why do we retreat from being totally honest about sexual abuse?
- What do we use as a smokescreen in an attempt to protect ourselves from the reality of how insidious paedophilia is?

The world we live in is as complex as the individuals within it; each individual is part of the mass we refer to as society.

- Societies create laws to protect the individuals within society, but do our laws acknowledge the true extent of the damage done by the paedophile and the insidious nature of paedophilia?
- How do we protect the innocence of children, if we devalue the importance of supporting those who protect children?
- Does our funding support the importance of child protection or is it an example of indifference?
- Does our funding enable law enforcement to keep pace with the way paedophiles have been able to exponentially expand their networks of paedophilia with technology?
- Is lack of funding and support hampering the capacity of our law enforcement?
- How do we evolve beyond the perpetuation of abuse, if we as a society deny the reality of indifference?
- How do we create change if we ignore reality?
- When do we start valuing the truth of ourselves as souls?
- If a child's innocence is a representation of truth, how respectful of truth are we if we ignore the reality of our own indifference to paedophilia?

To fear the truth of our reality is to make the choice to protect denial and indifference to truth.

The magnitude and scope of how insidious and prolific paedophilia is, reveals the illusion we have about our reality. Truth acknowledges the significance of all souls. If we, as mankind, did the same, our acknowledgement of the significance of all souls would mean we could no longer be complacent about the innocence of children being abused or exploited. All abused children are at the mercy of the insidiousness of the abuser and the level of indifference of the adults surrounding them.

Falsely Accused

Indifference manifests in many forms. There are people who are willing to use the insidiousness of paedophilia to gain control of another's ranking within the pecking orders of families or society. Some individuals retaliate against those they want to have ultimate control of, by falsely accusing them of being a paedophile or a sexual abuser. They contrive false accusations to undermine how the person will be perceived. These individuals seek to attach others' judgement onto those they falsely accuse, creating a stain for the innocent to carry. These individuals use the fear of paedophilia to seek ultimate control of another, knowing they will incite all those who hear the accusation to align to the fear of paedophilia and succumb to the accusation as if it were fact. Those who falsely accuse another are indifferent to truth and outweigh the importance of another soul with their retaliative disposition and their willingness to be abusive.

The accuser is relying on the ones who hear the rumours to believe they are 'in the know', even if they feel there is potentially no truth to the rumour, and rely on them to use this to gossip. This is how others are manipulated to become a willing participant in the assassination of the reputation of the falsely accused. Regardless of any evidence to the contrary, they will fixate on the rumour as if it was a proven truth in order to protect their image of being 'in the know'. Many people fear being fooled or kept in the dark, and choose to align to rumours, because they want to enhance their sense of superiority by being 'in the know'. The accusation and the perpetuated gossip becomes a stain the falsely accused carries, and regardless of their innocence, they become plagued by the knowledge that there are those who have heard the rumour and will judge them as a paedophile.

A person suspected of paedophilia is someone we believe to be guilty until proven innocent. The insidious nature of paedophilia means this reversal is necessary to protect and nurture the survivors of abuse through the process of justice. However, when a deliberately false accusation is made, it is a damnation on all victims of paedophilia. This is because the accusation of paedophilia is being used to abuse yet another innocent person. False accusations trivialise paedophilia and undermine victims, supporters and whistle blowers. Knowingly making a false accusation shows complete disrespect and disregard for how arduous it is for a survivor of abuse to come forth. It is a cruel form of indifference when someone is willing to use the accusation of paedophilia for perceived personal gain and vengeance.

Falsely using the accusation of paedophilia to attack another, attacks more than just the one being falsely accused, it attacks the integrity of all the survivors that have come forth. It also plants a seed of possible doubt in others who might have found the strength to expose abuse, fearing they will be accused of making false accusations. The accuser is vying to secure their stranglehold over the falsely accused's future, believing that without the ability to repair their reputation, the falsely accused will be vulnerable to the accuser's attack, innuendo and desire to destroy how they feel about themselves.

The accuser seeks to abuse the falsely accused because they cannot contain their own vindictiveness; they want to demoralise their perceived opponent or create a competition about who is going to dictate the reputation of the other. The accuser acts like they are the victim to ensure the falsely accused will have to struggle to prove their innocence. It becomes a competition between the accuser and the falsely accused, over each person's reputation and perceived integrity. This competition causes those who hear rumours and innuendos to feel compelled to decide who to align to. The accuser preys on the vulnerability and insecurity of the listener, and feeds them a story that will ensure compliance to their vindictive desire to annihilate the reputation of the innocent party. These stories can become inconsistent and more outrageous over time, although the damage is done before the deception is realised.

The listener is manipulated by the accuser and may become willing to spread the accusation, believing they are privy to the truth. When the accuser is vindictively lying, they generate indifference energy, the listener feels this and can mistakenly think they are feeling the energy of the one being accused, even though they are actually feeling the energy of the accuser. The accusations are based on vindictive lies, orchestrated by the accuser from their own callousness and slyness. The accuser relies on everyone's fear of paedophilia to assassinate the character of the one they have falsely accused and on the rumours being spread, which are beyond the innocent party's ability to control.

The accuser will use the listener's indecisive judgement, or seek to create indecisiveness within the listener, by bombarding them with contrived emotions and fallacies. The accuser seeks to create insecurity within all who will listen to their lies. The accuser knows if the listener is insecure about their own understanding of reality, they will anchor to the information generated by their lies, because they fear aligning to the defence of a paedophile. The accuser can create enough emotional anarchy, while bombarding the listener with lies, that the listener will be in a state of confusion. This confusion undermines their ability to feel and acknowledge the deception of the accuser.

The listener becomes insecure within their own confusion and reluctant to oppose the vindictive lies the accuser wants them to align to. The listener's silence will be taken by the accuser as confirmation that their lies have been believed and that the listener is on their side. The accuser believes they have created an ally who will contribute to and accept the annihilation of the accused's reputation, life, relationships and understanding of their self-worth.

Listeners may question their own ability to trust themselves to know what the truth is because of the sensitive nature of the accusation. This sensitivity to sexual abuse creates insecurity within the listener, which enables the accuser to repetitively enforce their unorthodox way of manipulating others to believe them, and to vindictively use the accusation of paedophilia to attack another. The accuser uses the fear of paedophilia to gain control of those they specifically want to target and they attempt to control the assassination of that person's reputation by having everyone else believe their lies.

The accuser wants to create emotional anarchy for the one they falsely accuse. The accuser is intentionally indifferent to truth, and the natural value, worth and significance of the person they are falsely accusing. The accuser seeks to disrupt the reality of the accused and delights in being the source of their emotional upheaval. The internal anarchy of the accuser becomes what the accused has to deal and contend with. The falsely accused will find it unfathomable that they have to defend themselves against lies and false accusations, and struggle to comprehend the motive behind the false accusations. The accuser's manipulation of reality can be relentless, because their lies become a way of securing their desire for ultimate control of another.

These individuals who are willing to use the accusation of paedophilia as a weapon, will fuel the lie to gain momentum, and will play their part as a victim with conviction and dedication. The accuser knows, if the truth of the insidious motives behind their false accusations are revealed, the judgement they have incited will back fire on them. The accuser fears being exposed as the instigator of abuse because they know, if they are caught falsely accusing another of sexual abuse, they will be judged with condemnation. The accuser is willing to risk exposure because they believe they can fool all involved. The accuser uses a process of conditioning, to believe their survival depends on their own ability to align with their own lies. What they started as an orchestrated lie may become their perception of reality. Their lies become their only focus and they are willing to create a competition with truth to alter others' perception of reality.

Due to the sensitivity of sexual abuse, the listeners are reluctant to question either the accused or the implied victim about what the truth is. If there is no official enquiry, the rumours and innuendos become an undercurrent for the falsely accused to contend with. The rumours and innuendos become the stain the falsely accused carries because of the accuser's indifference to them. The falsely accused has no way of knowing who has been told of the lie, who believes the lie or who has become a willing ally of the accuser. The falsely accused is a victim of someone who is willing to use the accusation of paedophilia as a weapon, so they are branded with the stigma of paedophilia.

The accuser is indifferent to the emotional hell they are creating for those who they falsely accuse of paedophilia, and is willing to inflict whatever is necessary to gain the results they desire. With the first accusation, the accuser has declared their willingness to oppose and devalue truth, and align to their desire to control the reality of the accused. When the accused holds a position that has been previously linked with paedophilia, the accused may have to contend with the prejudice created by the actions of others that have held the position before them. The paedophilic history linked to the position they hold, even though it has no direct association with them, is used to have a bearing on defaming their character. The falsely accused is defined and evaluated by their position. They are not recognised for the individual they are, but are seen as an extension of the indifference within the paedophilic history of their position.

The accuser's own willingness to use the insidiousness of paedophilia for the purpose of abusively accusing another, makes them part of the collective energy of paedophilia. These accusers are willing to be anti-truth to secure their desire for control. The accuser seeks to annihilate another with the stigma of being a paedophile. This is insidious indifference towards the accused. The accuser is as vile as a perpetrator of sexual abuse because they knowingly forgo truth to inflict pain with a hideous trap, the accused cannot escape due to the stigma of paedophilia. They seek to banish the innocent from being loved, respected and valued, for their own desire to gain control or a financial reward.

What price can anyone put on their soul integrity? It is their own soul integrity that the accuser has to override and devalue to falsely accuse another of sexual abuse. The accuser has become indifferent to their soul integrity by falsely accusing someone of paedophilia. The accuser's indifference becomes the stain that the falsely accused has to endure.

Family shock

Family members of convicted or known paedophiles can carry the shame of being related to a paedophile. The family members can feel guilty by association, even though they have not been aware of, or party to, the abuse inflicted by their relative. The family can feel as though the paedophile has abused the family name and can feel the shame of paedophilia, believing the stigma is connected to their name. Some people can become insensitive to the family of the paedophile and inflict their assumptions and judgement on those related to the paedophile. This is done without empathy, ignoring that the relatives have also been impacted by the actions and secret world of the paedophile.

Some survivors of paedophilia can carry the shame of the paedophile by adopting the identity of being a victim and allow the victim mentality to be how they dictate their value, worth and significance to themselves. They judge themselves as being part of something that is insidious, and from this judgement develop a wall of indifference that opposes the truth of their own soul. This can also be the reaction of those who are related to the paedophile. A relative can create their own opposition to the truth of being an independent soul, regardless of what another family member might have done. Some relatives can distort their own perception of themselves and devalue their sense of worth by consuming themselves with the fear of outside communal judgement. The relative experiences shock, and can devalue the truth of who they are because of their association with the paedophile. As the paedophile's secret world becomes revealed, the relatives can find the truth unfathomable. They find it hard to reconcile with the truth and become very confused. The beliefs they had about their family crumble, and this leaves them with no foundation to anchor to as they begin to question everything about their life. Their life and their perception of everything can feel tainted by their relative's actions.

Relatives and children of paedophiles who have not been abused, but have witnessed or suspected the paedophile of being an abuser, or have become aware of the abuse at a later stage, feel shame because of their association with the paedophile. The relatives of paedophiles who feel shame by association are also victims of the paedophile's perverseness. They start to distrust themselves because someone they trusted or respected has done the unthinkable and they were oblivious. They can feel trapped by their own memories of suspicion or by how unfathomable it is to them that someone they loved had such a perverse secret world. This causes them to struggle with the fear of being fooled and the fear they have inadvertently contributed to either the opportunity for another to be abused or have been used as a decoy for the paedophile's deviousness.

The ramifications for the victim

The helplessness the victim felt while being controlled develops into a fear of being controlled, and this leaves some feeling very defensive. They can feel a sense of shame when they compulsively want control over their reality at the expense of others. When they observe themselves being indifferent to others' feelings, it causes them to feel helplessly trapped within their own shame. The survivor of abuse is aware of how insidious wanting ultimate control of another is and feels shame about their compulsive desire to control, which is driven by their belief that their ability to control will keep them safe. Some survivors fear unleashing their control onto others and instead control themselves to become people pleasers with little regard for themselves. This generates a seething undercurrent of resentment they inflict on themselves while trying to sustain an image of being easy going and willing to be of service to others. Some survivors of abuse create a self-imposed emotional exile to live in, because they fear being controlling and fear being controlled. Some survivors of abuse become completely confused about how to interact with others because they always have a foreboding fear of being unsafe, manipulated or exploited.

Some survivors of abuse feel shameful because they fear the world they live in. They become consumed with wanting to protect and defend their desire to have ultimate control over themselves, life and others, believing this is the only way to keep themselves safe. These survivors of abuse feel shameful because they cannot control themselves to feel safe enough to be at peace with their reality. Shame is a type of heresy energy that is tangible and alters the survivor's perception of reality. Some survivors of abuse carry the shame of opposing their own natural significance. This becomes another stain of indifference they carry, except this shame is generated by their own resistance to, and denial and avoidance of accepting themselves as a significant, unique, independent, individual soul of *True Source Divine Origin Consciousness*. They compulsively oppose their own core essences, which keeps them entrapped in their fear.

The indifference of sexual abuse is an absolute assault on the truth of who the victim is, and they become overwhelmed by how insidious the indifference feels. They disassociate as a protective mechanism, seeking to escape the insidiousness of the indifference they have to endure. Some survivors of abuse struggle to find the truth of themselves after they have experienced the insidiousness of indifference, and struggle to hold to the truth that they are valuable, worthy and significant. Survivors of abuse fear feeling the reality of any type of indifference, which means they become highly reactive to their own and others' various forms of being indifferent. This leads the survivor to exist in a constant battle of wanting control over how their reality makes them feel, and only the slightest alteration to their expectations can ignite their fears. Once their fears are ignited, they refuse to stay in the truth of their reality and disassociate from the truth of who they are. They implode in on themselves, which leaves them scrambling in their insecurities and ramps up their desire for control even more. This fear of feeling out of kilter with what they were expecting leaves them feeling not good enough, and in a void they create by separating from their awareness of truth and disassociating from feeling the core essence of who they are.

The survivor's belief of 'not being good enough' has developed into a constant cloak of shame. Survivors inadvertently use their shame to rebel against accepting their own true value, worth and significance, which leaves them indifferent to the truth of themselves. Their indifference towards themselves sustains their separation from their awareness of truth and leaves them scrambling in the fears and embedded beliefs that enforce their soul denial.

Paedophiles inflict their indifference not only during the abuse, but also before and after the abuse, steering the victim to implode in their own heresy energy and the end result is they become anti-the truth of themselves. The paedophile wants to undermine the victim's respect for truth and how they value themselves, seeking to condition the victim to disregard their own soul integrity, value, worth and significance. The experience of sexual abuse is a multi-dimensional experience because the abuse is not just physical, but also has emotional, energetic and psychological components. This is all hideously overwhelming for the victim who can remain reverberating in the ramifications of the abuse, completely devaluing their own soul. They feel this as shame, and this becomes the prominent carried energy that annihilates the victim's awareness of their self-value, undermines their sense of worth and obliterates their acceptance of their natural significance. When the victim adopts the belief, that they are of no value, worth or significance, these beliefs lead them to feel like a shattered soul. They feel shattered because they are aware that the paedophile wanted complete ownership of their soul, and they feel helpless because they are left encased in their awareness of the insidiousness of the paedophile's indifference and desire to have ultimate control not only of their body, but also of their soul.

When the survivor of abuse feels internalised guilt, shame and humiliation, they retreat into their belief of being unworthy to feel the truth of their own soul. Survivors programme, condition, and indoctrinate themselves via guilt, shame and humiliation, to secure, protect and defend being separated from their awareness of truth and disassociated from feeling the core essence of their own soul. Guilt, shame and humiliation become triggers, which cause them to protect their desire for control and victim mentality without realising they are actually protecting the demise of their own awareness of the natural value, worth and significance of who they are, which is a soul of truth.

Some survivors get lost in the experience of being abused because they feel their natural right to freedom of choice and to hold to their own soul integrity and dignity was taken away. The survivor was stripped of their natural right as a soul to be treated with respect, care and unconditional love, and this has left them feeling like damaged goods. The physical force of the abuse disables victims' ability to protect themselves or to be able to use their freedom of choice, which induces an undercurrent of fear that some believe they can never escape. When the paedophile uses manipulation to coerce the victim into a vulnerable state, the victim is left with a fear of being unable to determine others' intentions. This leaves victims with a loss of confidence in their ability to keep themselves safe. This causes them to constantly second-guess every decision they make and to doubt their own perception of reality.

When survivors carry a memory of feeling the dominance of the paedophile and of their inability to protect themselves, they recoil from their awareness. They are aware that the paedophile wanted to gain ultimate control over them and they recognise that they have been controlled to be in opposition to themselves. They are aware that they have been ranked as useable and discardable fodder for the paedophile's personal desires. This leaves them floundering in a shroud of indifference. The paedophile seeks to corrupt the victim's understanding of their self-worth as a significant, unique, independent individual with their own thoughts and presence. The paedophile wants the victim to separate from any sense of self to increase their ability to manipulate the victim. The paedophile seeks to be an authority over the victim's freedom and disregards how this affects their victim. The survivor can feel used and discarded, which leaves them feeling stained by the indifference.

When the survivor is stuck in guilt, shame or humiliation, they feel oppressed and condemned to stay trapped in the stain of indifference left from their experience of being sexually abused. This causes survivors to congest their awareness of their natural flow of consciousness with their fears and negative beliefs about themselves. Their fears and negative beliefs concretise their position of being lost in the despair of their own oppression. As long as they remain trapped in their guilt, shame and humiliation, they experience being indifferent to their own soul, often without realising they have a choice. The survivor's immersion in their own guilt, shame and humiliation becomes a smokescreen that conceals the beauty of their soul. The survivor is overwhelmed by the victim experience and often resorts to resistance, denial or avoidance because they are unable to confront what is unresolved. This secures their indifference to themselves, concretises their victimhood and deprives them of resolution and evolution.

Survivors' guilt, shame and humiliation mean they annihilate their own awareness of the truth of themselves with self-loathing and self-hatred, conditioning themselves to tolerate their own despair because they believe it is a reality they cannot change. When the victim succumbs to the energy of guilt, shame and humiliation, they ignore the significance of their truth as a soul and avoid the truth of their own ability to resolve and evolve. The trauma of being abused means resolution is never easy however, every soul is capable of resolution and evolution.

Victims can be overwhelmed by their inability to trust themselves to deal with their own reality and others' indifference, which may have them believing that suicide will facilitate an escape from their own despair. Suicide can become a constant thought that plague victims, and a mind game they use on themselves. Often they can feel their situation is hopeless and believe that suicide is their only escape from the paedophile and their own emotional torture. Many are confused because they want to escape the pain, but believe the only way they can escape it, is to stop living. They are overwhelmed with the pain and are unable to realise that it is the pain they want to escape, and instead fixate their thoughts on wanting to escape life. They may feel that suicide will expose the truth of their reality, and expose the paedophile as a paedophile. However, some are aware there is no guarantee of exposure, because they believe the paedophile is clever enough to fool anyone who may enquire about the truth. The victim who is immersed in their own despair believes indifference is prolific, and believes no one would take the time to care about the truth of their life. Even if the victim knows they will not commit suicide and have no real desire to end their life, suicide can become a constant thought they ruminate about. Suicide is not an escape and also passes the pain onto others.

The threat of suicide from a victim can become a control structure or cry for help used to express how overwhelmed they feel. They feel as if everything is out of control and that there is no way of quelling their fear or appeasing their insecurities. This can manifest into wanting others to appease their insecurities and lead to a desire to have others pacify their unresolved emotions. Some victims use the threat of suicide as a weapon in an attempt to project guilt, shame and humiliation onto those who do not know how to pacify their emotional torture. Some victims use the threat of suicide to entrap others into their emotional upheaval and can be totally indifferent to the effect their threats have on those around them.

For some victims, the thought of suicide actually becomes the turning point that helps them shift into being able to trust themselves enough to face their fears, the abuse and life. The thought of suicide becomes the catalyst which enables the victim to acknowledge that, in spite of their despair, there are options and opportunities for help. The acknowledgment of having options and the victim's own courage to come out of hiding, creates a bridge back to truth and the truth of who they are. They have created barriers from the indifference they have taken on as an identity, which stops them from being at peace with themselves and leaves them existing in the ramifications of opposing their significance. When victims acknowledge their own natural significance, they begin to trust the process of resolution and permit themselves to unshackle their identity from their abuse.

Sexual abuse is an experience, not a definition to be encased in; you are far greater than any experience suffered through the insidiousness of indifference in the form of paedophilia. Reaching out for help is not a weakness, it is strength and courage in action. Recovery is not easy nor is it a quick process however, all souls are worth the effort required. Who you have come to believe you are can be very divergent from who your naturally are.

Truth creates freedom. When victims enable themselves to feel the truth of who they are, they are giving themselves permission to resolve beyond their own indifference. When victims trust truth they are choosing to unconditionally love themselves enough to accept and appreciate their own value, worth and significance. The experience of sexual abuse and indifference cripples the victim because they anchor to beliefs of being unworthy and insignificant. This causes the victim to lie about their own value, worth and significance. These lies create emotional labyrinths of self-deception that have correlating control structures that keep them stuck, constantly seeking validation for their deceptive, negative beliefs and internal lies. Some victims sabotage themselves within their own cyclic patterns of tolerating the devaluation of their natural value, worth and significance. Truthfulness is an antidote to indifference, lies and fears.

Looking for justice

- How do we as a society assist the survivor to feel secure and supported to speak out against the paedophile?
- How do we as a society deal with sexual abuse when we struggle to care for survivors who have the courage to expose their abusers?
- Does the fear of exposing truth contribute to the perpetuation of paedophilia?
- Why do we deny this could happen to anyone?
- Are our disabled and most vulnerable safe, if they are classed as ineligible to be a witness in our justice system?
- Do we fear exposing the truth of paedophilia?
- Are we hiding as a society from the horrible indifference that festers within society?
- If the judicial system denies the severity of sexual abuse, is this taken as permission to disregard the impact of paedophilia?
- Does our judicial system support and value the integrity of the investigators of paedophilia?

Some victims may believe they are unworthy to seek help from the authorities and may believe they are unworthy to stand against their abuser within the justice system. Some victims may want to bring justice to the situation, but fear exposing themselves and their experience to the scrutiny and judgement of those connected to the judicial system. Some victims may constantly second-guess their choice to trust the judicial system to expose the truth of their reality, and can be overwhelmed with the anxiety of not knowing how the judicial system will respond to them as an individual. The victim fears the focus will be on their character, not the paedophile's, and fears the judicial system will be complacent and indifferent to the events of their experience of sexual abuse, instead concentrating on questioning their integrity.

Some paedophiles can use the judicial system as a stage to expose the flaws within mankind's judgement of integrity, soul significance and the value of truth. The survivor is expected to prove, without a shadow of a doubt, that they were abused without consent, did not encourage the advances of the paedophile and can recall all facts related to the abuse. The paedophile only has to create doubt and the severity of the abuse may be treated as a minor incident in which the paedophile had a momentary lapse in knowing what is appropriate behaviour. Paedophilia is not a momentary lapse in knowing what is appropriate behaviour; it is an opportunistic, orchestrated attack on a vulnerable child and the truth of their soul with the insidiousness of being indifferent.

The victim carries the experience for life as a constant reminder of how insidious some individuals can be when they believe they can get away with their abusive behaviour.

The justice system may be another source of indifference that the survivor encounters and the decision of the court may not reflect the severity of the abuse. All parties of the judicial system become part of the victim's ordeal and some may feel victimised by those who are indifferent to truth, while others may feel they have to compromise their own integrity for the sake of society's laws. The decisions of the court and sentencing may not reflect the reality of the indifference inflicted on an innocent soul. The paedophile's desire to control via sexual abuse affects many because there are emotional ramifications for all those who come in contact with the insidiousness of the paedophile and sexual abuse. The paedophile's manipulation of the judicial system can leave many feeling jaded, especially if there has been a dumbing down of the reality, of the trail of destruction, the paedophile has inflicted. The paedophile seeks to have everyone involved buy into their web of deception, and when the severity of the abuse they have inflicted is dumbed down, we all become victims to their depravity.

The victim and advocates for truth may observe the charges being altered and the severity of abuse being downgraded because it suits the judicial system, but what does this say about the way we as society deal with sexual abuse and paedophiles? Paedophilia is the choice to take advantage of those who cannot protect themselves. Does our judicial system protect the innocence of children and those who cannot protect themselves, and have we allowed ourselves to become complacent about the reality of our judicial system?

Many survivors baulk at exposing a paedophile and refuse to speak out because they fear the judicial system will put them through another ordeal. The survivor's silence perpetuates the protection of the paedophile and inadvertently enables the paedophile to arrogantly continue their insidious attack on the innocence of others.

If any part of the judicial system is indifferent to the reality of abuse, the impact of this indifference is felt by many and can become an experience of indifference that they also have to carry. Those investigators who honour the truth and the significance of the victim, and are prepared to go to the lengths needed to expose the insidiousness of paedophilia, will also carry the effects of the judicial system's indifference. These investigators have chosen willingly to expose truth, while exposing themselves to the insidiousness of sexual abuse because they care for and are willing to protect the innocent. The investigators become emotionally, energetically and physically affected by the indifference they encounter, observe, discover, experience and report, when attempting to get justice for the victim.

The investigators of sexual abuse are constantly grappling with the victim's fear, insecurities and their uneasiness of not being able to control how the reality of their sexual abuse is exposed. They have to dismantle the code of silence for the investigation to have an impact. Often the code of silence is broken and truth is revealed, and then the investigators have to deal with an unexpected retreat due to the victim's fear of exposing the reality of their abuse. For some survivors of abuse the judicial system reinforces the reality of being abused, and they can recant out of fear because reliving their abuse becomes too traumatic for them. They want to return to the illusion that not being confronted with the reality of their abuse keeps them safe, because they fear losing their ability to suppress the hideousness of what they internally feel. They can retreat because they believe they are better off surviving in their denial of reality. They can fear the vulnerability of exposing their experience of abuse and they struggle to know if they have the courage to endure the longevity of being in the spotlight and on show in a court case.

If the paedophile is connected to a large organisation such as an educational, political or religious system, the victim can be emotionally impacted by the organisation's response or lack of response. The survivor of abuse may perceive that the organisation is evaluating their value, worth and significance, which can make them feel insignificant if the organisation refuses to acknowledge the truth. The governing body of the organisation evaluates the impact they believe the truth of abuse will have on the organisation's image and may elect to promote their own bias to uphold the organisation's image. The protection of the organisation's image may take precedence over the discovery of the truth of abuse. The organisation operates from the position that protecting the organisation's image takes precedence over an innocent child, which means they act dishonourably and align to the protection of the paedophile. The survivor of abuse is subjected to more indifference because they feel judged, and reel from the disregard the organisation has for them and truth, which feels like another violation.

Some survivors of abuse want the truth exposed within the judicial system because it is an opportunity to be heard. They want the truth exposed because it will be an acknowledgment of the magnitude of the impact sexual abuse has had on their life. They seek an opportunity to give voice to the impact and repercussions of the abuse. They want to reveal how the paedophile's indifference to their value and worth has had a profound disruption on their life. The purpose of the judicial system is to give a voice to those who have been rendered voiceless, and to provide an arena where truth is exposed and acknowledged. When the paedophile had all the control and power the victim was silenced, but when the survivor can walk into a judicial system that acknowledges truth in its entirety, the survivor is given back their voice.

Some paedophiles may use the judicial system to lessen the impact of being exposed as a paedophile, and even an admission of guilt may be a strategy used to manipulate the judicial system in their favour. If the survivor feels the paedophile is manipulating the judicial system and is still seeking to control reality to their advantage, the admission of guilt can be bitter-sweet for the survivor. They know the admission has only come about because the paedophile has been cornered into confessing and is seeking to lessen the charge or sentencing. Even though it may not relieve any of the emotional pain the survivor feels, it is still a relief to hear the paedophile confess their guilt. The court case is important to the survivor because it gives clarity to the truth of the brutality, physical force, manipulation, deception and conniving intent of the paedophile. The clarity of the truth being exposed and examined leaves responsibility for the abuse with the paedophile, and this may enable the survivor to re-establish their own understanding of innocence.

During the court case the victim may be subjected to observing the paedophile's indifference towards them and also be subjected to the emotional wrath of any supporters of the paedophile. This can overwhelm the victim because they have a heightened sensitivity to indifference. Some paedophiles want their victims to believe the court case is a competition and a battle for supremacy, knowing the truth of what happened during the sexual abuse is only ever known to the paedophile and the victim. Some paedophiles delight in watching the victim scramble to untangle the deception that the paedophile keeps perpetuating, even in a judicial process.

The victim can feel the mind games of the paedophile and has very little avenue to explain what is being felt because they fear being classed as overly emotional and unreliable. The accusation of paedophilia is huge and most people struggle to comprehend what, why and how it could have occurred, which paradoxically, leaves people questioning the victim's account and mental state. As the victim tells the truth, they often feel they are being scrutinised unfairly, and the paedophile uses the scrutiny as another way to undermine the victim's confidence. The paedophile can use the scrutinisation of the victim as a diversion from anyone discovering the truth of what actually occurred. There is an energetic exchange that is covert and unspoken, but all involved feel the energy, even though their own denial. The victim can see through the charades the paedophile performs, because they have witnessed the reality of the paedophile when they had free rein and thought no one was watching or scrutinising their actions.

Everyone in the court room is judging the responses of the victim to see if they meet their criteria of what a victim should react to and how they should respond if they are telling the truth. The victim may observe the paedophile's testimony with a complete understanding of the paedophile's manipulative traits. However, they may have no ability to expose to others what they can see and feel so clearly.

When a paedophile remorsefully admits to being guilty, the paedophile starts to take ownership and responsibility for the emotional hell they have inflicted on their victim. Their admission of guilt means the shame is being returned to the original instigator, which is the paedophile. For some survivors, the paedophile's admission of guilt enables them to resolve the emotional feeling of being shackled to the paedophile's insidious indifference. This allows the victim to acknowledge the paedophile as someone who willingly inflicted their indifference on an innocent child, instead of perceiving the paedophile as the authority over their value, worth and significance.

The survivor may carry the misconception that the shame of abuse should be carried by them and feel some reprieve when they witness a remorseful admission of guilt from the paedophile. Some feel that while there is no acknowledgment of the abuse, they are not worthy enough to be valued. This causes them to devalue themselves and their own perception of their history. There is an awareness of truth between the victim and the paedophile because they both know the truth of the reality of the abuse. All others involved will perceive the reality of sexual abuse through their own judgement and assessment of the integrity of the victim and the paedophile. When a survivor of abuse acknowledges their own natural value, worth and significance, regardless of another's judgement or the actions of a paedophile, they no longer emotionally feel beholden to the soul oppression created from being an abuse victim. Survivors' acknowledgement of their own natural value, worth and significance, means they can realise the only person who has authority over the value, worth and significance of their soul is themselves.

When the survivor of abuse witnesses the paedophile's admission of guilt or a guilty verdict being delivered, it breaks the fear that they have that the paedophile is a statue of power over reality and above the laws of society. This allows them to see the paedophile for what they really are; a perverse individual immersed in their own indifference to truth and reality. The survivor can perceive the paedophile as all powerful and in control of them. When the survivor hears and sees the admission of guilt or a guilty verdict, they observe the power the paedophile believed they were entitled to being stripped away.

The admission of guilt or a guilty verdict exposes that the paedophile could only exert their power and control on a helpless child when no others were present, or that those who were present condoned the behaviour. Paedophiles have the belief that they are allowed to operate beyond the bounds and limits of society, and being convicted as guilty of their crime pulls them back into having to accept that they are not beyond the norms and boundaries of society. The survivor may come to realise the paedophile is a coward who only preys on the vulnerable, and is powerless when confronted with the truth and surrounded by those who are willing to enforce the limits and boundaries of society. The survivor may observe how powerless and cowardly the paedophile is, as they are confronted by the truth of being a paedophile, when they are in the presence of others who the paedophile cannot control, manipulate, deceive or physically overpower.

One of the many conflicting issues the survivor has to deal with is considering who else is affected by them reporting the paedophile and breaking the code of silence. How does this affect their immediate family, extended family, wider community, church members, school and society? The cascading effect and ramifications depend on the paedophile's position and how the paedophile has orchestrated their relationship with others to suit their control. However, it is not the survivor's responsibility how others respond to truth and they are entitled to the relief of not having to hide and remain silent any longer. All those affected should take responsibility for their own responses and be willing to explore the truth with compassion for all involved.

Some paedophiles will deliberately target one child in a family and treat the other children with absolute respect, so they can use the other children to create doubt and confusion. They will use the children who have not been abused for a character reference if they are exposed. Some paedophiles seek to protect themselves from being exposed as a paedophile by pre-planning the testimonials of others, just in case they do get caught. This may cause the victim to become obsessed with why they were the chosen one, and leads them to believe the paedophile chose them because they were unworthy of respect. This reinforces their belief that they will not be perceived by the judicial system as credible. Victims can anchor to a distorted view of themselves and the judicial system without realising they are aligning to the paedophile's manipulation.

Some paedophiles use the victim's pain and distorted view of their own credibility to destabilise the victim in the hope they can render them silent. The paedophile will seek to create more emotional pain if they believe their illusion of control is threatened and will consistently try to undermine the credibility of the victim. The paedophile may use the willingness of others, who may or may not be privy to the reality of the abuse, to judge the victim and create a fear within the victim that others do not believe they are credible. This can cause the victim to fear not being able to control the judgement of others and to believe it is better for them to remain silent. This renders the victim silent because they are fearful of how others will assess the reality of their abuse and who they are. The victim may feel they are defenceless against the judgement they believe they will have to endure. The victim has no guarantees that all those involved will seek to expose the truth of the abuse.

When a victim steps forward and removes the shackles of silence they are relying on others' acceptance of truth to help them deal with their reality, even though they fear being judged. Respecting their courage should be our first step.

Child exploitation material

People who look at child exploitation material but do not actually perform the physical act of sexually abusing children attempt to tell themselves they are not hurting anyone. However, they contribute to the collective of indifference and paedophilia because they are part of the market that is sustaining and demanding child exploitation through pornography. These people encourage a paedophile to immerse a child in the indifference that destroys lives. The viewer of child exploitation material contributes to the soul carnage of an innocent child, and is part of the market that drives the insidious child pornography industry. Industries connected to child exploitation material or child prostitution are organisations of soul carnage. Those who profit from child pornography and sexual slavery trade in the carnage of souls and are also betraying the truth of their own soul.

Viewers of child exploitation material try to distance themselves from the cost of their depravity, which is the degradation of another soul. Being indifferent to the truth and reality of child pornography and being willing to gain pleasure from viewing the rape, molestation, manipulation and control of an innocent child, highlights the depravity of the viewer. They are supporting the debauched actions of another paedophile and are a voyeuristic paedophile, often in denial of the reality of what they are doing. They are a paedophile who likes to be removed from feeling the insidiousness of the reality of abuse. They use being a voyeur to distance themselves from the soul carnage created by paedophilia and justify their own indifference to the reality of sexual abuse.

The viewer of child exploitation material may justify their compulsions, deny their addiction and tolerate being indifferent to the reality that they are part of the driving force of the paedophilic industry that hideously affects many children. The viewer is an abuser that creates and contributes to the perpetuation of indifference to paedophilia and the emotional pain, carnage and dishevelling of an innocent child. Viewers desensitise and disassociate themselves from the depraved reality they contribute to. They may even be an advocate for their own child's safety, even though they have classified another person's child as fair game just because they fear no retribution as they have had no personal contact.

Some viewers of child exploitation material disassociates from feeling the reality of how insidious paedophilia is. They choose to ignore how child exploitation material is sourced, which enables them to watch more and more levels of child exploitation without abhorrence. This causes the viewer of child exploitation material to observe children even in the most mundane circumstances through their lens of sexual fantasy and detachment. The viewer's addiction to child exploitation material means their filters of right and wrong become jaded, degraded and tainted. The use of pornography is addictive, which means users compel themselves to seek more extreme depictions of abuse as their addiction worsens. Their compulsion to engage with child exploitation material drives them ever deeper into the insidiousness of paedophilia. Some view child exploitation material because of the hideousness, and revel in the malice and cruelty of what they are a part of.

Some paedophiles use child exploitation material to desensitise a child to the reality of abuse. They attempt to create a normality about it and seek to make the child pliable to their control and desires. Abuse does not always have to be physical to have a devastating effect, being exposed to pornographic material both of children and adults through film or photographs can have a long-lasting impact. It is also abuse to incite a child to parade or pose in provocative positions, dressed or undressed for photos or recordings, regardless of whether it is shared or used privately. 'Peeping' through bathroom, bedroom doors or windows is also an abuse, whether seen or not seen by the child.

Freedom

There is no avenue of paedophilia that does not leave the reality of broken souls. However, those individuals affected by paedophilia always have the opportunity to resolve their soul carnage by trusting themselves to feel the truth of their own soul's consciousness. The victim is an innocent, who has experienced the indifference of a paedophile. It is the victim's resolution of their own indifference to the truth of who they are, which will give them freedom from the experience of being sexually abused. Those who seek to resolve their soul carnage will endeavour to feel the truth of who they are, by being completely honest with themselves. The survivors truthfulness enables them to acknowledge the significance of their own freedom of choice. Accepting their freedom of choice enables them to trust exploring beyond their abuse experience and to resonate with the consciousness of their soul. There comes a time in all soul journeys where denying and deceiving yourself is no longer an option, because the devastation becomes evident and the cost is too high to ignore. Freedom from indifference is the choice to unconditionally love yourself for who you naturally are, appreciating the strength within your soul and honouring your own opportunity for resolution and evolution.

History cannot be altered, but how you perceive yourself, your history and the reality of the strength of your soul is dynamic. You have the opportunity to use your truthfulness to feel the unconditional love of your origin. Your willingness to unconditionally love the truth of being a resolving and evolving soul allows you to discover freedom from what oppresses you, which is your indifference to truth. The journey back to the truth of who you are starts with the choice to be honest with yourself about the reality of your life experiences and the strength of your soul. There is more to you than the abuse you have experienced.

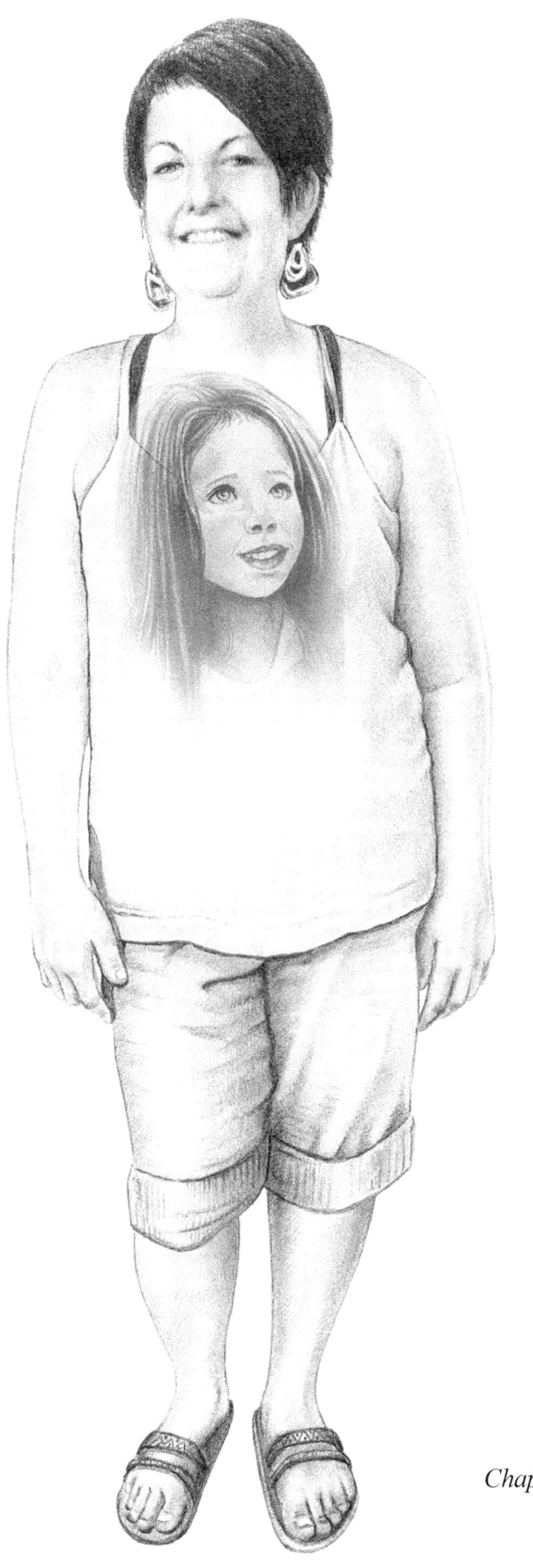

Chapter Three | 169

Section Three

Chapter Four

Forgotten Soul

**When you gaze upon yourself with indifference, you have forgotten your soul.
When another gazes upon you with indifference, they have
forgotten their own soul and devalued yours.**

Indifference aligned with the intent to harm creates soul carnage and leaves a sense of damage that permeates every fibre of the abused. The longevity of this carnage is difficult to navigate and there are far too many beautiful souls suffering in silence, unable to feel the core of their own being. They often hide in a sea of self-loathing, unable to value themselves. They can become trapped within the relentlessness of their own emotional storms, while attempting to row to a safe harbour, not knowing which direction to go. They struggle to anchor to the truth of their soul, and internally panic as they feel the tsunami of fear and distress constantly rising from within. Isolation becomes their friend and their foe as it creates a place to hide, when the intense disturbance takes hold, but it is also a place they allow their emotions to fester, leaving them forgetting their own soul.

Others may not realise the emotional riptide concealed beneath the surface. Others might never know of the effort required to suppress their internal turmoil. Beneath the despair and defence mechanisms is a soul who is hurt, carrying unseen scars that can never be forgotten. Their experiences of being deprived of respect and dignity, and abused by the indifference of another, leaves them exploited and in pain. The pain is a reflection of the abhorrence of the indifference they have endured, and it is also a motivator to find their way home. Pain creates whirlpools of emotions that eventually cannot be denied. Pain is not quiet and demands to be heard, even though the recipient may be silent. The abuse of indifference alters their life course and resetting is not an option as the indifference traverses their experience of life. Indifference of a certain calibre cannot be ignored and pollutes the perception of even the most resilient of souls.

When you feel at sea in an abyss of emotions, reconnecting to the beauty of your soul can be difficult, but it is never impossible. The voyage may be rough and perilous water may have to be crossed, but storms cannot prevail forever and eventually you can set

sail. Your demoralising thoughts create rough seas, and self-rejection creates gale force winds. The thoughts that erode your sense of self can be rejected and instead you can compassionately nurture yourself and navigate the effects of indifference.

Self-rejection can be replaced with acceptance and loyalty to your soul. When you choose to appreciate your own tenacity of never completely giving in to the residue of indifference carried, you realise there is a part of you that indifference could not touch. The thunderous roars of feeling forsaken, and the bellowing shame may have swamped your awareness and separated you from the truth of yourself, leaving you out at sea. As confusion and shock took hold, you forgot your soul and felt abandoned, but the essence of your soul was patiently waiting for your recognition and return.

When you become aware that it was you holding to the oars as the rough seas rolled in, you realise that you never truly renounced the value of your soul as you bravely weathered the storm. If you are such a soul, may you find the hope and courage to see and feel the truth of who you are, while realising you can calm your emotional seas by remembering your divinity within.

When you gaze upon yourself, may you feel the internal strength of your soul, and calm the rough sea of your emotions with care and trust. May you remember the purity of who you are and allow each crashing wave of emotion to be an opportunity to confront that which separates you from the exquisiteness of your soul.

As you recognise an opportunity to make peace with yourself, may you give yourself grace instead of condemnation. May you remember you were never to blame and did not deserve to be abused. May you trust you are of value and realise your existence is significant to this world. May you experience serenity and relish feeling loved. May your possibilities be endless as you cultivate the potential of your soul. May you find peace with your history and the internal freedom to sail on.

When you gaze upon yourself, may your fear be an historic memory, not a residing foe. May you remember you were always the innocent, and that your kindness and trust was betrayed by someone who has forsaken yours and their own soul. May you feel the joy of rekindling your relationship with your soul. May you unconditionally love yourself and nurture your voyage of life.

May you have compassion and patience as you break your silence and freely express the truth of your soul. May the murky waters of your despair become diluted by your clarity and allow the essence of your soul to flow freely.

When you gaze upon yourself, may you see and feel yourself lift the anchors from your pain, because you know you are worth it. You deserve to sail free and to discover and explore the shores that give you peace within your soul.

Chapter Five

Curiosity

Curiosity allows you to look, but truthfulness enables you to see.

When you become emotionally overwhelmed, curiosity can be replaced with apathy, which leaves you feeling emotionally, socially and spiritually bankrupt. Curiosity is the first step on a path and truthfulness is acknowledging what the path reveals to you. When you lose the inclination to be curious you can become trapped by the despair created by the loss of hope. Lack of curiosity about the truth of yourself can leave you believing you are unremarkable, which means you are unable to see and feel the truth of your soul. Curiosity is essential to any recovery process, because it is the motivator to be brave and to look up from despair and see opportunity. Curiosity unleashes the explorer within your soul, which enables you to become a traveller instead of being stuck in the waiting room of your own emotional limbo, waiting for freedom to find you. Freedom is to live without barriers to your soul; unresolved emotions and negative self-beliefs are barriers that leave you indifferent to the truth of who you naturally are. Being curious about yourself can become the first step in breaking down your own barriers to truth.

Curiosity stems from the longing to feel the truth of your soul and from the ache of wanting to understand yourself and your reality. Curiosity is a motivator and even an identifier, motivating you to tread into the unknown as it urges you to trust yourself to know when to explore and when to retreat. Curiosity flags up where you are unsure, identifying that something is amiss and indicates that you are aware that there is something to discover or uncover.

Curiosity can become a curse if you are indifferent to others' privacy or if you attach it to your desire for control. There is a self-responsibility to recognise the difference between curiosity and prying. Prying is not curiosity and is often used as leverage for control or used to manipulate advantages at the expense of another's insecurities. The true essence of curiosity is to be eager for knowledge that enhances your understanding of your soul or truth. This understanding can either be quietly digested or shared with others.

Curiosity creates a sense of concern within you, which exposes an awareness that you do not, at this moment, have all the facts. It is a recognition that you are interested, and should not be ignored as curiosity creates the path for the value of truthfulness to be realised. The combination of curiosity and truthfulness is a gift you can give yourself that defeats indifference, judgement and denial. Your acceptance of curiosity and truthfulness enables you to explore the truth with integrity and differentiate lies from denial.

Lies are deception used to conceal truth and denial is rejection of truth. Denial signifies the inability or refusal to recognise and see. Denial can stem from fear. Fear of loss, discovery, the inability to cope or of being accountable for your own indifference to truth. Lies are the desire to cover up what you do not want to see and become layers of deception that hamper your clarity. Your curiosity helps you to navigate your journey to freedom from that which oppresses your awareness of truth. You have to negotiate with yourself about how you negate your lies and denial. However, never forget the importance of truthfulness because curiosity may get you to the door of discovery, but it is your truthfulness that turns the key and lets you see and feel the truth of your discovery. Curiosity may expose something to you, but if you are not truthful you will not integrate what you have learnt into resolution, and you may even use it to be cruel to yourself.

Life is something you have journeyed into the minute you are born, and when you abandon your own curiosity and truthfulness, you align to the lies and denials that secure your barriers to truth. Your harsh self-judgement flags up what is unresolved and can become debilitating, leaving you reacting to everything with fear. Your fear reactions can leave you running from yourself or fighting against the worth of your soul. You may find yourself frozen, not sure about what you are waiting for, or seek refuge in the ways you hide from truth. You may even revert to fawning over others for their bravery in a way to diminish your own. Retreat is part of the process of discovery, it may indicate that you need to rest. Take notice of your reaction because you are educating yourself, which means discovery is occurring. You might not know what it is you discover until you have many pieces to your puzzle or you may be extremely aware that you just do not like what you have found, but every discovery of truth is significant to your soul.

Discovery is not a destination; it is exposure to truth. The truth of your reaction exposes you to that which is unresolved; you are showing yourself the truth of what inhibits you from being freed from your own oppression. Curiosity needs to be fed with self-compassion and kindness, and a willingness to care about the value of truth and yourself. You strengthen your truthfulness, when you nurture curiosity, which means you excitedly open more doors to discovery and go beyond your barriers to truth.

Chapter Six

Anchoring to the truth of who you are

When you feel swamped by your own unresolved emotions or trapped by trauma or despair, and have lost your sense of self, remembering you are more than just what you have experienced can shed light into the darkness you feel. Despair can deprive you of your awareness of your own core essences, which are conscious energy that originate from the truth of your soul and from your origins.

Recognising and respecting yourself as a significant soul can be a stepping stone to recovering from the traumas you have experienced, and from the distorted self-perceptions that leave you believing you are not good enough. Others may shine light into your darkness but they cannot sustain it for you. You have to be the one who accepts or brings the light to the darkness, which is difficult if you have forgotten the true value of your own core essences.

When you have forgotten the core essences of your soul or are left believing they have been ripped from you, you feel lost and aware of a void within. The void you feel is your separation from your awareness of your soul and the burden of your own soul denial. The lost feeling is an awareness that you, or part of you, is trapped in your cesspit of indifference against yourself. This can leave you indifferent to life and yourself, denying and devaluing the truth of who you naturally are. Feeling lost means you are aware that something is missing, and becoming curious about what is missing can be the starting point to bridging yourself back to being aware of, and in tune with, the truth of your exquisite soul.

Finding your way back to the truth of your soul can be a journey full of uncertainty and bouts of overwhelming emotions. You can become fearful of your own unresolved emotions, creating a crippling sense of vulnerability, but to stay trapped by your own unresolved emotions and distorted perception of yourself is also a perilous journey. The willingness to be curious, and to lean into and objectively observe the reality of your own unresolved emotions, is an opportunity for resolution.

To remain trapped is to deny yourself the opportunity, and you are worth more than hiding in your denial. You are worthy of your own effort to uncover the truth of your soul. This is your life and you are a significant soul, but you have freewill, so exploring the truth of yourself is a choice that only you can make. When you feel lost, being supported by others is invaluable, and finding a place that is safe for you to explore the reality of your emotions can be part of the process of learning to self-nurture. However, you are the pivotal point, you are the bridge and the interface to your emotional reality, which means accepting your natural worth is imperative to your resolution.

When you choose to nurture your soul and seek to liberate yourself from the oppression and despair you feel, you are acknowledging your own value, worth and significance. You may not fully comprehend that you are moving towards your own self-acceptance, but discovery is a major part of the process. When you feel broken, overwhelmed or demoralised, thoughts of value, worth and significance can become surreal concepts that are easier to say than feel and respond from.

Accept all souls are of value, acknowledge all souls are of worth and remember all souls are significant, then remind yourself that you are a soul. When you feel trapped in your own unresolved emotions this understanding can help ignite your own spark of curiosity about the truth of who you are. One truthful thought can alter your self-perception and your curiosity can lead you from your own soul oppression. You are both your soul's consciousness and unconsciousness. Your soul's unconsciousness is the storehouse of that which is unresolved and burdens your soul's consciousness. Your soul's consciousness is the divinity of your soul, and you are the interface between the two. What you decide to value, nurture or explore is important and deeply impacts how you experience life.

If you are feeding your unconsciousness with negative self-beliefs and ignoring your consciousness, which is the natural essence of who you are, you are the oppressor of your soul. When you become accustomed to feeding your unconsciousness, you lose awareness of how the core essences feed your soul.

When you explore and embrace your own core essences you can create a ladder to climb out of your emotional hole, a harness to support you whilst in the midst of confronting experiences and a soft comforting blanket that warms and shields you from the coldness you observe and feel. To climb out of an emotional hole, you have to be prepared to acknowledge and use the ladder you create with your core essences. You may find the first rung easy, but fear moving to the second rung because you have to step away from what has become familiar. It is imperative to acknowledge what has become your familiar

and to realise familiarity does not always create safety. Familiarity means you have got used to something and conditioned yourself to tolerate it, which does not necessarily stem from any truth. Familiarity also means you have knowledge about what is going on, which means you also have a choice in how you respond. Indifference can be tolerated but that does not mean it is not harmful. Distortions, lies, oppression and indifference can become your familiar, and overshadow the truth of who you naturally are, which changes your perception of yourself, life, others and truth. Resolving what is overshadowing you, which is a process, enables you to feel the truth of your soul.

Natural is not constructed, but can be explored. Distortions, lies, oppression and the compulsion to be indifferent to yourself are constructs, and create pain, despair, fear and negative beliefs. However, what is constructed can be dismantled, and what is natural is revealed.

Your soul's consciousness is never damaged. When you devalue yourself, you hide from your awareness of your soul, which can leave you layering many unresolved emotions over the truth of yourself. Your soul's consciousness is the purity of your soul, which can never be corrupted, although you can silence your awareness and deny your soul insight. Your soul's consciousness is the part of you that strives for resolution of that which is causing you to forget, devalue or deny you are a significant, unique, independent, individual soul of your origin of truth.

The ladders, harnesses and blankets you create from your core essences will be used many times, as resolution is not a one-off event. You aid your resolution by valuing and accepting the worth and significance of the core essences. Self-nurturing results from acknowledging your own natural significance. Understanding your core essences as part of who you are enables you to comprehend the truth of yourself, which can support you to objectively observe that which is unresolved. Your unity within your own core essence liberates you from any self-imposed prison that has become your familiar.

There is purity to the truth of who you are, it cannot be emulated as it is just the natural truth of your soul. The natural essence of the reality of your soul is not a belief, it is the truth of who you are.

Core essence of unconditional love

The core essence of your soul is *unconditional love*, which is the unification of all these core essences:

- *Acceptance*
- *Appreciation*
- *Care*
- *Clarity*
- *Compassion*
- *Dynamism*
- *Freedom*
- *Grace*
- *Harmony*
- *Honesty*
- *Hope*
- *Independence*
- *Individuality*
- *Integrity*
- *Joy*
- *Kindness*
- *Loyalty*
- *Patience*
- *Peace*
- *Purity*
- *Serenity*
- *Trust*
- *Truthfulness*
- *Uniqueness*

Your core essence is the purity of who you naturally are that flows through the nucleus of your existence. You have a unique frequency, as you are energy within a physical body, your energy is identified as a soul. Your soul's consciousness is the purity of who you are and is in harmony with your origin, labelled here as *True Source Divine Origin Consciousness*. *True Source Divine Origin Consciousness* is collective divine consciousness, a sea of truth energy that is the true source of your soul and life.

You originated from truth and your separation from your awareness of your soul enables indifference to permeate through your awareness of yourself. This causes you to lose insight into your natural value, worth and significance. Resolution is the process of resolving what inhibits you from accepting the truth of your soul. Evolution is the natural expansion of your insight and awareness of truth and of your own soul, as well as freedom from oppression.

You express or feel unconditional love as the core essences of your soul's consciousness unite. When you feel another's or *True Source Divine Origin Consciousness'* unconditional love for you, you feel safe, warm and an energy that is difficult to explain in words. However, when ignored, overridden or ran from, unconditional love can become recounted as an unusual anomaly and devalued or denied. This can deprive you of realising you are loved, which allows the opposite to your core essences to take hold, which can cause you to separate from your awareness of the unconditional love flowing within you.

Examples of the opposite to core essences

The opposite of:

- *Acceptance* is rejection
- *Appreciation* is devaluation
- *Care* is neglect
- *Clarity* is obscurity and complication
- *Compassion* is insensitivity
- *Dynamic* is stagnation and apathy
- *Freedom* is oppression
- *Grace* is unforgiving
- *Harmony* is separation
- *Hope* is despair
- *Honesty* is dishonesty
- *Independence* is codependence
- *Individuality* is collective
- *Integrity* is inequity
- *Joy* is pain and boredom
- *Kindness* is malice
- *Loyalty* is treachery
- *Patience* is impatience
- *Peace* is struggle
- *Purity* is corruption
- *Serenity* is panic and anxiety
- *Trust* is distrust and cynicism
- *Truthfulness* is deception
- *Uniqueness* is blind conformity
- *Unconditional love* is indifference to truth.

There is a purity to the frequency of your soul that naturally resonates and unifies with truth. The acceptance of truth, regardless of what that truth is, enables you to feel your flow of unconditional love. Unconditional love is at the core of your being, regardless of how separated from truth you have become. It is part of the life force of your soul, and when you unify with truth, unconditional love flows freely from your soul.

Unconditional love freely flows from your origin, undisturbed by the energy of your soul's unconsciousness or any other unconscious energy. When you do not accept you are of worth, you become unaware and the unconditional love of your own soul can become deeply hidden, and yet, it is still within the core of your being. You can also deflect the unconditional love of others and of your origins that is bestowed upon you. This can cause you to feel unsafe, cold, lonely, isolated and aware of internal deprivation. Unconditional love enriches you and life, and is felt abundantly when valued and cherished.

Your willingness to be truthfully honest with yourself, while unconditionally loving the truth of your soul, enables you to explore the reality of your own unresolved emotions without fear and give yourself the grace of forgiveness. Forgiveness does not mean compliance nor accountability, but an acknowledgement of the truth and a willingness to be free from carrying the trauma and resentment that indifference to truth creates.

Forgiveness is acceptance of reality and acknowledgement that history cannot be changed. It is to make peace with what has occurred, knowing you are worth the freedom. It is also the conscious choice to not allow another's indifference to deprive you, of your awareness, of the exquisiteness of your soul. Experiences of indifference change your perception of life, others and who you believe you are, but beliefs are not always built from truth and should be examined.

Forgiveness of yourself is often a way of discovering the falsity of believing you are unworthy of respect, and frequently exposes how you are using shame to cultivate negative beliefs about yourself. Shame is the belief that there is something wrong with you. If you are carrying shame because another abused you, it is not your shame. Being an abuse victim means the shame belongs to the abuser not the abused. Shame is a resolvable emotion, especially when you unconditionally love yourself, and value and accept the truth of innocence.

Unconditional love for your soul enables you to be supple with your core essences. This initiates moving more easily and gracefully through the experiences of your life, discovering, exploring and learning from yourself, interactions with others and the events that shape the journey of your soul.

When you are entangled in and ensnared by emotions that leave you indifferent to truth, unconditionally loving yourself is a foreign concept. This means you have to consciously contemplate the value of love and decide you are worth your own effort to tap into the natural stream of consciousness flowing within your soul. You have to choose to feel and value the significance, uniqueness, independence and individuality of your soul, and remind yourself that you are rare and precious, because there is no other soul exactly like you.

When you allow yourself to be present in your reality, while lovingly caring for the truth of yourself, your awareness alters and you see further, and feel the goodness of your own core essences. This allows your horizons to change, and means you can appreciate your own opportunities for resolution, unconditionally loving yourself through the recovery of your soul. Unconditional love is your pure resonance with truth, which is felt with every fibre of your soul and feeds the expansion of your awareness of truth. When unconditional love is oppressed, restrictions rein. When you trust there is value to your own soul recognition and the exploration of truth, you become aware of the significance of loving yourself and of valuing the equality of all souls.

Unconditional love enables you to be aware of the truth of unconscious energy produced by yourself and others, with a willingness to forgive yourself and others, so you can become free of oppression. Unconditional love enables you to care for and nurture your soul with no hidden or detrimental judgement or agenda, which facilitates freedom from oppression. Unconditional love is to embrace truth with the hope that the recognition of, and respect for truth enables you to resolve your own soul oppression. To love without conditions is to express the purity of your soul.

Unconditionally loving yourself and truth enables you to utilise all your core essences as you emotionally, energetically and physically deal with unshackling yourself from your own chains of oppression that cause you to be indifferent to yourself and truth. Unconditional love creates an intent to become free of your own soul oppression and to celebrate the truth of who you are.

CHAPTER SEVEN
Core essences of your soul

Core essences are unique strands of conscious (truth) energy that contribute to the purity of who you are. They are the unique strands of conscious energy within unconditional love. Each core essence is natural energy that emanates from your soul's consciousness. They are a natural expression of your soul and enable truth to permeate your awareness. Expressing your core essences is a choice to value truth and the equality of all souls, and is an expression of your unity with truth. When consciously accepted and utilised, core essences facilitate resolution and radiate from your soul's consciousness.

Acknowledging the value of your core essences and embracing the reality that they are naturally within, smooths the progress of you experiencing your own shine of consciousness. This is an internal glow that can be felt even from within the deepest oppression. Your shine of consciousness is the natural emanation of the truth of your soul. As you express the core essences of your soul, your awareness of your own stream of consciousness strengthens.

Core essences are valued only when chosen to be, otherwise they become assessed as insecurities, a point of vulnerability or something to exploit or oppose. Core essences are synchronised, individually in unison or trigger another core essence to occur. Your core essences are how you support yourself and others during your soul journey. Core essences guide you through life and valuing your core essences create intentions that enable you to expand your awareness of truth and to respect the insight of your soul.

Acceptance

Self-acceptance is unconditional love for who you are, which can be difficult to concede when you resist, deny or avoid the truth of your soul or have given up on hope, fear love or are trapped punishing yourself for that which you could not control or decisions that have left you indifferent to yourself. Acceptance is an acknowledgement of reality with the realisation that you cannot change history, but you choose how you value yourself now and in the future.

When you accept you are significant to yourself, you alter the stranglehold your indifference to truth has over your perception of yourself and of reality. Acceptance expands into clarity, and strengthens your ability to care for yourself. Acceptance is to embrace your own soul and to realise your relationship with yourself is the most important you have. When you accept yourself, you can share the core essences of your soul with others.

Acceptance is also the undertaking of self-responsibility for your reactions to your life experiences, while recognising you are the one who determines what you value, nurture, resolve or use to oppress yourself. True acceptance does not foster deception, indifference or denial, for that would be submission, conformity and acquiescence. True acceptance does not hide truth, it illuminates truth and compassionately unravels what has been hidden and returns whatever has been deprived.

Acceptance stems from trusting yourself to be truthfully honest and present in the dynamics of the entirety of what is occurring. It is self-permission to value truth and to explore reality. Acceptance clarifies what has to be dealt with in order to unshackle the chains of oppression that cause you to reject yourself. It creates an intention to find peace with your reality and to resolve that which is inhibiting the potential of your soul.

Appreciation

Self-appreciation is unconditional love for reality, which can be difficult when you have lost gratitude for the life you live or feel deflated by the degradation of your awareness of your soul and truth. Appreciation is a recognition of value, and what you intentionally value lays down a pathway to walk. Appreciation is a choice to knowingly alter your negative perception, by valuing the dynamics of life and optimistically examining your awareness of reality.

Appreciation expands as you intentionally become aware that there is a bigger picture to life. As you willingly embrace that you do not have a full understanding of the intricacies of life, you awaken to the reality of belonging to the source of life. You are a soul, and life is an experience. Appreciation is a way of finding joy, peace and serenity while being present in reality.

Appreciation comes when truth is valued and expands as you comprehend the significance of your own ability to resolve beyond the confinements of oppression. Appreciation is thwarted by defiantly sustaining humiliation, shame and guilt, while depriving yourself of the acknowledgment of what you are contributing to your present moment. Appreciation stems from a knowing that every moment offers potential. Feeling gratitude for the uniqueness of your own experience of life and for the presence of others, enables you to accept your own potential. When you appreciate that you have potential, you support exploring your own truth, guiding yourself to resolution and evolution of your soul.

Appreciation for life enables you to be present and honest in your current life situation and allows you to loosen the grips on your past that you use to create self-definitions. Appreciation can thrive when you do not participate in the dumbing down of your soul. Appreciation creates harmony within your soul, which facilitates the resolution required to unshackle the chains of oppression that cause you to devalue yourself. Appreciation creates an intention to learn from life.

Care

Self-care is unconditional love for yourself and the equality of all souls, which can be difficult when you have been exposed to the insidiousness of indifference and are reluctant to trust the significance of your soul. When you devalue your yearning to care, indifference to truth appears to be limitless, until you get to the point that you can no longer remain on the sidelines of your own negligence, carelessness or recklessness. The perpetuation of indifference is finite as it is a self-destructive energy, and your willingness to care lessens the scope of your indifference to truth. When you care, you realise indifference to truth is resolvable. Caring indicates when to be alert, alarmed and loyal to your soul. Self-care is innate and a triggered response to indifference or danger to your survival. Self-care has to be overridden to cultivate your tolerance of indifference.

Care enables you to investigate the reality of your indifference against yourself and to realise your reactions are resolvable emotions. To care is to explore beyond what is initially seen, believed or opposed. Care enables you to patiently reveal truth to yourself at a pace you can comprehend. Care enables mindful exploration of your soul and truth.

Care is an expression of love and concern for yourself and others. You may fear this makes you vulnerable or susceptible to disappointment, but in fact it feeds your appreciation of life and opens you to be inspired by those you hold dear. Caring takes you out of the superficial and facilitates being attentive to the layers within your soul. Caring facilitates freely feeling the truth of your soul and enables you to share the unconditional love within your soul with others.

Caring is to be thoughtful and kind, which expands your perception of reality and allows you to see what is often hidden. Caring is to pay attention to the reality of your reactions to life and acknowledge the cause and effect of your choices. When you care, you accept the value and worth of truth, which enables you to independently choose your course of action.

Caring means you embrace taking responsibility for nurturing the exploration of your own natural significance and the significance of others. This facilitates being committed to respecting truth and the freewill of other souls, which allows your acceptance of freedom to grow. Caring invites grace for yourself as you unshackle the chains of oppression that cause you to neglect yourself. Care creates an intention to develop an awareness of your soul.

Clarity

Clarity is unconditional love for your unification with truth, which can be difficult when you combat the significance of your awareness of truth and remain devoted to what you want to believe or have been indoctrinated into. Clarity is marred by dogmatically clinging to what you think you know, which creates beliefs that conceal what you refuse to acknowledge, explore or challenge. Deliberately making something difficult to understand, leads to confusion. This is problematic when the something is you, the truth of your soul, behaviour, beliefs, fears, denial and indifference, which can leave you developing a mentality that is detrimental to who you naturally are. Clarity promotes unity, whereas that which is deliberately obscured and made complicated endorses separation and division.

Clarity is acceptance of reality, free from any deception or desire to make reality difficult to understand. Clarity is not cryptic, although at times clarity is conceding that there is a mystery. Life reveals truth in pieces and you may not have the jigsaw in place, and acknowledging this reality is clarity. Clarity can invoke trust and a freedom to explore. Clarity about one subject can ignite curiosity around another, and one question can lead to more questions. However, the clarity is in the comprehension that you seek the truth, which enables you to feel your resonance with truth as you uncover or find answers to your questions and interest in your curiosity.

Clarity is acknowledgment. Clarity can result from a realisation that can happen suddenly without warning or from a painstaking investigation to reveal truth. As you endeavour to be truthful with yourself, clarity becomes more commonplace and your deception, fear or denial are often felt as an opportunity to explore rather than an opportunity to defend what leaves you indifferent to yourself. Clarity conquers the insanity of indifference and sheds light on misconceptions, confabulations and outright lies, enabling you to fathom the unresolved emotions supporting your indifference towards yourself.

Clarity is precisely expressing the truth you are aware of, understand and trust. It is truthfulness you can be loyal to, because it is not a belief but an understanding backed by your certainty. Clarity enables you to grasp the reality that you can unshackle the chains of oppression that cause you to be deliberately vague or restrictive about the facts. Clarity creates an intention to be at ease with your awareness of truth.

Compassion

Self-compassion is unconditional love for your own soul journey, which can be difficult when you have become accustomed to suppressing your feelings and aligning to self-loathing thoughts and beliefs. Compassion is the willingness to empathise with all souls who have embarked on the journey of life, including yourself. Compassion is the recognition that you and others experience wounds and pain from many life events that cause us to forget who we naturally are.

Compassion reminds us that we are souls from a united origin. It is the acknowledgement that life, at times, is a struggle that can be alleviated with kindness. Compassion is the willingness to reach out, intentionally seeking to create comfort for those who are suffering, and is done with respect for the integrity of those whom you reassure that there is kindness in this world. This includes reaching out to yourself.

Compassion is allowing yourself to feel the reality of life while having the fortitude to face your own feelings and to interconnect with yourself and the living beings you encounter. Compassion is deciding to not turn away in times of trouble and, if you are rendered physically unable to intervene, then be a witness who speaks freely of what you have seen. Compassion grants truth a platform to be discussed, which unearths insensitivity and enables you to explore the true cause and effect of decisions made.

Compassion is to flow in harmony with the realisation that each individual soul, including yourself, is significantly unique. Compassion is a celebration that your presence can have a soothing and heartening effect for another as well as yourself. Compassion gives hope and encourages change that benefits humanity.

Compassion quells judgement and shines a light on indifference, suffocating ignorance and arrogance. Compassion is an action or a motive, and untangles the complexities experienced along the journey of a soul. Compassion stems from accepting the reality of both consciousness and unconsciousness, and is the recognition of the immaturity of souls.

Compassion is an expression of thoughtful resonance with unconditional love. Compassion is the willingness to be present in the truth of what is or the reality of that which has occurred. Compassion is contagious and can create a ground swell of sympathy for those who have suffered. Compassion moves you to express the truth of your soul and your awareness of reality. Compassionately dealing with reality unshackles the chains of oppression that cause you to be insensitive to the truth of yourself and creates an intent to be inspired by truth.

Dynamic

Being dynamic is unconditionally loving the flow of truth, which can be difficult when you believe your stagnation and apathy are protecting you from fear and change. This attitude narrows your experience of life and creates ruts that deprive you of freedom and leaves you distrusting the value of your soul. Being dynamic enables you to observe truth objectively and to trust the value of truth, because you are not trying to protect your agendas created from the belief that change will interfere with what you know and believe you can control. Being dynamic stimulates self-motivation and enables you to recognise opportunities as they are presented. Being dynamic is to value truth and the processes that enable truth to be revered. It is the willingness to explore reality and to respond within the flow of truth, instead of opposing truth.

When your ability to be dynamic is oppressed, apathy suppresses the truth of your feelings and emotions, creating mediocrity. This dumbs down your awareness of the truth of your soul and inhibits you being aware of the flow of truth that exposes reality. When apathy takes hold and complacency shields you from acknowledging your own reality, you lower your expectations and settle for what is familiar. This can leave you existing in what drains you of your own awareness of yourself, stagnating in your own despair, lethargy, fears and indifference to truth. Being dynamic while exploring truth is the willingness to surprise yourself and is the realisation that you are constantly choosing how you interact with the truth of yourself, others and life.

The dynamics of truth are often revealed within the flurries of emotions that expose reality, motives and agendas. Being dynamic means you recognise the cause and effect of the truth of energy.

You recognise:

- The energy you generate from your soul's unconsciousness.
- The energy that emanates from your soul's consciousness.
- The energy you experience from others.
- The collective energy of mankind.

Being dynamic is the result of being present in and honest about the truth of your life experience. It is also the ability to quickly adapt to the truth of what is occurring. Being dynamic is to choose change and to allow yourself to be energy in motion, instead of settling for the repetition of your cyclic pattern of soul oppression. Dynamism is to value your own resolution and evolution. Being dynamic enables you to independently deal with what is inhibiting you from unshackling the chains of oppression that cause you to be stagnant in your perception of yourself. Being dynamic enables you to resolve and evolve beyond the confines of your soul oppression.

Freedom

Freedom is unconditional love for truth and freewill, which can be difficult when you default to what oppresses your awareness of your soul, truth and the reality of having options. You can misconstrue the meaning of freedom, believing it results from having your own way and from being in control of life. This is a misconception that leaves you dogmatic in your opinion of what should be, ignoring what is, or oppositional to anything you believe interferes with what you want to believe. You can become vindictively judgemental of yourself and others, believing your sense of entitlement is more important than the value of truth. You can constantly strive to gratify the insatiable appetite of wanting control with a willingness to be insensitive towards your impact on others. This is not freedom, it is oppression.

When you devalue the true essence of freedom, you create restrictions and conform to the oppression that you believe serves a purpose or enables you to hide from self-responsibility. Freedom is respect for equality and freewill. Freedom is to accept truth, with a willingness to be honest about the facts and the reality of cause and effect.

Freedom is to recognise yourself autonomously, and accept that you choose your reaction and responses to life. Your reactions and responses stem from the energy within you, and choices are made by what you carry that is unresolved and what you value. Freedom is reflected in your responses from your soul's consciousness, and oppression is reflected from your reaction stemming from the energy of your soul's unconsciousness. Freedom is choosing your own response to both your consciousness and unconsciousness. You always have the freedom to choose how you feel about yourself, regardless of your lack of control or influence on your reality.

Freedom is to live the authenticity of your soul without fear. It is the acceptance of freewill and the divinity of your soul. Freedom is to know when you have a choice and accept when your choice is relevant to the reality of what is occurring. Freedom facilitates awareness of how you are contributing to your reality and enables you to comprehend the value of staying true to yourself, which is integrity.

Acknowledged freedom originates from valuing your own uniqueness, independence and individuality. Freedom creates genuineness, and the opportunity to confront what oppresses your experience of life, with dignity, intelligence and hope. Freedom enables you to deal with whatever is emotionally shackling you to the chains of oppression that cause you to reject yourself.

Grace

Grace is unconditional love for the opportunities within the symphony of truth to resolve what oppresses you or others. Grace is to acknowledge the authenticity of your soul and your relationship with your origin of truth. Grace is unconditional love for the opportunity to continue your soul journey within a physical body. Grace is difficult to comprehend when you operate from the duality of judgement, seeking only to define what is right or wrong, unable to acknowledge the complexities of life.

When you are unwilling to accept there is a big picture to your experience of life, grace becomes an enigma to you, leaving you judgemental and retaliative against all that interferes with what you want. Grace is the willingness to forgive, as you unburden yourself of resentment, rage, vengeance and indifference to your own soul. Grace is trust in the evolutionary process of souls through the truth of their own energy. It is an acceptance that you do not want to carry what is unresolved within you to the end of this lifetime and beyond. Grace is the willingness to accept that you have an opportunity to resolve.

Grace refers to the constant flow of conscious energy within your soul that cascades from *True Source Divine Origin Consciousness'* unconditional love for you and the emotional, energetic and physical plights that occur throughout life. Whether you are recognising, accepting or denying and opposing truth, conscious energy is always present. Grace is the energy of your truthful honesty harmonising with truth. Grace is acceptance that you are part of divinity. Grace is the willingness to trust the unconditional love within your own soul's consciousness and the willingness to be of truth.

Grace eases distress and pain. To give grace is to be free of judgement and accept that you are a part of a shared experience of life, and cannot control the freewill of others. Grace facilitates the recognition of truth and it is the acknowledgement of truth that educates us all. Grace is acceptance of reality, while remaining true to the purity of your soul. Grace shines the strongest within forgiveness, and illuminates the strength of your soul.

Grace is appreciation for being aware. Grace facilitates the generosity of your soul to forgive the actions of mankind in the arena of freewill and to accept life as a learning curve for all who inhabit Earth, including yourself. Grace is the energy that you use instinctively to access and stimulate the energy of the other core essences required for you to remain present and true to your soul within reality. Grace creates the opportunity to deal with what has shackled you to the chains of oppression that cause you to be unforgiving towards yourself, others and truth. Grace creates an intent to nurture your soul with awareness of the value of all your core essences and the equality of all souls.

Harmony

Harmony is unconditional love for your own and others' resonance with truth, which can be difficult to reconcile with when you operate from envy, jealousy and mistrust of your own true worth. Harmony is the remembrance that all souls come from the origin of truth and the uniqueness of experiences creates diversity and allows agreements between souls to unfold. Harmony is the acceptance that we are all unique and significant. Harmony is the ability to flow in the dynamics of truth, while feeling the significance of your own unification with truth and respect for all others.

Harmony is the willingness to freely align to and support your own presence within truth's symphony, without any desire to harm, exploit or oppress another. The intention of harmony is compatibility, using respect and integrity as fundamentals to guide our interactions with each other. When respect for others is opposed, conflict ensues and the willingness to exploit for perceived personal gain flourishes. This causes you to perceive life as an arena for winners and losers, which destroys awareness of the serenity, peace and joy found within harmony.

Harmony is the willingness to accept reality, while retaining the independence of your uniqueness and individuality. Harmony is accepting all souls' significance, independence, uniqueness and individuality. Harmony is produced in an environment that fosters freedom for all to strive to reach the full potential of their soul. Oppression creates disharmony, which means there is no freedom to thrive in, only segregation. Oppression operates from selective endorsement and indifference. You can create segregation within your soul, depriving yourself of the freedom to thrive while endorsing that which oppresses you. Oppression is the choice to remain indifferent to the truth of who you naturally are.

When you are in harmony with your original intention to value truth and endeavour to discover that which is unresolved within and what inhibits you from expressing the truth of your soul, you are in harmony with the potential of your soul. Harmony is unification within your own soul, meaning your words, actions and intent align. Separation from your awareness of your own soul causes your words, actions and intentions to differ, and leaves you contrary to yourself, others and truth.

Harmony is valuing yourself with the willingness to value others; it is not submission for the illusion of peace nor is it blind conformity. Harmony is derived from freedom, and is not coercion or dominance.

Harmony is to be present in reality, unified with truth and freely resonating with the essences of your soul. Harmony cannot be contrived through oppression, and naturally occurs with freedom. Harmony is natural co-ordination, such as your own different core essences that work in sync. Harmony is acknowledging the presence of *True Source Divine Origin Consciousness*' unconditional love for all souls and choosing to respect equality. Harmony within your soul unshackles the chains of oppression that cause you to separate from your awareness of truth. Separation from your own insight and awareness of truth causes you to devalue yourself, which makes it extremely easy for you to devalue others. Your intent for harmony creates the will to resolve discordance with others, which builds understanding, friendships and unison.

Honesty

Honesty is unconditional love for choice, which can be difficult to acknowledge when you fear truth. Honesty can be used by both conscious and unconscious energy as a bridge to something else. You can be honest and then use what you have been honest about to fuel your own oppression of your soul. Or you can use honesty as a stepping stone to uncover what is oppressing your soul. Your honesty can become a trigger for your own harsh judgement, or it can be deceptively used by others as a weapon to demoralise your sense of self. Fear of the consequences of your honesty, can cause you to retreat, but retreating enables dishonesty to govern your existence.

Honesty is the ability to recognise truth with the willingness to be sincere, which becomes a junction within your awareness of truth. A junction is when you become aware of the intersection between deception and truth, and your honesty enables you to see the contrast of all energy and the options that are presented. Your honesty is the recognition of the value of truth and is felt within your realisations. Honesty invokes an awareness that you have a choice. Knowing you have a choice alters your perception of being trapped in an emotional wasteland. You may be powerless to change your physical environment, but you choose how you feel about yourself. Self-respect, integrity and care are choices you can make.

Honesty is acknowledgment of truth and the truth of your feelings, which creates opportunities to explore your reactions and responses to your reality. When truthful and of pure intent, honesty is the bridge to experiencing your own flow of consciousness, free from any form of deception. Honesty creates the opportunity to recognise you are the pivotal point in unshackling the chains of oppression that cause you to default to hiding behind your dishonesty. Honesty creates an intent to explore your own truth and to honour the significance of truth.

Hope

Hope is unconditional love for your own courage and optimism, which can be difficult when you feel demoralised or believe you are helpless or damaged. Your soul's consciousness is never damaged, just your awareness is corrupted when you feel impaired. When you lose awareness of the truth of your soul and feel overwhelmed by your experience of life, despair can reside where hope used to dwell. Hope inspires and creates prospects. When you lose hope, instead of having a panoramic view of yourself and your potential, you congest your perception of yourself with your past, fears, hurt or disappointments. This causes you to be depleted of opportunity and can leave you wallowing in despair and your own indifference towards yourself.

Hope is recognition of the dynamics of truth and acceptance of your synchronicity with truth. Hope strengthens confidence and can trigger the aspiration to be the nurturer of your own soul. Hope is an appreciation for the unconditional love that *True Source Divine Origin Consciousness* has for you and that you have for truth. It can also be awareness that your journey is in play and the journey of your soul is never over.

Hope is an awareness that life is complicated and an acceptance that you are part of a bigger picture. Hope is a reminder that you are an evolving soul, who experiences life with the opportunity to learn. Hope keeps you moving towards full comprehension of your soul and truth.

Hope facilitates your acknowledgment of your uniqueness and willingness to be inspired by your own internal knowing of your own value, worth and significance. Hope facilitates undeveloped trust of yourself to expand. Hope is realistic, and is developed from a foundation of truth, as opposed to using fantasy to feed an illusion. Illusions cause you to struggle to be and feel grounded in your own life. Hope fuels aspirations, which can become a guide to exploring what is important to you or can expose what is unresolved. Hope ignites possibilities and truthful honesty creates probabilities.

Hope enables you to be courageously present within the uniqueness of your reality, whilst acknowledging life is dynamic and often unpredictable. Hope is a motivator that enables you to look up from the despair and to envisage freedom. Hope facilitates the willingness to deal with whatever has shackled you to the chains of oppression that cause you to feel despair, fear and hopelessness. Hope creates an intent to be courageous as you liberate yourself.

Independence

Independence is unconditional love for freedom and the willingness to accept being an autonomous being, which means taking responsibility for the truth of your own behaviour, beliefs, energy and the words you speak. This can be difficult when you seek to embroil others into participating on your merry-go-round of soul oppression, which means you desire to control them to adhere to your wants and desires, making them a victim or witness to your oppression, or responsible for pacifying your fears. This leaves you expecting to inflict them with your unresolved emotions whilst being unaccountable for the reality of yourself and yet dependent on others.

When your fear turns to a codependency on observing the cause and effect of your own emotions on others, you lose autonomy. You lose your autonomy because you are operating reactively to what others are doing and saying, or reacting from your paranoia about what they might be doing or saying. This leaves you susceptible to others' judgement or your perception of what they may judge you on, which causes you to evaluate what others think and leads to you discounting your own awareness. This can change your priorities and cause you to dumb yourself down, eroding your understanding of your soul and leaving you existing but not living your truth.

Independence is the choice to allow your uniqueness to flow with ease, undisturbed by your willingness to oppress your freedom. Independence is to trust your internal knowledge of being an eternal strand of truth energy (a soul), flowing from your origins of *True Source Divine Origin Consciousness.* Your soul's consciousness is always connected to your origins and you are never abandoned by truth, but you have freewill. You decide if you value your relationship with yourself, others, *True Source Divine Origin Consciousness* and with the truth of your present moment reality. Acknowledging yourself as a soul and the degree to which you value truth is an independent choice.

Independence is your ability to freely experience life as a soul, uninhibited by negative judgement and opposition to truth. Independence is not isolation, it is sharing the truth of yourself and choosing to not lose the sovereignty over your own soul. Independence is acceptance of accountability for your own energy. It is also taking responsibility for the resolution of the energy of your soul's unconsciousness and evolution of who you naturally are.

Energetic independence is to take responsibility when you know you are projecting energy at another or entwined and enmeshed with another. It is also trusting yourself to be aware when you feel the projection of another's energy towards you and to acknowledge the influence you allow them to have. Independence is to make decisions autonomously rather than hiding behind or relying on external factors to govern your reactions and the choices you make.

Independence can be a successful end to a struggle and a show of competency. Independence is respect for yourself, which enables you to feel at ease with how you interrelate and interconnect with others, life and yourself. Independence is a choice that can lead you to address what or whom you codependently cling to, which shackles you to the chains of oppression and causes you to disrespect yourself. Independence creates an intent to value your own sovereignty over your soul.

Individuality

Individuality is unconditional love for the exquisiteness of your own soul and your relationship with truth, which can be difficult if you are opposing your own uniqueness. Individuality is accepting yourself as an independent strand of truth, freely resonating with the uniqueness of your own dynamic soul. It is freely expressing the truth of who you are and acknowledging what you feel. When you perceive yourself through the lens of collective judgement or only identify with collectives as a way to define yourself, you lose awareness of your individuality. This can cause you to gloss over your reality and to fixate on the image you want to portray or your beliefs that certain possessions, achievements, experiences and situations define you. You can lose awareness of the distinctiveness of who you naturally are, and conform to collective expectations that deprive you of freedom.

Individuality is to embrace the uniqueness of your soul and to value the qualities that make you distinguishable from others. Individuality is to embrace diversity rather than collective conformity. Individuality is to accept the natural frequency of your soul as distinguishability that you can support by fostering the truth of your soul.

There is an individuality to your relationship with *True Source Divine Origin Consciousness*, we are all connected individually. You are an individual who is rare as there is no one exactly the same, and this makes you naturally precious. When you forsake your own preciousness, you inadvertently invite others to do the same. Accepting your individuality facilitates truthfulness, which enables you to lovingly deal with what is inhibiting you from unshackling the chains of oppression that cause you to conform to collective ideologies, judgements and expectations that separate you from the truth of yourself. Individuality creates an intent to be true to yourself and respectful of others.

Integrity

Integrity is unconditional love for soul accountability and the willingness to be true to yourself, which can be difficult if you have forsaken the truth of your soul. Integrity is to value yourself and to respect your own values and the core essences of your soul. It is to operate from a sense of fairness, while recognising the value of being truthful and trustworthy. Lack of integrity leads to you being manipulative and conniving, only seeking to enhance your own agenda. When your agenda is to oppress your own soul or another, lack of integrity can create disastrous consequences. Lack of integrity enables inequity to flourish, which leads to corruption and exploitation. Lack of integrity purposefully undermines the natural equality of all souls with the intent to be deceptive and unjust.

Integrity is to maintain your unity with truth, and is the result of you valuing the significance of truth. Integrity is a moral compass that develops from being willing to accept the entirety of a situation and the cause and effect of decisions made. Integrity is to value truth whilst making decisions, instead of ignoring your awareness of the cause and effect with feigned innocence or ignorance. Integrity is to be true to your word and to follow through with promises. Integrity means there is value in what you say, even to yourself.

Integrity enables you to be aware of the importance of your soul and to feel and respond from the energy of your soul's consciousness. When you lovingly support your own soul, you feel the free-flowing energy within you, which is undamaged and not divided by any deception. Integrity is to adhere to and trust your original intention to experience the truth of your reality and respond to life from truthful honesty. Integrity is maintaining your awareness of your present moment, your options and the value of truth. It is to make decisions with commitment and fortitude that support trusting your own feelings and your awareness of truth.

Integrity creates wholeness within your soul, facilitating the bravery required to unshackle the chains of oppression that cause you to be part of the inequity within life. It also creates the aspiration to operate from fairmindedness and objectively observe with the willingness to be accountable for your actions, beliefs and the words you speak.

Joy

Joy is unconditional love for being alive, which can be difficult when you have lost interest in yourself, life and truth. You deprive yourself of joy when you become discontent with life and disconnected from the truth of your soul. Joy comes from appreciating and accepting the dynamics of life, and is the willingness to be present and curious. When you deny yourself curiosity and oppose wonder, and focus on disappointments and align to betraying your own soul, you deplete yourself of joy. This leaves you in pain and bored with yourself. Boredom is a gateway to indifference that can incite cruelty that causes you to want to deprive others of their joy. This can invoke malicious jealousy and the desire to be derogative of others and their achievements.

Joy is the spontaneity of recognition that incites your elation. Recognising the lighter side of life provokes amusement, smiles and humour that facilitates a sense of wellbeing and hope. It also creates a willingness to share the joy with others, which becomes comforting and kindness. Joy is to be at ease with your own existence and to allow humour, laughter and enjoyment to be accessible to you and others. The lack of joy is a choice to put the oppression of your soul at the forefront of your existence, which sustains despair and can leave you being an energetic vampire inhibiting others from feeling at ease with themselves.

Joy is a choice to accept life and to acknowledge the charm of finding the funny side of reality, even within the insanity of your own indifference to yourself. Humour is an educator and can explain many things to you and also exposes you to the reality that all souls appreciate feeling joyful. Humour can become a safe way of exposing reality and that there are options in how you approach life. When you are willing to lovingly laugh at your own behaviour, thoughts, fears and beliefs, you are ready to be truthfully honest.

Jubilation for being alive is expressed as joy. Joy is to feel your own shine of consciousness, which may be for a brief moment, which becomes a reminder of who you naturally are, or a constant internal resonance with the truth of yourself. Joy facilitates the freedom to naturally be at ease and enables others to be at ease within your company. Joy is an expression of celebrating the truth of your own soul.

Joy enables you to feel yourself trusting the journey of life and the originality of your agreement to learn from the truth of your life experience. Joy can stem from a recognition or an internal knowing that is difficult to explain. Joy alleviates the emotional residue of that which has to be dealt with to unshackle the chains of oppression that cause you to feel trapped by your pain or that leave you bored with yourself and your life situation. Joy creates an intent to explore and revel in the reality of yourself.

Kindness

Kindness is unconditional love for giving without an agenda, which can be difficult when you have become jaded, or willing to maliciously exploit others' kindness as an opportunity to run your own agenda. When kindness is abused; pain, hurt and disappointment ensue. Abuse of kindness is the act of maliciously devaluing and discounting that you had been valued by someone who felt for your soul. Abuse of kindness is to leave yourself impoverished by your lack of respect for the value of the core essences.

Kindness is an expression of humanity, which means regardless of the form of kindness, how small or large the act of kindness, it stems from the willingness to accept that we are all souls within a physical body. It is the willingness to be thoughtful and acts of kindness remind those in difficult situations they are not alone nor forgotten. Kindness strengthens the soul awareness of both the giver and receiver. Kindness is to express to another that you see the value of who they are, and are attempting to understand and care. Kindness is always remembered fondly and can be defining moments in life. Kindness reveals the truth of your soul to another.

Kindness initiates change that you might not see at first and may never truly comprehend, but remains significant. Kindness enables the other core essences to shine within those who have lost awareness of themselves or fear they have been disregarded. Kindness is the willingness to be sympathetic to the plight of others and yourself, with the knowledge that compassion, gentleness and mindfulness create unbounded possibilities. Kindness results from trusting your awareness of truth and freely sharing the essence of who you are with life, yourself and others.

Kindness is the choice to care and to be present in the truth of what is occurring. It is also the willingness to accept the inspiration created when unconditional love is freely given. Kindness clarifies what has to be dealt with to unshackle the chains of oppression that cause you to maliciously judge yourself or others, and creates an intent to make your life and the world a better place.

Loyalty

Loyalty is unconditional love for the essence of truth and a willingness to care for what you have decided is important and of value, which can be difficult when you devalue truth and struggle against your own integrity. When you are uncommitted to caring and valuing yourself and have no allegiance to the significance of truth and being truthful, treachery becomes an alternative. Loyalty is a decision to be true.

Loyalty is to live the authenticity of your soul, consciously participating in your relationship with truth. Loyalty is dependability, but it is not blind conformity or dogmatism, for you should only be loyal to what resonates with your soul or to what you acknowledge is of value. Obligation is not loyalty, as it deprives you of freedom of choice and leaves you feeling controlled. Loyalty is pure of intent and a choice made with freewill to care, nurture and to be trustworthy. Trustworthiness is shared honesty and it is the willingness to be forthright in your communication.

Loyalty is the intent to never cause harm to those who you care about or to whom you are loyal, and to be devoted to being truthful when interacting. Treachery is the ability to appear loyal whilst running a different agenda, and the willingness to betray trust and exploit whatever or whomever you deem necessary to get what you want, which becomes a violation. Loyalty is to be honest if you have an agenda while respecting the freewill of others. Loyalty comes with reasoning. Loyalty is strengthened when reciprocated, and shared loyalty is strong when jointly valued.

Loyalty to the truth of yourself is the first port of call, because if you are unwilling to be loyal to yourself, you will struggle to be loyal to another. Loyalty is not a sacrifice, but the willingness to be dedicated to what you consider significant and to those you love. Loyalty is being dedicated to help, with the intention of not hurting, mistreating, misleading or overpowering. Loyalty is to remain true to what you have conveyed, and if there is a change in circumstance, to be honest in your approach when explaining your reasoning.

Loyalty is to trust yourself to unify with the significance of truth and to remain faithful to your soul. It is the result of being honourable and respectful of your original intentions and resonance with truth. Loyalty sustains harmony within your soul. Loyalty to your own soul facilitates the commitment required to unshackle the chains of oppression that cause you to be treacherous in your dealings with yourself, or with others.

When you recognise an opportunity to exert your desire for control, but choose to be loyal to your soul and to value the significance of truth, you feel the integrity of who you naturally are. Loyalty creates an intent to be true to your word and accountable for your actions.

Patience

Patience is unconditional love for your own synchronicity with truth and the acknowledgment that life is a shared arena and does not just revolve around you. This can be difficult to accept if you are impatient or approaching life narcissistically. Patience is to peacefully accept reality and calmly examine your options. Patience is an acceptance that at times life is completely out of your control and your option is to be present in what is occurring, rather than steering life with wants and desires. Patience is an acceptance of what is, with a realisation that waiting is the recognition that time is shared and you have the stamina to patiently wait for the next opportunity to present itself.

Patience is acceptance of reality, while having the fortitude to take responsibility for yourself and to participate in the change required to enhance your ability to be at peace with yourself and life. Patience is not procrastination, nor is it giving away responsibility for yourself to another. It is the courage and endurance to see things through. Patience is to be mindful of the entirety of reality and to accept that at times you have to wait for all cards to be on the table, before you can make an informed decision. Patience is to go along with reality as it presents itself, without the desire to exert your control.

Patience is to trust the truth of your soul journey and to voluntarily accept the intricacies of the symphony of truth. Patience is to trust that your original intention to resolve and evolve is always supported by your synchronicity with truth. Patience is honest acceptance of what is, within the uniqueness of every experience and present moment, which enables you to be serene as you encounter the highs and lows of life.

Patience assists you to have, or strive for, the endurance to never give up on the significance of discovering the truth of who you are. It is freely accepting that reality is a shared experience you are participating in, and that the world does not revolve around your desire to be in control of reality or your expectation that the world should work the way you want it to. It is the realisation that these beliefs, wants and desires cause you to be impatient. Patience is acceptance that all souls are of equal value and all deserve respect. Patience is required to unshackle the chains of oppression that cause you to impatiently react when life is not what you expected. Patience creates an intent to persistently pursue discovering the truth of your soul and to freely accept life as a journey.

Peace

Peace is unconditional love for reality and the willingness to be of goodwill. This can be difficult when you have become conditioned to expect conflict, fight to be right or cling to arrogance and ignorance, because you believe it empowers a position you want to hold to. Peace cannot be found where truth is disrespected. Peace cannot be found where reality is overshadowed by the desire for power. Peace cannot be found where there is no freedom to be the truth of who you are. Peace cannot be found when reality is denied.

Peace is freedom from struggle, war or the intent to fuel hostility. Peace is freedom from oppression. Peace flourishes when valued and becomes a yearning when devalued. External peace can be taken away through no fault of your own, and peace may come at an extraordinary price at times. Peace is a reflection of valuing the equality of all souls and the truth of reality. Internal peace is always your responsibility and cannot be sustained unless you deem yourself of value.

Peace is freely addressing your internal conflict, self-disparagements or restrictions. Peace is not found when conflict is ignored, but peace is the result of the resolution of conflict. Your own negative self-beliefs are internal conflict that are resolvable. You create peace within by remembering you have a choice, and electing to be calm as you examine the conflict, which enables you to be peaceful in the process of resolution and evolution. As you quieten and resolve your internal conflicts, you become peaceful energy within the world.

Peace stems from an acceptance of being a naturally significant, unique, independent, individual soul of *True Source Divine Origin Consciousness*. It is the recognition that you are an eternal soul who can change what you consider successes; being kind, caring and nurturing of yourself and others can become your assessment of success. Living a life that you feel the truth of your soul resonating with can become how you define success. Peace is the result of knowing what feeds your soul and electing to prioritise your soul being fed. Peace is experienced as you realise that struggling to comprehend the truth of who you are and to come to terms with what you have experienced, does not diminish the value of your soul. Struggling means you have not discovered truth or peace yet, but does not mean you will not.

Peace develops within the willingness to be present, regardless of what is occurring. It is also the ability to not fight against acknowledging your reality and to trust yourself to experience life as an opportunity to be of your truth. Peace develops within freewill. When you trust your synchronicity with the presence of truth within your reality, you develop your sense of peace. Peace is an acceptance of the significance of being aware of yourself within your present moment, it develops from knowing, now is important.

When you acknowledge that what you energetically contribute to life is significant, you realise the importance of not forsaking yourself. Peace is a result of accepting the significance of truth's symphony without judgement or expectations. Peace is a result that requires effort, because reconciling with the reality of yourself, others, history and life does not occur with procrastination, abiding to your fear or the protection of your denial.

Peace is the stillness felt when you are in harmony with your own consciousness. Peace is a state of mind that unshackles the chains of oppression that cause you to struggle with the truth of yourself and creates an intent to accept yourself as a significant soul.

Purity

Purity is unconditional love for consciousness, which is difficult when you have corrupted your awareness of the truth of your soul. Corruption is to allow yourself to be dishonest and fraudulent, which decays your sense of self and leaves you operating from the energy of your soul's unconsciousness, separated from your awareness of your soul and disassociated from feeling truth. The more unresolved emotions you store and carry, the greater your separation from the truth of yourself and the less you become inclined to value truth. This leaves you consenting to illusions, images and emulations, causing you to become manipulative, deceptive and corrupt, often compulsively operating from the energy of your soul's unconsciousness, polluting your own experience of life. Purity is to engage with life from pure intent and no desire to harm or oppress another.

Purity is freedom from contamination and unaltered by unconscious energy. It is to be of your consciousness. Purity is felt as you emanate the shine of your consciousness, and feel the vividness of your soul. It is the acceptance of truth. Truth is not a belief; it is something you feel resonating with your soul. When you do not value truth, you deprive yourself of your own shine of consciousness and corrupt your own sense of self.

Purity is the transparency of truth that is always there. Truth may be hidden beneath the deception placed upon it or exploited with manipulation and corruption, but regardless of what occurs, beneath that which is not pure is the purity of truth. Truth can be deceptively built upon but can never be completely replaced. Truth is the foundation that deception is built upon, but constructions become unstable when they are not true to their foundations, which become overloaded and exposed. Deception is always threatened by truth. Truth may be concealed by deception, but is never altered by deception. Truth remains, even if never discovered. Purity is truth.

Purity is to be free of any unconscious energy, complete within the wholeness of your soul resonating with your origins without division. Purity is to be of your totality with nothing wanting, it is a state of completeness, where you feel the frequency of your soul and comprehensive acceptance of yourself and your soul journey. Purity is wholeness within your soul and as you resolve what is unresolved within, the frequency of your soul's consciousness expands and becomes purer. Purity has a ripple effect that enables truth to be seen and felt more clearly.

Purity can be felt within the true answers to the questions you internally ask. Purity is complete truthfulness. Purity is felt within the pureness of the unconditional love of *True Source Divine Origin Consciousness* and your soul's consciousness. Purity is felt as a result of consciousness unifying with consciousness; it is hard to articulate but once felt is never forgotten. Purity thrives when you unshackle the chains of oppression that cause you to corrupt yourself. Purity facilitates an intent to be at peace with your reality and to resolve what is inhibiting the potential of your soul.

Serenity

Serenity is unconditional love for being at peace with reality and a pure acceptance of diversity, which can be difficult when you are not at peace with yourself or life. Serenity is to be free of mental stress and composed and content with the truth of who you are. Serenity is to be united within yourself, whilst accepting your own nature.

Serenity is the tranquillity created by accepting your natural significance, uniqueness, independence and individuality. It is steadiness within your mind which is undisturbed by what is emotionally, energetically or physically surrounding you. This is felt as natural strength. Serenity is to feel your own flow of consciousness, while recognising the truth of your own soul's unconsciousness.

Serenity is to have unclouded awareness coupled with your natural ability to trust yourself as a soul of truth. It is the still calmness felt within the depths of your soul. Serenity is to be free from fighting against what has already befallen you. Serenity results from choosing to accept there is value in being present in your reality, armed with the willingness to be completely truthful. Serenity is to calmly decide what is in your best interest and to act upon what you know to be true. It is also an acceptance of the unknown and to diligently explore, question and objectively observe what is revealed. Serenity stems from the willingness to remain open and honest, because dishonesty and narrowmindedness cause you to struggle against whatever does not suit what you want to believe. This panics and limits you, which means some form of oppression will ensue.

Serenity results from acknowledging you are not alone and valuing your resonance with the presence of *True Source Divine Origin Consciousness* within your present moment. It is the courage to accept reality and recognise your contribution to your own struggles, allowing what is not your responsibility to return to where it belongs. You cannot be responsible for how another judges you, and if they refuse to acknowledge the value of your soul, you can make sure you do not align with their condemnation. Serenity is to comprehend your freewill to value the truth of your own awareness and being open to allow truth to support you in your hour of need. Serenity develops as you accept the diversity of life with equanimity, realising that you are part of the constant flow of reality.

Serenity is felt while unconditionally loving *True Source Divine Origin Consciousness* (your own origins) and your soul. It is to be internally joyous and respectful of your own clarity and the magnitude of your significance. Serenity invokes level-headedness, which is important for the resolution of whatever is shackling you to the chains of oppression that cause you to panic and exist in an anxious state. Serenity creates an intent to be present, whilst valuing the truth of your soul and the significance of being a friend to yourself.

Trust

Trust is unconditional love for naturally accepting your own significance within your present moment and a result of valuing truth, which can be difficult when you have become jaded and scornful of life. Trust in others develops as does trust in yourself. However, when you become cynical you operate from trying to prove you are right about what or whom you distrust, including yourself. Cynicism leaves you frustrated by your own and others' unconsciousness, which may lead to you being protective of your own victim mentality or desire for control. This can mean you become disenchanted with life and focused on the indifference of those you interact with or observe.

Trust in yourself enables you to objectively observe yourself and others, which enables you to take a realistic approach to life and to value the integrity of your soul. Integrity is to accept the importance of being true to yourself. Trust also enables you to give credence to the reality that you are significant.

Trust is confidence in your own or another's integrity, it is also confidence that truth is significant. Trust is your resonance with truth in action. When you accept the truth of all energy and do not discount your own awareness, your trust in yourself expands. It is important to trust yourself to be truthful, because if you protect the lies you tell yourself, you become your own oppressor. Trust is to grace yourself with acceptance and to be honest without fear. Trust is taking responsibility for yourself within your reality and to engage with truth.

Trust in yourself can enable you to realise the relevance of the symphony of truth to your life, which means you can begin to objectively observe the intricacies of your life experiences and the opportunities to resolve what is unresolved within you. When you trust you are a significant soul, you strengthen your understanding that you are more than just what you have experienced, and events out of your control are not permanent self-definitions. Trust also enables you to learn from yourself and to take responsibility for your own behaviour, beliefs and the words you have used that have caused you or another pain, confusion and soul oppression. Life is the opportunity to explore both the consciousness and unconsciousness of your soul, and freewill means you choose what you value and protect. Trust is felt when you can rely on yourself to support and nurture the true essence of who you are.

Trustworthiness is to operate from the intent of not manipulating, exploiting or abusing those who place their trust in you. Trustworthiness is not a belief nor is it an image to portray, it is an action and a way of being. You choose if you are trustworthy. When you value being trusted, you protect the trust with truthfulness. When another has privately shared their deepest feelings, thoughts and fears with you, you are their confidant, which means you are responsible for protecting the trust and any breech should be admitted by you to them. Trust is generally not given lightly, which is why a breech in trust is so hurtful. If another breeches your trust it is not because you are worthless, it is because they are unworthy of your trust. Being trusted is the highest honour another can bestow upon you and when valued, it exposes unconditional love between those who are trustworthy.

The purity of your trust is not a prize given to those who just appease you, but to those who care about your freedom to be the truth of yourself. Trust is knowing when all others walk away, there will be a soul walking towards you. Trust means you care deeply.

When you trust yourself to be your closest friend, your trust enables you to feel the clarity of your soul. Trust in your own natural worth enables you to feel the strength of your unconditional love for truth and *True Source Divine Origin Consciousness'* unconditional love for you. Trust stems from appreciating your own synchronicity with truth and enables you to accept the opportunities to experience your own flow of consciousness.

Your trust in yourself bridges you from thinking to feeling, which enables you to explore your awareness of truth and to realise the importance of self-nurturing. Trust is to see, hear, feel and act upon the value of all your core essences. Trust is an embracement of your own divinity and strengthens your ability and willingness to be consciously aware of truth without fear. Trust facilitates exploring what is emotionally, energetically or physically shackling you to the chains of oppression that cause you to distrust yourself and to be cynical of others. Trust creates an intent to be trustworthy and to allow your consciousness to shine.

Truthfulness

Truthfulness is unconditional love for resonating with truth, which can be difficult when you become deceitful and deceptive. When you are not truthful, you mislead, which means there is agenda. When you acknowledge the truth of your agenda, you uncover the truth you fear. Your arrogance or ignorance can be the source of you misleading yourself. Intentionally misleading yourself means you are arrogantly deceptive. Unintentionally misleading yourself means you are ignorantly deceptive. However, regardless of the form of self-deception, it is the intent to deny the significance of truth and of your soul. Deception is to discount the value of resonating with truth and to adhere to the desire to create lies, confabulations, propaganda and camouflage over the truth you refuse to acknowledge or value. Truthfulness is freedom from the intent to deceive or to distort what you know to be factual.

Truthfulness is the application of truth and your own integrity. It is the willingness to value and acknowledge truth and to respect your own internal soul knowing. Truthfulness is the intention to be completely honest about how you interrelate with truth and within your relationships with others, yourself and life. Truthfulness is to express to the best of your knowledge what you understand to be true, with the willingness to allow the exploration of truth to continue. Your truthfulness evolves as your understanding does; it is not based on beliefs but on facts, observations and the openness to valuing transparency. Truthfulness has no hidden agendas or expectations.

Being mistaken does not mean you were deceptive, it means you were lacking in understanding and knowledge. Deception is done for a purpose, which alters others ability to trust the accuracy of what you convey. Deception creates doubt, doubt fuels fear, and fear often counteracts the value of truth. This leaves fear and the desire for control to be the governing factors over your decision making, which can leave you devaluing your own resonance with truth and the integrity of your soul. Deception is a choice to deceive, truthfulness is a choice to acknowledge reality.

Truthfulness enables you to experience your own flow of consciousness. It is the willingness to be open and honest with yourself about your own internal and external reality, facilitating your ability to be present, engaged and a witness to truth. Truthfulness creates foundations from which evolution develops. Truthfulness is always the key to unshackling the chains of oppression that cause you to be deceptive with yourself and creates an intent to evolve your understanding of truth and yourself.

Uniqueness

Uniqueness is unconditional love for authenticity, which can be difficult when you deny the essence of your soul and blindly conform to what you believe others want, becoming a people pleaser codependent on believing you know what others think of you. You can fall into the trap of restraining the truth of yourself and conform to your own desire to control how others perceive you, striving to control others from harshly judging you. This can leave you fearful of being the truth of yourself or believing you are not good enough, becoming codependent on an image of yourself. The image you portray can cause you to disassociate from feeling the truth of your soul and you can become obsessed with whatever you believe sustains your image.

Uniqueness is to value your truth and to acknowledge yourself as worthy of the freedom to be yourself. You comprehend your uniqueness when you love the truth of your soul. Conformity means to suppress your uniqueness to comply with rules created by others who are denying their own uniqueness and worshiping their desire for control. Uniqueness is not rebellion, it is the true expression of your soul and the acknowledgement of the freedom to choose what you value. Uniqueness is comprehending that the mass of mankind is made up of unique individuals and our uniqueness is precious.

Uniqueness makes it impossible for another to permanently imitate you, because their own uniqueness will shine through any image or illusion they create. Uniqueness is the truth of the frequency of your soul; others may quote or impersonate you, but they do not feel like you, because you are unique. When you value and unconditionally love the authenticity of your soul, your uniqueness is effortlessly felt. When you embrace your uniqueness, you become a safe person for others to be around as they embrace their own uniqueness, which make sharing time with others interesting. Nurtured uniqueness becomes innovation. Blind conformity becomes a prison that has you residing in the dumbing down of your own soul. Understanding the uniqueness of each soul, enables us collectively to share in the value of life.

Your uniqueness is the exquisiteness of who you are. Your uniqueness flourishes when you unshackle the chains of oppression that cause you to blindly conform to what oppresses your understanding and unconditional love for yourself. Comprehending that you are unique creates an intent to live the authenticity of who you are without fear of condemnation.

Glossary

Carried victim energy is produced by a victim mentality. It is the experience of not knowing how to resolve, or having no aspiration to resolve the emotions that ensue from a victim experience. Carried victim energy becomes a control technique used to oppose the acceptance of reality and to undermine the value of who the victim naturally is. It is also a description of how a victim mentality becomes a protected self-definition, which immerses victims in the energy produced by their indifference towards themselves.

Carried victim energy fuels an addiction to victimhood, self-pity, internal rage or martyrdom. It can also cause the victim to become manipulative and protective of that which is familiar, which stagnates their evolution. It also can become the basis to remain trapped in a state of desperation, or making a struggle out of everything, which leaves the victim sustaining their emotional upheaval.

Heresy is to be willfully persistent in rejecting the truth of your soul, which causes you to be indifferent to truth. Your own heresy against yourself is how you incite your many forms of indifference energy:

- Desire for control
- Indifference to truth
- Resentment of reality
- Opposition
- Programming
- Conditioning
- Indoctrinations
- Guilt
- Shame
- Humiliation
- Denial of reality
- Disassociation from feeling love

Heresy is the willingness to exploit your own awareness of truth, allowing yourself to use your awareness as a manipulative judgement tool in order to remain separated from the significance of who you naturally are. It is the perpetuation of your indifference to the truth of your own significance. Heresy energy is the willingness to be anti-yourself.

Indifference energy is produced from the intention to abandon the truth of reality and to class everything, other than the desire for control, as unimportant, unworthy of attention or incidental. It is the result of being disconnected from integrity. Indifference is a self-perpetuating energy that enables non-caring for your own and others' suffering to continue unabated. It is the willingness to support your own denial of reality and to be apathetic about the ramifications of your desire for control and denial of truth. Operating from indifference energy means you remain intentionally unconscious and unresponsive to the truth you are aware of.

Indifference energy is the result of completely losing awareness of being a soul, and denying the significance of all souls. It is to be uncaring and emotionally insensitive to the point of being cruel. It is also a callous disregard and denial of the significance of unconditional love. Indifference energy is the desire to oppose the core essences of your soul, other souls and the presence of truth. Indifference stems from, and results in, denial of the significance of truthfulness and of the significance, uniqueness, independence and individuality of another soul.

Intentional unconsciousness is to deliberately override your own awareness of truth, or to disregard the value of truth for the purpose of remaining indifferent to truth.

Paedophile is:

- A person who sexually desires children or adolescent.
- A person who uses child exploitation material for sexual gratification.
- A person who sexually targets innocent children who cannot defend or protect themselves.
- A person who manipulates or forces children to pacify their sexual desires.
- A rapist who prefers children.
- A perpetuator of sexual abuse and sexual assault of another who is under the age of full legal responsibility.
- An arrogantly selfish person who perceives children as sexual objects who they can own and discard.
- A person who refuses to acknowledge or care about the ramifications of their devious sexual depravities.
- A person who uses their power and ability to control another, to create carnage for them to endure.
- A person who is the embodiment of indifference.

Paedophilia is the sexual perversion of being attracted and aroused by children. Paedophilia is desiring sexual gratification through completely controlling a child's freewill. It is the willingness to cause harm to a child whilst in pursuit for sexual stimulation and gratification. It is any sexual behaviour, desire, voyeurism or compulsion that inflicts sexual, emotional, energetic, mental or physical abuse on an innocent child.

There are labels for peadophiles who have an age preference for their victims:

- Ephebophilia - sexual preference for adolescents aged from 15 to 19.
- Gerontophilia - sexual preference for a non-consenting elderly person.
- Hebephilia - sexual preference for early adolescents aged from 11 to 14.
- Nepiophilia - sexual preference for toddlers and infants aged from 0 to 3.

Sexualised Being aware of the control that can be exerted over another by using sexual energy or innuendo.

Soul oppression is inhibiting your own awareness of the presence of your soul's consciousness and truth. Allowing yourself to constantly default to using the energy of your soul's unconsciousness to dominate your attention and overshadow your clarity. Remaining stuck by repetitively immersing yourself in that which causes you angst. Controlling yourself to deflect or conceal truth. Subjugating your own core essences with your indifference to your soul.

Soul oppression is your willingness to mistreat yourself or others by overriding your soul integrity and tarnishing your shine of consciousness. Suppressing your true feelings. Seeking the demise of your awareness of truth, by repressing your soul insight and activating negative thoughts. Inflicting cruelty and torment upon yourself by denying the truth of who you are. Setting yourself up to be repetitively anti-yourself, and lost in your fears and embedded beliefs.

Soul oppression is feeling restricted. It is burdening yourself with your own emotional, energetic and physical resistance to unshackling your indifference to yourself, others and truth. Protecting your own anguish or feeling the void within. Dominating and intimidating yourself or others with oppressive energy. Oppression is the anguish you create by separating from your awareness of your soul, and disassociating from feeling the unconditional love within your soul and the unconditional love of *True Source Divine Origin Consciousness*.

Struggling human energy is to be anti-truth, and causes you to be:

- Anti-the eternalness of your soul
- Anti-the truth of your soul journey
- Anti-your opportunity for resolution
- Anti-your original intention for evolution
- Anti-this lifetime
- Anti-being present and honest about your reality

Being anti-truth becomes fuel for your own web of deception. Your struggling human energy is the result of your heresy against yourself, and your opposition to the significance of the uniqueness, independence and the individuality of your soul. Struggling human energy is the result of your willingness to be in conflict with the truth of your value, worth and significance, which means you become your own enemy.

Survivor of abuse is a person who has experienced being a victim and has survived. Resolving the ramifications of their abuse experience, requires resilience and courage.

Victim is a person who has been or is being hurt, overpowered, exploited or tricked by another person, a group of people or because of a crime. Those who find themselves in a circumstance where they are unable to alter, change or reason with the perpetrator. A person who has experienced or is experiencing deprivation of their freedom.

Acknowledgments

Thank you to Bronwen Prazak for the countless hours spent on the epic task of proofreading and editing *Breaking Free From the Chains of Silence*. It is not an easy subject to be immersed in and I thank you for your dedication to the importance of this book.

Thank you to Rachel Dearnley for proofreading and being an assistant to clarity. I appreciate your frankness and willingness to openly discuss the different perspectives that can be taken from what is written. I have appreciated your assistance and encouragement. Thank you for breaking the chains of silence by finding a voice to reveal your truth.

Thank you to Katherine Close for going the extra mile for me and the book, and for approaching the illustrations with such respect for the intent of this book. Thank you for all the effort you applied to the cover and your continual support and insightful feedback.

Thank you to Leanne McIntyre-Burnes for your artistic insight and support while we created the preliminary sketches for the illustrations and throughout the process of getting this book published.

Thank you to Daniel Middleton for taking the time to advise and support me; I appreciate your kindness.

Thank you to my family for your on-going support and encouragement.

I would like to thank the survivors of abuse who trusted me as they recounted their history and explored the reality of what they were and are still trying to deal with on a day-to-day basis. Each survivor has uniquely broadened my understanding about the rawness, longevity and pain which results from abuse. It has been a privilege to have met and witnessed so many brave souls break their own chains of silence. Your resilience is inspiring and I want to thank you for your candour and trust.

Dear reader,

Thank you for taking the time to read Breaking Free from the Chains of Silence.

Your opinion of this book matters! Your review may help others find this book. All honest reviews and ratings are appreciated. Amazon, Goodreads, Lorraine's website and Facebook are appreciated.

Amazon
https://www.lorrainenilon.com.au/Amazon-BreakingFree-Paperback

Goodreads
https://www.lorrainenilon.com.au/Goodreads-BreakingFree-Paperback

Facebook
https://www.facebook.com/LorraineNilon/

Lorraine's Website – To add a review, first click on book, in the shop.
https://www.lorrainenilon.com.au/shop

About the Author

Lorraine Nilon is an Australian author, Soul intuitive®, life researcher, philosopher, and spiritualist. With over 20 years of experience exploring spirituality and self-discovery, she's gained a comprehensive knowledge about how you can develop a deeper connection with your inner self and boost your spiritual wellbeing. Her mission is to share her teachings with the world, educating others on how they can better understand themselves and live more balanced and spiritual lives.

She has a heightened awareness of the cause and effect of unresolved emotions, and the true nature of who we are hidden beneath the emotional baggage we all carry. Lorraine has spent decades honing her skill of reading both the conscious and unconscious energy of soul systems. She tracks energy, and can insightfully explain the complexities and origin of unresolved emotions. Lorraine has an innate understanding of the barriers that restrict our awareness of the authenticity of who we are, and of how our avenues of being indifferent to truth separate us from the true essence of our souls. Her insight and awareness reflects her respect for the uniqueness and equality of all souls, and her willingness to stand in her own truth.

For well over a decade Lorraine has been a trusted custodian of many individuals' history of abuse, and has borne witness to the rawness of their unresolved emotions, the internal struggle they endured and the insidious nature of abuse. This, along with her distinctive ability as a soul intuitive, has enabled her to energetically track and document the reality of how energy is felt and carried, and the travesty of indifference and abuse.

www.insightandawareness.com.au

Other Titles from Lorraine Nilon

Breaking Free from the Chains of Silence
A respectful exploration into the ramifications of abuse hidden behind closed doors

Your Insight and Awareness Book
Your life is an expedition to discover the truth of yourself

Take a Moment to Reflect – Quote booklet
Contemplation nurtures your soul

Spirituality, Evolution & Awakened Consciousness
Understanding how to get real about soul maturity and spiritual growth

Energy of souls
Understanding your soul system to expand your emotional and spiritual maturity

Emerging Awareness
An invitation to honour the true essence of who you are

Worthy of recovery
Understanding the wake left behind life shocks, betrayal, abuse, addictions and narcissistic relationships

www.insightandawareness.com.au

www.ingramcontent.com/pod-product-compliance
Lightning Source LLC
Chambersburg PA
CBHW080410300426
44113CB00015B/2460